Crumbs from the Table of Joy

and Other Plays

Lynn Nottage

Theatre Communications Group
New York
2004

Crumbs from the Table of Joy and Other Plays is published by Theatre Communications Group, Inc., 520 8th Ave., 24th Floor, New York, NY 10018-4156.

"Luck" from *Distance Nowhere*, by Langston Hughes, published in *Selected Poems of Langston Hughes*, Vintage, New York, 1990.

This publication is made possible in part with funds from the New York State Council on the Arts, a State Agency.

TCG books are exclusively distributed to the book trade by Consortium Book Sales and Distribution, 1045 Westgate Dr., St. Paul, MN 55114

LIBRARY OF CONGRESS CATALOGING-IN-PUBLICATION DATA
Nottage, Lynn.
Crumbs from the table of joy, and other plays / by lynn Nottage.
    p.cm.
ISBN 1-55936-214-6 (Paperback : alk. paper)
1. African Americans—Drama. 2. Africa—Drama. I.Title.
PS3564.O795 C78 2003
812'.54—dc21
2003000816

Cover design by Mark Melnick
Book design and composition by Lisa Govan
Author photo by Tony Gerber

First Edition, May 2004
Fourth Printing, August 2022

In memory of Ruby Nottage,
my mother and inspiration.

Table of Contents

Preface   ix

Crumbs from the Table of Joy   1

POOF!   89

Por'knockers   105

Mud, River, Stone   163

Las Meninas   245

Preface

My plays were born in an orange-colored kitchen with a group of women seated around a mod Formica countertop, but my plays are not "kitchen sink dramas." My playwriting began inside my mother's gaze—that provocative way her eyes smiled after two glasses of Mondavi. Her gaze was warm, it was distant, magical, quixotic and at times even impenetrable; it embodied her paradoxical nature. I knew it would take my lifetime to decipher and understand the story behind my mother's gaze, but I didn't know that this nomadic search would take me to Brooklyn in the 1950s, to the court of Louis the XIV, to a terrorist cell in Bushwick, into the thick, dense forests of Mozambique, and through the boudoirs of old New York. The path would be paved with humor, at times difficult and even unpalatable; it would be provocative, political, but never without irony. As it turned out, my mother's gaze, her reflective eyes, became my own looking glass.

I don't know whether it's an overstatement to say that my writing is an outgrowth of my curiosity. But I hope that it's true, because the magnificent thing about curiosity is that it's limitless. It is not bound by convention; it is not confined or predictable. In fact it has taken me in inexplicable directions, and given shape to the cantilevered architecture of my work.

It's perhaps the reason my characters are always questioning and challenging the world within which they live. They are unsettled souls, striving to make sense of their surroundings, and ultimately refusing to surrender to expectations. And as such, I offer my curiosity as an open-ended question, a challenge, a reflection, a belch, a whisper, a scream, a laugh, a paradox, a play.

—*Lynn Nottage*
Brooklyn, New York
March 2004

Acknowledgments

A special thanks to the following people for helping me bring to the stage the plays included in this anthology: Carole Rothman, Tim Sanford, Doug Aibel, Timothy Near, Gavin Cameron-Webb, Margot Harley, Michael Bigelow Dixon, Seret Scott, Roger Rees, Michael Rogers, Michael Donald Edwards, Jerry Patch, Erin Sanders, Chiori Miyagawa, George Emilio Sanchez, John Emigh, Nakissa Etemad, Peter Hagan, Joe Morton, Daniela Varon, Lenora Brown, Thulani Davis, Martin Benson, David Emmes, Paula Vogel, Ruth Maleczech and members of the Mabou Mines Suite and, in particular, Tony Gerber.

Crumbs from the Table of Joy

Sometimes a crumb falls from the table of joy,
Sometimes a bone is flung.
To some people love is given,
To others only heaven.

—*Langston Hughes*
"Luck"

Production History

Crumbs from the Table of Joy received its world premiere at Second Stage Theatre in New York City (Carole Rothman, Artistic Director; Suzanne Schwartz Davidson, Producing Director) in May 1995 under the direction of Joe Morton. The set design was by Myung Hee Cho, the lights by Donald Holder, the sound by Mark Bennett and the costumes by Karen Perry. The dramaturg was Erin Sanders, the production stage manager was Delicia Turner and the stage manager was David Sugarman. The cast was as follows:

ERNESTINE CRUMP	Kisha Howard
ERMINA CRUMP	Nicole Leach
GODFREY CRUMP	Daryl Edwards
LILY ANN GREEN	Ella Joyce
GERTE SCHULTE	Stephanie Roth

Crumbs from the Table of Joy received its West Coast premiere at South Coast Repertory in Costa Mesa, California (David Emmes, Producing Artistic Director; Martin Benson, Artistic Director) on September, 17, 1996, under the direction of Seret Scott. The set design was by Michael Vaughn Sims, the lights by Paulie Jenkins, the sound by Garth Hemphill, the costumes by Susan Denison Geller and the vocal/dialect consultant was Lynn Watson. The dramaturg was Jerry Patch, the production manager was Michael Mora and the stage manager was Randall K. Lum.

The cast was as follows:

ERNESTINE CRUMP	Karen Malina White
ERMINA CRUMP	Susan Patterson
GODFREY CRUMP	Dorian Harewood
LILY ANN GREEN	Ella Joyce
GERTE SCHULTE	Nancy Harewood

Characters

ERNESTINE CRUMP, African-American, seventeen

ERMINA CRUMP, African-American, fifteen

GODFREY CRUMP, African-American, Ernestine and Ermina's father, thirty-five

LILY ANN GREEN, African-American, Ernestine and Ermina's aunt, thirty-five

GERTE SCHULTE, German, Caucasian, thirty

Time

Fall

Place

Brooklyn, 1950

✳ Prologue

1950. Ermina, Ernestine and Godfrey Crump sit on a bench with their heads slightly bowed. Ernestine is a slightly plump seventeen year old. She wears her hair pulled tight into tiny mismatched pigtails. Her diction is crisp from practice and has the gentle inflections learned from her favorite screen actresses. Godfrey, a lean, handsome thirty-five-year-old man, wears an impeccably pressed suit. His appearance is always neat and well assembled. Ermina is an attractive, slim fifteen year old; she also wears her hair in mismatched pigtails

ERNESTINE: Death nearly crippled my father, slipping beneath the soles of his feet and taking away his ability to walk at will. Death made him wail like a god-awful banshee.

(Godfrey wails like a god-awful banshee.)

Like the 12:01 steamboat mooring.

(Godfrey continues to wail.)

Death made strangers take hold of our hands and recount endless stories of Mommy. In church, at work, strolling, laughing, eating and of course at that infamous picnic in the park where half the town fell ill to Cyrinthia Bowers's potato salad.

(They all laugh and shake their heads.)

Death made us nauseous with regret. It clipped Daddy's tongue and put his temper to rest. Made folks shuffle and bow their heads. But it wouldn't leave us be, tugging at our stomachs and our throats. And then one day it stopped and we took the train north to New York City.

(The family stands in unison. Ermina stands with her arms folded and her lips pursed in disgust.)

(To audience) Death brought us to Brooklyn, the Nostrand Avenue stop on the A line . . . A basement apartment, kind of romantic, like a Parisian artist's flat.

ERMINA: If Parisian mean ugly.

ERNESTINE: Daddy worked the late shift at a bakery downtown. He'd leave every night two hours after dinner, tip his hat to Father Divine and return the next morning as we'd rise to go to school.

(Godfrey tips his hat and walks slowly, as if making his way to work. The girls walk the Brooklyn streets.)

And then we'd walk exactly fourteen blocks to school . . . Always thought of myself as being smart. Down home, smart meant you got homework done in time. Not so smart in . . . Brooklyn. They put Ermina back one grade.

ERMINA: So? *(Shrugs her shoulders and sticks out her buttocks defiantly)*

ERNESTINE: They . . . them . . . the gals laughed at us the first day at school, with our country braids and simple dresses my mommy had sewn.

(The sound of girls' laughter surrounds Ernestine and Ermina. Ermina rolls her eyes.)

ERMINA: Least they clean, which is more than I can say for your tired bag of rags.

ERNESTINE *(To audience)*: Our dresses were sewn with love, each stitch. But them, they couldn't appreciate it!

(The laughter grows. Ermina prepares herself for a fight. She slicks back her hair and hitches up her dress around her thighs.)

So Ermina fought like a wild animal.

(Ermina swings wildly in the air.)

Scratched and tore at their cashmere cardigans and matching skirts. She walked home with a handful of greasy relaxed hair and a piece of gray cashmere stuffed in her pocket.

(Ermina basks in triumph. Ernestine strolls the streets of Brooklyn.)

Brooklyn . . . everything you'd ever need not more than a few blocks away. Streets of jagged slate, pennies stuck in the crevices; I collected over ten cents one day. Still, it wasn't any place to live . . .

(She sits down. She is swathed in the brilliant, blue flickering light from a motion-picture projector.)

. . . until I sat in the cinema, The Fox, right smack between two white gals. Oh yes! *(Looks from side to side)* Practically touching shoulders. And we all wept. Wept unabashedly.

(Ermina joins Ernestine. They take each other's hands.)

Watching our beautiful and wretched Joan Crawford's eyebrows and lips battle their way through one hundred and three minutes of pure unadulterated drama, we could be tragic in Brooklyn.

(Ernestine and Ermina weep softly. The sound of the projector rolling gives way to a distant radio.)

RADIO BROADCASTER *(Offstage)*: Today Senator McCarthy began—

(In the distance the radio dial is switched and "Some Enchanted Evening" plays. It continues to play softly throughout the duration of the scene.

Lights rise on a sparsely decorated living room punctuated with an old standing radio/phonograph. On the mantle is a photograph of Sandra Crump, Ernestine and Ermina's mother, smiling gloriously. Over the mantle hangs a huge photograph of Father Divine, the charismatic leader of the waning Peace Mission Movement, in his prime. Godfrey sits in an armchair reading the daily newspaper with a magnifying glass, chuckling. The music from another apartment is barely audible, taunting the girls with possibility.)

ERMINA: Now? Well?

(Ermina awaits a response. Godfrey doesn't bother to look up from his newspaper.)

GODFREY: Ain't listening!

(Ermina walks tentatively over to the radio and flicks it on. She shoots a quick, wide-eyed glance at Godfrey. Radio laughter fills the room.)

Off!

ERMINA: Ah!

(Ermina flips off the radio. Silence, except the distant music of "Some Enchanted Evening.")

GODFREY: It's Sunday, gal!

(Ermina's leg shakes wildly, a nervous tic that is triggered when she becomes agitated. Godfrey still doesn't look up.)

Leg's gonna fall off.

ERNESTINE *(To audience)*: Almost did, but that comes later.

ERMINA *(Ventures)*: Ain't no use in having a radio. Might as well be a log, 'least we could burn it to keep warm.

GODFREY: You sassing.

ERMINA: Nah, sir!

GODFREY: Could have sworn you was.

ERMINA: Really? Well, I ain't.

ERNESTINE *(To audience)*: Tomorrow we'll have nothing to talk about in school. Again, we will miss *Amos 'n Andy.*

ERMINA: Again ruined by Father Divine. *(Rolls her eyes and turns toward the portrait of Father Divine hanging over the mantle)*

ERNESTINE *(Whispered, to audience)*: Father Divine . . . Ever since Mommy passed on, he stands between us and our enjoyment. Daddy discovered Father Divine when he was searching to cure "the ailments of the heart," those terrible fits of mourning that set in.

(Godfrey begins to weep loudly.)

Father Divine, the great provider, sent his blessing via mail. And shortly thereafter Daddy was cured.

(Godfrey stops weeping and returns to reading his newspaper.)

He vowed to move nearer to Divine, to be close to God, devote his waking hours to the righteousness "Divinely" ordained. Daddy thought Divine's Peace Mission was in Brooklyn, 'cause of a return address on a miracle elixir boasting to induce "peace of mind." Divine was not in Brooklyn or New York City. But that didn't diminish Daddy's love. No, he let Divine strip away his desire and demand of him a monk's devotion. This a man who never went to church and never tipped his hat to a woman, until we got to . . . Brooklyn.

GODFREY: What would Sweet Father say if he knew his rose-buds, on a Sunday no less, didn't have the strength or conviction to honor and respect his wishes.

ERNESTINE *(To audience)*: Daddy wanted us to wear the "V."

ERMINA AND ERNESTINE: Virtue, Victory and Virginity.

GODFREY: Yes indeed. Peace and blessings.

ERNESTINE *(To audience)*: His words now for everything, good, bad or indifferent.

GODFREY *(By rote)*: I ain't doing this 'cause I like to, I'm doing this 'cause I got to. Appreciation is like all other subtle pleasures in life, it comes with age.

(A moment.)

ERMINA: Well, could we at least go up to the Levys' to listen the radio? They says so. We'd appreciate this moment all the more.

(Ernestine perks up with anticipation.)

GODFREY: They's being polite . . . Running up there to them white peoples every time you get a chance, they're gonna think you don't got a proper home.

ERMINA: They old! . . . They don't think nothing.

GODFREY: Oh you God now, you knows what they think!

ERMINA: Nah, sir! *(Wrinkles her nose)*

ERNESTINE *(To audience)*: Mr. Levy gives us a quarter on the Sabbath to turn on the lights, the stove and of course his smacking-new television.

ERMINA: It's practically the size of a car. For real.

GODFREY: They white people, don't know any better than to spend their money on foolishness.

ERNESTINE *(To audience)*: There you have it! "They white" — with those two words he can dismiss our wants, our desires, even our simplest pleasures. "They white."

(Ermina sits down and mopes, her leg shaking furiously.)

It doesn't matter that his Father Divine has gone off and married himself a "spotless white virgin," who remains untarnished despite marital vows. Oh yes! There'll always be that great divide between us and them. Divine was God, and God was liable do as he pleased, but you see Daddy was just a poor colored man —

(Godfrey looks up from his newspaper.)

GODFREY AND ERNESTINE: . . . from Pensacola, and I gone out my way to keep trouble a few arms' lengths 'way. I don' want to wind up like them Scottsboro boys, but you wouldn't remember.

(Godfrey continues to speak; Ernestine mouths the words:)

GODFREY: Terrible mess, terrible mess.

(Godfrey takes out a little notepad and takes notes. He then returns to reading with his magnifying glass. Ernestine runs her hands across the chair as if she could feel the memory coming to life. Godfrey becomes choked up; he tries to restrain his sobs, but is unable to do so.)

ERNESTINE *(To audience)*: Brooklyn . . . Evenings; listening to Daddy weep, missing Mommy and staring at the radio. A Radiola Mommy won, she guessed the number of marbles in a jar: seven hundred and two. Daddy will win playing that number some years from now. Only number he will ever play.

(She and Ermina stare at the radio longingly. Laughter fills the stage.)

Can hear Mrs. Levy upstairs in her rocking chair shifting back and forth from laughter. Can hear the television in the Friedlanders' apartment. We sit and listen to all the white laughter. Seems to us only white folks can laugh on Sunday.

(Laughter fills the stage. The three stare out into space. Silence.)

GODFREY: I almost forgot, *(Singsong)* something in my pocket for my babies.

(Ermina and Ernestine rush over to Godfrey's worn over-coat hanging over the chair. Ernestine pulls out a handful of cookies.)

ERNESTINE *(To audience)*: Again, he's bought us off with cookies and shortcake. *(Savoring the words)* Love is candied peanuts and sugar babies, day-old cinnamon buns and peach cobbler.

GODFREY: Well, maybe when I find me a "better" job we'll, we'll, take a walk maybe, and maybe look at some television sets. I do want the best for my babies.

ERNESTINE *(To audience)*: Something better is always on the horizon.

(Ernestine stuffs her mouth with sugar cookies, gobbling them down obsessively.)

🌿 Act One

Scene 1

The Crumps' living room. Lights rise on Ernestine. She sits hemming a pair of her father's slacks. The radio can ever so faintly be heard through the walls.

Lights rise on Godfrey sitting in his armchair shining his shoes; for him, it is an act of love performed with meticulous care. In the absence of a cloth he uses a piece of newspaper to buff his shoes.

GODFREY: Ernie, wouldn't know these was old, would ya? Would ya now? Hey, hey, the boys at the job can't help eyeing them, smart shoes like these make 'em think you more important than you is.

ERNESTINE: That so? *(To audience)* It's Thursday. Last night a madman went on a rampage in South Brooklyn, killed a Mohawk Indian and stabbed four others with a bread knife. We're staying in.

(Godfrey shakes his head and glances at the newspaper.)

GODFREY: No reason to go out. Remember what happened to that Johnston family gal, shipped home seven of her fingers.

15

ERNESTINE: Nah!

GODFREY: Hear that's all that was left, no thumbs or nothing. Her mama threw herself into the baptismal waters and nearly drowned two men when they tried to rescue her. Can't even help out folks these days. *(Again, he glances down at the newspaper. He goes over to the front door and checks the lock)* Pity! Country folk come up here and turn on each other. That's what happens when you live piled up on top of each other day in and day out. Ain't natural. *(Balls up the newspaper. In a soothing tone)* God's done retreated from this city, I can tell you that much without being a scientist.

ERNESTINE: Where'd God go?

GODFREY *(Thinks)*: Philadelphia, my rosebud. *(Takes a small pad out of his pocket and jots down notes. He places the notes in a box and shoves the box beneath his chair)*

ERNESTINE *(To audience)*: We're locked inside awaiting word from Father Divine. The mailman is our deliverer.

(Godfrey stands, alert.)

GODFREY *(Anxious)*: The mailman here yet?

ERNESTINE: That's the third time you asked me today, sir.

GODFREY: I thought I heard you say so —

ERNESTINE: Nah, sir.

GODFREY *(Excited)*: Well now, I's expecting the *New Day* paper and a little word from Sweet Father. Been putting all these questions to him, it's only a matter of time before he answers. *(Earnestly)* Peace will come.

(The sound of the Levys turning the radio dial. Laughter, then gunshots, emanate from behind the wall.)

We all know who done it, Mrs. Levy. It's the doctor. I wish she'd turn it down, can't concentrate. It ain't good enough for white folks just to have a television, they got to let the whole neighborhood know.

(Ermina enters casually with the mail. She thumbs through the pile.)

ERMINA: Mailman says if you leave 'im a dollar in the box he'll make sure you git your mail in the mornings like the white folk do.

GODFREY: Morning. Evening. Ain't a dollar difference to me. Whatcha got? The *New Day* come?

(Ermina slowly picks through the mail.)

ERMINA: Look here! From home for me. *(Takes a deep whiff of the envelope, then tucks it lovingly into her skirt)*

GODFREY: Smells good now, he won't remember your name by summer.

(Ermina continues picking through the mail. Godfrey laughs to himself.)

The *New Day* come?

ERMINA: Oooo! Ernie! What I got? Look like that pattern for your graduation dress finally here. Bet you dying to see it. I bet it pretty. *(Examines the envelope. She keeps it away from Ernestine)* It feel nice. Feel expensive.

ERNESTINE: Give me!

GODFREY: Expensive? What's that there?

(Ermina tosses the pattern to Ernestine.)

ERMINA: You gonna tell him? . . . Well, if you ain't, I will. *(Defiantly)* Mommy promised Ernie a graduation dress and she gonna need some money for the fabric. *(To Ernestine)* All right, it been said!

ERNESTINE: Ermina!
GODFREY: You graduating?

(Ernestine nods. Godfrey breaks into a smile.)

Nah . . . A first. You really gonna graduate? You're gonna be a high-school graduate like Percy Duncan, Roberta Miles, Sarah Dickerson, Elmore Sinclair, Chappy Phillips and Ernestine Crump. Lawd, I got a high-school graduate in my living room.

(Ernestine, bashful, covers her face.)

ERNESTINE: Not quite yet!
GODFREY: Why didn't you say something?
ERNESTINE: Didn't I?

(A moment. Godfrey, embarrassed, takes out his notepad.)

GODFREY: . . . The *New Day* come?

(Ernestine expectantly tears open the envelope. Delighted, she inspects the pattern. Ermina holds up an official-looking envelope.)

ERMINA: The *New Day* come.

(Godfrey breaks into a broad smile. Ermina passes Godfrey the envelope.)

GODFREY: Glory be! Been expecting this for a week now. Gals, gather round. *(Takes in a deep breath, then rips into the envelope with an unbridled pleasure. He pulls the huge magnifying glass from his jacket pocket and begins to read with difficulty)* Peace Angel . . . *(Beaming)* He called me

18

an angel. *(Basks in the heavenly glow of the Peace Mission. Reading)* Peace Angel . . . You-are-one-of-the bl-bl-ess. *(Hands the letter to Ernestine)*

ERNESTINE *(Reading)*: Blessed. Peace Angel, you are one of the blessed. Your positive visu . . . visu . . . visual-i-zation has materialized into a response to your letter. Your honesty touched me. STRENGTH! You speak of being a poor man, being a colored man, being a man without prospects.

(Godfrey nods emphatically.)

You speak of Jim Crow. COURAGE!

GODFREY: COURAGE!

ERNESTINE *(Reading)*: We know that there are no differences between the races in this Kingdom, and that segregation is the creation of the ignorant to punish those who are in touch with God—

GODFREY: What's that?

(Ermina rips open her letter.)

ERNESTINE *(Reading)*: . . . segregation is the creation of the ignorant to punish those who are in touch with God. That God who is a living vital force moving through you.

GODFREY: Oh yes. Go on. Go on.

ERNESTINE *(Reading)*: ATONE! You, who have escaped the hold of passion and other temptations that corrupt the purity of the spirit. Remember celibacy, peace and Godliness are all that I ask of you! ABSTAIN! *(A moment)* ALERT! I have considered your request and decided to bestow upon one of my devoted disciples beautiful names for your family. Names that God will immediately recognize and open up to a direct line of communication. All that said and done, I give you the names Godfrey Goodness—

GODFREY *(Tries it on)*: Godfrey Goodness!

ERNESTINE *(Reading)*: For your eldest, Darling Angel. And your baby, Devout Mary.

(Godfrey smiles at Ermina; horrified, she mouths the name.)

JOIN US AT THE HOLY COMMUNION BANQUET! The Kingdom awaits you. REMEMBER! HEED! VIRTUE! Life is a feast, but unfortunately, food still costs money and I know you won't let us starve. Peace and Blessings, Father Divine, Philadelphia, Pennsylvania, United States of America.

GODFREY: Ain't that beautiful? THERE! He speaks the truth! From God's mouth to our ears.

ERMINA: Not me, Miss Devout Mary. *(Sucks her teeth)* What's wrong with Ermina Crump? No way I's gonna be called Miss Devout Mary. What kinda first name is Devout? What sorta boy is gonna wanna ask out a gal named Devout Mary?

GODFREY: Well, you know where Father stands on that.

ERNESTINE *(To audience)*: Is he speaking for himself or Father Divine? Ain't always clear. I like being a Crump, was just getting used to being a Crump.

GODFREY *(Flabbergasted)*: We're now part of his flock, we're capable of entering the Kingdom. *(In a heavenly daze, he reaches into his wallet and counts out his money)* This is just about the best news I've heard. *(A moment. In a broad, theatrical gesture)* My Angels, this calls for a celebration. What are you waiting for, go on and get dressed up, we're going out . . . to the movies!

ERNESTINE *(To audience)*: At least I wish he had said that, but he sat and counted his money until it was time to go to work.

(Godfrey sits down and counts his money.)

(To audience) You ever have the feeling of floating out of your body, entering the Milky Way and getting stuck in it just as it's curdling? *(Tucks the pattern under her arm)*

Scene 2

Lights rise on Lily Ann "Sister" Green standing in the Crumps' doorway; she is wearing a smartly tailored suit and sparkling white gloves. Her hat is cocked to the side and she smokes a cigarette. Her eyes are concealed behind the thick-rimmed bebop sunglasses popular at the time. She is a nonconformist, a "dangerous woman." Lily takes out a tissue, spits into it and extinguishes her cigarette.

Lights rise on the living room. Ermina stands by the open door; Ernestine is sitting.

LILY: Didn't you hear me ringing the bell, nearly froze my ass out there. *(She displays her legs)* These stockings, thank God for 'em, just ain't no competition for this weather. Remind me, take a note, need for weather-resistant stockings. Period. Stop! *(To Ermina)* Ernestine, is that my gal?

ERNESTINE *(To audience)*: And there now is Aunt Lily, the first colored woman we'd seen dressed up like a white lady. Smart looking and posture straight. She'd been to Harlem . . . For us country folk that is the equivalent of reaching the promised land.

LILY: Ernestine, is that my gal?

ERMINA: Ermina! *(Shuts the door)*

LILY: But haven't you grown. Ladyish and whatnot. How's my baby doing? Where's my hug?

ERMINA: Don't know who you is. Can't be giving out loving to anybody that ask.

(Lily laughs. Godfrey enters to investigate the noise.)

21

LILY: Ain't that the truth. *(Strikes a pose, then takes off her coat and throws it across the chair)*

ERMINA: Who you?

LILY: Who I? Precious! If that ain't a question! It's me, your Aunt Lily, Sister.

(Ermina takes a long hard look. Godfrey gawks.)

(Tentatively) Now Godfrey, ain't you got words for me?

GODFREY: Sister Lily? Sister Lily Ann Green?

LILY: Who else? Never thought you'd bring your country ass on up here. You ole alligator bait. But don't you look . . . good, Daddy.

(Lily walks over and embraces Godfrey. He stiffens awkwardly, uncomfortable with the display of affection. Godfrey takes a few steps backward and looks down at the ground.)

GODFREY: I'll be damned! This here is your Mama's sister. Remember?

(The girls do not respond.)

LILY: That's all right. Memories need maintenance. I won't hold it against y'all. You're still "y'all," 'cause some folks come North get all siddity on *(Relishes)* "y'all."

(Godfrey sits, then stands.)

GODFREY: Lawd, I've gotten so used to seeing strangers, barely know what to do with a familiar face. You're looking . . . smart, Sister Lily.

LILY: Now don't tell me you're surprised!

GODFREY *(Jokes in a familiar way)*: Used up all my surprise on the first day in Brooklyn. Ain't surprised, pleased though. Some pleasures you never stop looking forward to.

LILY *(Flirtatiously)*: Well now! That tongue still got a taste of honey.

(An awkward moment. Godfrey looks away from Lily, who smiles seductively.)

GODFREY: Ain't heard no word from you since . . . since . . . Well. *(Bows his head, unable to continue)* We tried to track you down up there in Harlem. Ain't like a small town where your bizness is a matter of public record.

LILY *(Amused)*: This the big city, Godfrey, don't want everybody to know ya. They got names for women like that. Oh hell, that's why there's the telephone . . . But I forgot ya from the country, probably don't know how to use the telephone. *(Cackles)* And don't think it was easy to find "y'all." Do like to say it, "y'all." I can smell the orange blossom and the pig roasting on the spit . . . Look at ya, I can track down a fine-looking Negro halfway across the state.

GODFREY: Now . . . don't . . . don't—

LILY: Don't get bashful on me. Gals, me and your daddy go back to—

GODFREY: It's been quite a—

LILY: Still wearing them shoes.

(Godfrey peers down at his perfectly shined shoes.)

I must admit they sure do have a fine shine.

(Lily winks at the girls. They giggle.)

GODFREY: I keep 'em up.

(Laughing, Lily takes off her gloves and tosses them on the table.)

Why don't you take a load off your feet?

LILY: Thank ya, I thought you had lost your manners. *(As she prepares to sit, she notices the picture of Sandra over the mantle. She goes over to the picture. Suddenly sober:)* Sandra. *(Takes off her hat)* I'm sorry. I couldn't make it down for the funeral. My heart was there with "y'all." I cried for nearly two weeks straight. She was a special woman, I always said that. *(A moment, as she covers her eyes. She whimpers, then recovers her composure)*

GODFREY: Great loss . . .

(Lily forces out a smile. Ernestine studies her aunt.)

I told you about staring, Darling.

(Lily notices and shows off her outfit.)

LILY *(Breaking the silence)*: Ya like my suit?

(Ernestine nods.)

I bought it on Fifth Avenue, sure did, to spite those white gals. You know how they hate to see a Negro woman look better than they do. It's my own little subversive mission to outdress them whenever possible. Envy is my secret weapon, babies. If ya learn anything from your auntie, let it be that.

GODFREY: So, how come you ain't stopped over sooner?

LILY: Well, ya know how it gets! *(Lights up another cigarette as she takes a perfunctory look about the apartment)*

GODFREY: Thought you was lost up in Harlem. Selling books and whatnot.

LILY: Was. Changed my plans. Books, with the television I'm told there's no future in them. I'm . . . an "etymologist" now.

GODFREY: You don't say!

ERNESTINE: Really?

LILY: Nearly broke my neck with the studies. Well, somebody had to break the barrier, let those white boys know we saying what we please.

GODFREY: How about that. Always said you was the clever one.

ERMINA: What do a et—

LILY: I ain't gonna bore you with the details. I'll leave it at that.

(She grabs her stomach. Godfrey takes out his little pad and jots down some notes.)

Oh chile, listen to it, if that ain't my stomach saying hello.

GODFREY: Oh well, we . . . we ain't prepared nothing for dinner yet. As a matter of fact, you . . . you our first visitor . . . *(A moment. He impulsively straightens the furniture. Stops)* Darling Angel! We got any fixings for Sister?

ERNESTINE: I'm sure I can find something, Daddy.

LILY: Chile, don't go out your way. I ain't that hungry. *(A beat)* Whatever ya got will be fine.

(Ernestine turns to leave. Lily reaches out to Ernestine.)

Ernestine, you better not leave this room without giving your aunt some sugar.

(Ernestine bashfully approaches Lily and gives her a hug. Lily pinches Ernestine's buttocks.)

What's that? I don't remember that being there last time. But haven't you gotten big! And look at those boobies! Bigger than mine and ya how old? Ya better watch yourself, you're liable to attract ya a grown-up man.

(Lily shimmies, shaking her shoulders and breasts. Aghast, Ernestine covers her breasts with her arms. Lily laughs. Godfrey laughs with discomfort.)

ERNESTINE: I'm gonna go and see what's in the kitchen.

LILY: Now gal, don't want to have to take out this suit another inch . . . Something light.

(Ernestine exits into the kitchen with her arms covering her breasts.)

And Godfrey, you going to leave my bags out in the hallway?

GODFREY: Bags? You going somewhere?

LILY: Not anymore.

GODFREY: Whatcha mean?

LILY: Oh hell, Godfrey, you know what I mean.

(She chuckles to herself. Ermina gawks.)

It do seem colder in Brooklyn, but don't it though? . . . Didn't see a Negro face between here and 116th. HELLO white peoples! *(Waves. A moment)* Living in their midst do have a way of wearing down your stamina. *(Pats Ermina on the shoulder, then strolls around the apartment. She runs her hand across the furniture)* Never did have taste, Godfrey.

(Lily sinks into the chair. Ermina plops down next to her. Lily swings her arm around Ermina.)

GODFREY: But I see it's good enough to sit on.

LILY: You know how it is! These tired hams. And look at you, just standing there like you lost your tongue. What you got to sip on? I need a drink.

GODFREY: We . . . we don't keep liquor in this house.

(Lily bursts into laughter.)

LILY: Oh ya a Christian now?

GODFREY: Well—

LILY: Oh please, Godfrey, don't make me sick. Gimme a drink, will ya, goddamnit!

(Ermina's eyes grow big. Lily continues to laugh. Godfrey is horrified.)

You really a Christian? *(She peers at the portrait of Father Divine)* Oh I see, the Peace Mission, Father Divine. He still alive and playing God?

GODFREY: Sweet Father Divine, he found me down in Florida and his word carried us up here. I'd still be mourning over my biscuits in the Nortons' kitchen if—

(Lily straightens her clothing.)

LILY: I'm touched, Mr. Crump—

ERMINA: Goodness.

LILY: Goodness. I recall a certain Saturday at the juke—

GODFREY: Please.

LILY: Please, nonsense. You do remember the juke joint. Don't tell me you've given up everything? Everything? Hell, I'm surprised.

(A moment.)

GODFREY: Now we both been surprised. And you? You still up there fooling with—

LILY: Go on say it, tongue won't fall out. The communist party, amongst other things.

(Ermina giggles.)

Oh, you find that funny? *(Earnestly)* I ain't laughing. I suppose ya happy with what you got, a bit of nothing. Sure, I was happy at your age, "a little pickaninny" selling hotcakes to the fishermen. Taking pennies from poor people ain't a job, it's a chore. This may be New York, but this still the basement. Don't none of those crackers want to share any bit of power with us. That's what it's about. Red Scare, should be called Black Scare.

GODFREY: I wish you wouldn't conniggerate in front of the gal.

LILY: You act like I'm saying dirty words. Worker! Revolution! Proletariat! There! Christian!

GODFREY: This communism thing a bit frightening to this young one.

LILY: Ain't no more frightening than Jim Crow. I said my "peace."

GODFREY: Go on! 'Cause talk like that keeps company with the door closing behind you. You know something about that.

LILY: Watch yourself! I promised Nana I'd look after these gals for her. She don't think it's proper that a man be living alone with his daughters once they sprung bosom. I'm here out of sense of duty. So relax, you've always been tight in the chest. Breathe, breathe. There you go. God won't strike you down for relaxing. *(A moment. Smiling)* Well, could I get a soda pop at least, spent half the day underground.

ERMINA *(Cheerfully)*: I'll get it. *(She exits)*

LILY *(Yelling after)*: Thank you, sweet thing.

(She and Godfrey have a tense, awkward moment, not quite sure what to say to each other.)

Nice-looking gal. Precious.

(Lily smiles seductively; Godfrey looks away, then takes out his little pad and jots down some notes.)

LILY: What do you keep writing down?

GODFREY: Oh, nothing, just questions. Things I want to ask Father Divine when he comes to New York for the Holy Communion.

LILY: Oh! And I thought it was something interesting.

(*Unnoticed, Ernestine reenters the room with a sandwich.*)

GODFREY: You ain't changed a bit.
LILY: Thank ya.
GODFREY: That ain't how I meant it.

(*Lily flicks her ashes on top of an old magazine. Godfrey retrieves an ashtray for her.*)

LILY (*Noticing Ernestine*): Oh, there ya go.

(*Ernestine places the sandwich on the table. Lily greedily examines the sandwich, not entirely pleased with the offerings, but nevertheless hungry.*)

Let me see what you got me to eat. Didn't have no mayonnaise?

(*Ermina returns with a glass of soda. Lily drinks it down, then ravenously bites into the sandwich, fighting to force down the half-chewed chunks of food.*)

MMMMmmm. That hit the spot. (*Embarrassed, she looks Ermina over. To Ermina*) Thank you, sweet-smelling thing, that's nice at your age. You must be fifteen.

(*Ermina nods.*)

How'd I know? Prescience is what carried me up here. Prescience, my dear chile. It runs deep through our African veins; take a note, tell family story one day, period, stop! Ain't ya pretty. She looks just like Sandra. Don't she?
ERMINA: You think so?

ERNESTINE: Back home everybody say I look like my mother also.

LILY: That so? . . . Are my bags okay in the hallway?

(She bites into the sandwich. Godfrey reluctantly exits to retrieve Lily's bags from the hallway. Ernestine studies her aunt with a childlike infatuation.)

ERNESTINE: You really my mommy's sister?

(Lily nods.)

I don't see it.

LILY: It ain't the first time I heard that. But I am your mama's sister, don't let the style fool ya, take away this suit and there's still a little country.

(Godfrey reenters with three enormous suitcases. He drops the suitcases at Lily's feet.)

GODFREY: What you got in here anyway?

LILY: My life, darling, and when ya look at it in those terms them bags ain't that heavy. Are they now? *(She cracks up)*

GODFREY *(Mumbled)*: I suppose ya gonna stay. *(He carries Lily's bags into the bedroom)*

LILY: Only if you insist.

(Lights fade on everyone but Ernestine.)

ERNESTINE *(To audience)*: Down home when Rosalind's mother came back from New York smoking cigarettes and her face painted up, the minister declared it the end of the world, oh, I remember the horror he instilled. He preached his longest sermon on the nature of sin. But I'd confronted sin tonight and it didn't seem half bad.

Scene 3

The Crumps' kitchen. Ermina sits in a straight-back chair. Lily heats a hot iron comb on the stove; she takes it off, then wipes the hot comb in a towel and applies it to Ermina's head. Ernestine reads a magazine.

ERNESTINE *(To audience)*: You place two single beds together it becomes big enough for three. The mathematics of the Crump household. I don't know how I got pushed to the middle, stuck on the crack. Just like down home, where the Hendersons were known to squeeze seven to a bed. Many a night we did ponder that puzzle.

ERMINA: Why'd you lose your job?

LILY: Well, babies, a Negro woman with my gumption don't keep work so easily. It's one of the hazards of being an independent thinker. If I've ever had me a job for more than a few weeks then I knew it was beneath me. You see what I'm saying?

ERMINA: Ernie wanna be a movie star.

ERNESTINE: Hush up!

LILY: "Darling Angel, the star of stage and screen, the virginal vixen." *(Laughs)*

ERNESTINE: But I'd change my name to something special. Like "Sylvie Montgomery." Or "Laura Saint Germaine"; that's French.

LILY: Well, pardon me, Miss Bette Davis, when'd you git to be so big and black?

ERMINA: Ooooooo.

(Ernestine wraps a towel around her hair, feigning brushing long silky hair.)

ERNESTINE *(Playfully)*: It runs in the family. But don't you worry yourself. When I'm onscreen I sure can act very white. That's why I'm a star.

LILY: If only they knew you began as a poor colored child.
ERNESTINE: Imagine that.

(Lily laughs.)

LILY: Imagine that. Miss Bette, I must say, I like ya a wee bit better, just a wee bit now, as a colored child. When's your next picture? I hear it's a romance.

(A moment.)

ERMINA: She ain't never gonna make no romance until she get rid of some of the butt.

(Ernestine sucks her teeth.)

LILY: Hush! Romance is overrated. I've known too many women who relinquished their common sense for a dose of . . . romance.
ERMINA: Sister, why ain't you been married?

(Lily laughs long and hard.)

LILY: You're just filled with questions. 'Cause I ain't. *(Tugs Ermina's head straight, wielding the hot comb like a weapon)*
ERMINA: Nobody ask you?
LILY: Nobody ask me . . . Besides, I never plan to marry. How you like that? I'm exerting my own will, and since the only thing ever willed for me was marriage, I choose not to do it. And why take just one man, when you can have a lifetime full of so many. Listen up, that may be the best advice I give you babies. And you needn't share that little pearl of wisdom with your daddy. Now, Ermina, sit still!
ERNESTINE *(To audience)*: We were Lily's family now, kinda like buying flowers from a store without having to plant the seeds.

(Ermina squirms in the chair.)

LILY: Sit still, don't fight me on this. Choose your battles carefully, chile, a nappy head in this world might as well fly the white flag and surrender!

ERNESTINE *(To audience)*: She'd talk constantly about "a revolution" from the kitchen. I's always wondered when this revolution was going to begin and would I have to leave school to fight along her side.

LILY: We're at war, babies. You don't want to be walking around school with a scar across your forehead. You want people to think your hair's naturally straight. That it flows in the wind.

ERNESTINE: How are they gonna think that?

LILY: Pass me the Dixie Peach. When I'm finished you're gonna look just like a little Indian girl.

(Ermestine reaches under the chair and passes Lily the jar of Dixie Peach hair pomade. Lily rolls up her sleeves.)

ERNESTINE *(To audience)*: Would this revolution pit Negro against white, rich against poor? And just how many would die?

LILY: If Jennifer Johnson—

ERNESTINE: Jones.

LILY: Well, that white lady star walked through that door right now, she wouldn't look no better than you or I. She'd look just like them cracker women with their bad teeth and gutter ways. Frankly, I git tired of them telling you how you supposed to look good. I can turn a man's head in any part of this country, hairpiece or not. Ermina, sit still and maybe I can take a little bit of the nap out this kitchen.

(Lily presses the hot comb against the back of Ermina's hair. Ermina lets out a terrible wail.)

ERNESTINE: Just like Mommy used to do.

LILY: She never could handle a hot comb, bless her heart.

(Lily presses the comb to Ermina's head; Ermina wails.)

ERMINA: You trying to kill me?

LILY: Vanity is a weapon. I'm not trying to kill ya, I'm trying to make ya beautiful enough to kill others. There's the difference. *(Lights a cigarette)*

ERMINA: My hair's gonna smell like smoke.

LILY: Hush up, it's good for it, adds texture. Sweetness, open the door so your daddy won't smell the smoke. He can sniff it out hours later like a goddamn hound dog.

(Lights fade on all but Ernestine.)

ERNESTINE *(To audience)*: Smothered in gossamer smoke and dizzying assertions, I wondered, had her revolution already begun? So I went down to the public library round my way, "Revolution, American; Revolutionary War; Revolution, French." But no Negro Revolution. I did find twenty entries on communism in the card catalog, but no books on the shelves. The teacher said, "Select a topic that's close to you." My essay was entitled "The Colored Worker in the United States"; the mistake was using the word "worker" too liberally. The principal called in Daddy Goodness and told him to stop mingling with the Jews at his job and everything would be all right. Daddy didn't bother to tell him that his coworkers were all colored. And the Jews on our block won't speak to us. Well, except the Levys, who if they didn't talk to us they'd have to sit in the darkness on Friday night.

(Lights rise on Godfrey shining his shoes in the living room. Lily sits in the armchair reading a movie magazine.)

GODFREY *(Hushed)*: Whole school thinks I'm a communist. It's all your fault, ya know.

LILY: And I suppose I'm to blame for segregation, war and polio as well.

GODFREY: You can't ever leave well enough alone. It's fine for you and your smart set, but I'm a working man gotta ride the bus each morning.

LILY: Surprised you ain't walking as tight as you are.

GODFREY: Don't change the subject on me.

LILY: Well, hell, Godfrey I ain't said nothing about nothing. I can't help it if that child got eyes and ears, and a mind that ain't limited to a few pages in the Bible. I ain't seen you this spirited since I got here . . . in fact, I think being a communist agrees with you.

(Lily gives Godfrey a few playful jabs. Godfrey feigns laughter.)

GODFREY: That's funny! Try telling that to the fellas at work, ain't none of them speaking to me. *(Pointing to Lily)* This is your doing. Got that old bad magic rubbing off on us.

LILY: Don't get superstitious on me. *(Laughs)*

GODFREY: My little voice told me something like this could happen.

LILY: That little voice got you wound too tight! Shucks, I think you need to come uptown with me and get a little taste of reality.

GODFREY: Sister, I don't care what you think, that's the honest-to-God truth. But I do care what my gals think. *(To Ernestine)* Darling, you gonna have to go up to school and apologize.

ERNESTINE: Why's that, Daddy?

LILY: Ya gonna make the chile do that? Punish her for having thoughts. How are we ever gonna get ahead? Have you read it? It might be a fine piece of writing, Godfrey. Look here, it says—

GODFREY: I don't care what it say, but it upset that white teacher and she seemed like a smart lady.

(Lily makes a show of sitting down to read the essay.)

LILY: I like the way it starts already. Simple, don't bother with them highfalutin words.

(Godfrey snatches the essay out of Lily's hand.)

GODFREY: She gonna apologize!

(Ernestine shakes her head furiously.)

And I'm going to tell you once, then I'm gonna leave it alone: we were doing just fine without your sorta learning. We don't want and we don't need it.

LILY: Well, I promised my mama I'd look after these babies. They need a woman's voice in this house, that's what they need.

GODFREY: Maybe you ain't the right woman.

(Lily stares long and hard, fighting back the urge to respond. Godfrey turns away from her and jots down some notes in his pad.)

LILY: That's right! Go on, ask Father Divine! Ask him what to think.

(Lights begin to fade on a simmering Godfrey, leaving Ernestine and a laughing Lily in separate pools of light.)

ERNESTINE: I . . . Darling Angel, apologize for anything in my essay that might suggest that communism is a good thing. My intent was to deal with the labor movement in the United States, which primarily consists of God-fearing patriotic Americans dedicated to improving the conditions for the working man.

(She crosses her heart. The National Anthem plays.)

I pledge allegiance to the flag of the United States of America . . . *(Her eyes cloud over with tears)*

LILY: I never stand for the National Anthem, don't even know the words. But ya know the tune that git me to my feet every time, that Charlie Parker playing "Salt peanuts, salt peanuts." Chile, I practically conceded to God when he took his sax on up that scale.

(A bebop version of "Salt Peanuts" plays. Lily exits. Lights continue to fade on Godfrey.)

ERNESTINE *(To audience)*: Daddy had become a communist by inference. His fear of God replaced by the fear of the government. If he'd read the essay, then he might have fought a little harder when he was passed over for the promotion and we'd be watching television in the evenings. Down home he fought only once, when he got drunk on a barrel of sour whiskey and went on a drunken tirade. Beaten nearly senseless, he accused the white man who sold him the liquor of allowing the devil to slip into his soul. Mommy calmed his brow with witch hazel and talked him into a gentle sleep. His anger a faint memory at rest.

Scene 4

The living room. Ermina is dressed for a visit to the Peace Mission in a pristine white pinafore. A very drunk and disheveled Lily enters. She accidentally knocks into Ernestine's dressmaker's dummy, which displays the beginnings of a white graduation dress. Lily catches it just as it's toppling over and does a halfhearted cha-cha with the dummy as her partner.

LILY *(Seeing Ermina)*: Oh! YOU STILL UP!

ERMINA: Shh!

LILY: WHY YA UP SO LATE?

ERMINA: It's morning.

LILY: That's what I told 'em. *(A moment)* Where ya going? You playing doctor or something?

ERMINA: We're going to the Peace Mission. Help get ready for Sweet Father's visit.

LILY: He's finally letting you out of the house, and you're going out dressed like that. Little pixies. Oh no, not me. *(Plops down)*

ERMINA: I don't wanna go, but Ernie won't say nothing to Daddy.

LILY: THEN WHY GO?

(Ernestine rushes in. She is also dressed in a pristine white pinafore.)

ERMINA: Shh! Daddy here.

(Lily cackles.)

ERNESTINE: You wanna lie down? Please Sister, wish ya would . . . Don't let Daddy find you this way.

LILY: He's the one that talk to me first. He was leaning against the window smiling at me. He says he's from Cuba, but he sure didn't look like no Desi Arnaz. Black like coal . . . But he do speak Spanish, of course he could have learned it from a correspondence book. Right? Like my friend Janice did. He could of been right from Florida, I'm telling you. He was splendid to look at, hair like a wave breaking, good hair. It just fall flat by itself. And he wasn't no good-time boy, a real gentleman like from your movies, Ernie.

(A slow mambo begins to play.)

He tipped his hat and everything, asked if he could escort me home. I told him up front, "I ain't like those gals standing big-bellied in a state line 'cause they gave themselves for an evening at the Savoy and a pair of silk stockings. I'm a grown woman with a different set of requirements. You see, Mr. Cuba, I'm a thinking woman, I'm communist!" He laughed and said, "Baby, so am I, tonight."

(She stands up. The girls look on with disbelief.)

I danced the mambo. Our hips pressed together. Me and Papo.

ERNESTINE: You did what?

LILY: I danced the mambo. *(Demonstrates the steps)* Oh, gimme your hand, *(Teasing)* Darling Angel.

ERNESTINE: Please don't call me that.

LILY: Hell, ya dressed for the part.

(The mambo music grows louder. Lily grabs Ernestine, wrapping her wiry arm around her niece's thick frame.)

Ya stiffer than a board. Ain't you never danced up close with somebody?

ERNESTINE: Why would I want to do that?

(Lily draws Ernestine in close.)

ERMINA: Daddy ain't gonna like the mambo!

LILY: He a man, I imagine a man invented the mambo.

ERMINA: What about me? I want to do the mambo.

LILY: You too young yet, ain't supposed to get that close to a man's privates, might be a little surprise ya ain't ready for.

(Ermina sucks her teeth.)

ERMINA: Been closer up to a boy than Ernie ever been.

ERNESTINE: You better not have.

(*Lily swings Ernestine around. They continue their dance.*)

LILY: Papo was all shiny and black like a new pair of patent
leather shoes. He kept whispering in my ear, "*Que Linda!
Que Linda!*" How beautiful I was.

(*She and Ernestine dance the mambo, their cheeks pressed
together.*)

How beautiful I was.

(*Blue projector light comes on and begins to flicker.*)

ERNESTINE (*To audience*): I want to cry. I want to be dancing
with Papo. He's slender and dark like the man at the watch
counter at Loesser's.

(*Lily and Ernestine continue to dance an elaborate
mambo. The music stops abruptly. Godfrey stands in the
doorway, horrified.*)

GODFREY: Darling, Devout, go on outside!

ERNESTINE (*To audience*): If this had been a movie, Papo would
have come to Sister's rescue. In the movies, he'd have
been a dashing young doctor, rather than a fishmonger.
He'd have asked my daddy for Sister's hand in marriage.

(*Ermina and Ernestine scramble for their coats.*)

LILY: Oh nigger, don't start with me.

GODFREY: I said, go!

(*Ernestine and Ermina stand by the door, poised to leave.*)

LILY: But we're doing the mambo.

(She reaches for Ernestine's hand. Ernestine is tempted to take it, but Godfrey gives her a look of condemnation.)

I danced with the man, Godfrey. Anything else done was imagined.

(Godfrey takes Lily's arm to lead her to the couch.)

Are ya asking me to dance?

(Lily dances a circle around a steadfast Godfrey.)

GODFREY: Where ya stockings?

(Lily isn't wearing stockings and laughs at the discovery.)

LILY: I don't know.
GODFREY *(Holding his notepad)*: You been drinking?
LILY: I'm drunk.
GODFREY: You know I don't permit drinking here.
LILY: I didn't drink here. I drank before I got here. So it don't count. And Mr. Goodness, don't you go off pretending like you ain't had a drink. *(To the girls)* I remember a particular batch of moonshine that blinded him. *(Back to Godfrey)* Groping in the darkness, I do remember ya gitting friendly with this-here thigh. *(Winks)*
GODFREY: Hush up now, don't want the neighbors to hear. DARLING, DEVOUT, I said, go outside.
ERNESTINE: She's sorry, Daddy. She's just tired.
GODFREY: Tired my behind.

(Lily laughs again.)

Don't make this a joke. You'll git us all in trouble like—
LILY: That's what you'd have them believe. Tell them the truth . . . That's what this is about, ain't it? How come in your

version I always start the trouble, as though I alone single-handedly brought down the ancient walls of decorum and civility in Pensacola. Oh, for God's sake, I ain't the devil, I ain't paying ya sub-minimum wage, Mr. Goodness.

GODFREY: You ain't paying nothing period. And you know this wouldn't happen if you came on down to the Peace Mission; why, you'd understand that liquor and loose moral character are the cripplers of our race.

LILY: When did you get so self-righteous, Mr. Goodness? You used to be able to get a good laugh out of me. Now you're all peace and blessings. *(Directed toward the girls)* Passing judgment on me, like he's above it all. *(A moment)* You wanna know something, I got a secret for ya. *(Whispered)* I hate your Sweet Father.

ERNESTINE *(To audience)*: Oh, she did say "hate." I wish she hadn't, I wish she'd said, "I'm bothered by Father Divine" or "I'm sickened by Father Divine."

GODFREY *(Hushed)*: Pray for forgiveness, for peace of mind. You're lucky Sweet Father loves all, including those who have forsaken 'im. I wish you would go on inside and sleep off this bewitching.

LILY: Sleep it off. Damn it. I can't sleep off this bewitching any more than you can make Sandra rise from the dead or I can return home a virginal bride primed for marriage to an ignorant sharecropper. Picking fruit, damn, my fingers are hurting just thinking about it.

GODFREY: How can you be so disrespectful to Sandra's memory? *(Puts on his hat)*

LILY: I know a few folks that would testify to the fact that you drove poor Sandra into the grave. I can't say I blame her.

GODFREY: ERNESTINE, ERMINA! You heard what I said. GO!

(He grabs his daughters' arms and shoves them into the bedroom.)

NOT IN FRONT OF THEM, YOU DON'T! *(Angrily approaches Lily, thinks, then recomposes himself)* Were you at Sandra's side when she closed her eyes? Where were you when we put her in the ground?

LILY: I own part of that pain.

GODFREY: No, you were up North with your books and your friends and your party.

LILY: Sounds like you're jealous.

GODFREY: Not me!

LILY: Yes, I was up North with my books and friends. Why should I stay someplace that treated me like filth.

GODFREY: Treated you? And I was having a grand ole time baking cakes for Mr. and Mrs. Norton. *(Shaken)* And now you're gonna stand in my home and disrespect the choices I've made.

LILY: I ain't disrespecting ya, Godfrey. Honestly. Just having fun. What have I done, seriously? 'Cause you've purged your life of passion don't mean I got to. If I go to hell, I go of my own volition, not 'cause some preacherman's words sent me there. What have all your prayers brought you anyway? A sorry pair of shoes and an apartment barely fit for human beings.

GODFREY: It ain't enough that you got the whole neighborhood thinking I'm a . . . *(Whispered)* communist. Now you have to unsettle my home with your, your, your—

LILY: What would you like me to do? You want me to apologize?

(She moves toward Godfrey. She leans into him and plants a kiss. He momentarily gives in to the kiss.)

There. *(Breaks into a smile)*

GODFREY: My gals are going to have the best. They're gonna rise above you and I. When you're on my time clock, eating out of my icebox, sleeping under my roof, Father Divine is your leader. His word is grace. You don't like it you can git the . . . you can leave us at peace. I left Florida for a reason, couldn't breathe, couldn't think, couldn't do nothing but go to work, make my dime and drink it down on Friday night. Then I found something that gave me inspiration, gave me strength to make a change. May not be like your change, revolution! Oh, but it do feel that big to me. It soothed my pain and that's all I want right now. It took all the strength I had to take these gals on a train, out their wooden doors and place 'em here in brick and concrete. And I think I deserve some respect and you're trying me, you're trying me.

(He sniffs the air. Lily smiles seductively.)

I smell the liquor and the sweat. I see the jukebox swirling and the cats laughing. *(Begins to laugh, lost in the memory)* I can hear the big sister on stage hollering out her song. Go on, sing! *(Stomps his feet)* But I ain't going there. Taste my lips puffing on a Cuba, talking out my ass.

(He pulls Lily close to him and does a few quick dance steps, then releases her.)

Feel my hands 'round a woman's hips, swaying to the beat. But I ain't there!

(Godfrey storms out the door. Lights slowly fade on a dejected Lily as they rise on Ernestine, swathed in the blue glow of the cinema.)

ERNESTINE *(To audience)*: In the movies the clothing is always perfectly ironed, the seams even and pointed. In the movies, when families argue it is underscored by beautiful music and reconciliation. In the movies, men are heroes, broad-shouldered and impervious to danger. Their lives are perfect formulas resolved in ninety minutes. But as Daddy would say, "They white."

Scene 5

The blue, flickering light rises on Ernestine holding a pair of galoshes in her hand. She is on the stoop in front of the Crumps' apartment.

ERNESTINE *(To audience)*: So Daddy disappeared, went off with just a jacket and a hat. He didn't even take his rubbers and it's gonna rain. It's gonna rain furiously for the next few days. That's all that will be talked about on the radio.

(The blue, flickering light shifts into subway lights, which reveal Godfrey on the IRT train. He sits with his hat pulled over his eyes, asleep. Gerte, a thirty-year-old German woman, sits next to him with her luggage surrounding her feet. She nudges Godfrey. Gerte has the posture of a film star from the thirties and the waning beauty of a showgirl.)

GERTE: Is this the Bronx?

GODFREY: This may well be the Bronx.

GERTE *(German expletive)*: The gentlemen said, "Lady, if you reach the Bronx, you know you've gone too far."

(Godfrey pulls his hat over his eyes. Gerte laughs at her mistake.)

Do you know Pierre Boussard?

GODFREY: Should I?

GERTE: I have his address in New Orleans. I was told I must go to Pennsylvania Station to catch the train. *(Unfolds the address and shows it to Godfrey)*

GODFREY: Probably the case. I wouldn't know.

GERTE: It is far, New Orleans?

GODFREY: It far.

GERTE: I'm from Germany, I recently arr—

GODFREY: How about that, you the first German I seen that ain't in a newsreel.

(Gerte shuffles in her seat. Godfrey moves away slightly.)

GERTE: Do you mind if I talk with you?

GODFREY: We talking already.

GERTE *(Laughing)*: I guess we are.

GODFREY: What, ya trying to git me in trouble?

GERTE: Have I done something wrong?

GODFREY: Oh no! Shove on, sister, I ain't one of those uptown cats. I ain't like those adventurous colored fellas. I'm a family man.

(Godfrey stands up. Gerte self-consciously checks to make sure all of her clothing is in order. The train pulls into the station. Godfrey moves away.)

GERTE: Are you getting off?

(Godfrey does not respond.)

(Panicked) Should I get off here? Which way should I be going?

GODFREY: I don't know where it is ya going, ma'am.

(Gerte stands. The train pulls out. Gerte returns to her seat and begins to weep. Godfrey pulls his hat back over his eyes. A moment.)

(Lifting his hat) Are you all right?

GERTE: No.

(A moment.)

GODFREY: Ya want a cookie?
GERTE: Thank you.

(Godfrey hands her a cookie. She greedily stuffs it in her mouth.)

May I have another?

(Godfrey gives her another cookie.)

These are good . . . Your wife make?
GODFREY: I made.

(Gerte manages a smile.)

Ain't so bad, you'll find your way.

(Gerte nods; Godfrey moves away again. The train pulls into the station.)

GERTE: You're not getting off, are you?
GODFREY: Not yet.
GERTE: Good.

(Godfrey looks down at the bags. He sits back down next to Gerte.)

GODFREY: Looks like you got the world there.

(Darkness. The roar of the train. Gerte screams. Lights rise on Gerte clinging to Godfrey's arm. Godfrey looks at Gerte and untangles her from his arm.)

It's all right, gave me a little scare also. Look at that. Lights
back on.

GERTE: I am sorry. I thought. You don't want to know what
I thought.

GODFREY: It's all right, ma'am.

GERTE: Sorry . . . I'll stop talking to you.

(A moment.)

Please, may I have another cookie?

GODFREY: You hungry?

(Gerte nods.)

Well, over at the . . . Peace Mission. I think I'm heading
that way. They'll feed you if you're hungry.

GERTE: May I follow you? I am sorry. I shouldn't have asked.

(Godfrey looks from side to side.)

GODFREY: If you like, but it's not like we'd be going there
together.

*(Gerte tries to straighten her clothing. She takes a quick
sniff of her underarms, then returns to sitting quietly.)*

GERTE *(Suddenly)*: I am Gerte Schulte.

GODFREY: I am Godfrey Goodness.

*(They shake hands timidly. Gerte slowly retracts her hand.
They quickly look away from each other.)*

GERTE: I am so glad you spoke to me.

GODFREY: Well, it looks like we were looking for the same
place after all.

(Gerte and Godfrey are basked in a heavenly glow; then, the lights fade on them. Lights rise on Ernestine and Lily on the stoop. Lily wears a rain slicker and carries a bucket.)

ERNESTINE *(To audience)*: The water backed up in the yard. What a sight, Lily in her high heels trying to clear the drain, too proud to ask any of the neighbors for help.

LILY: Ya ask white folks for help, and they turn it 'round on ya in a second. Self-deter-ma-nision, there's an uptown word for ya to digest.

ERNESTINE *(To audience)*: Even the drainpipe had become part of the struggle. Then the oak tree at the corner blew down the telephone line and all the neighbors gathered to watch the workmen carve up the three-hundred-year-old tree. "If that ain't a sign," said Lily. It took them three days to clear it and still no sign of Daddy. Our tears salted over and caked our brown faces gray. Lily chipped away the bits of crust with a butter knife, soothing us with the hope that with the death of a great oak comes life.

Scene 6

The empty living room. The front door opens slowly. A cautious, nervous Godfrey steps in carrying a suitcase. He stands for a moment before speaking.

GODFREY *(Singsong)*: GOT SOMETHING IN MY POCKET FOR MY BABIES!

(A moment. Godfrey tips his hat to Father Divine. Ermina and Ernestine enter. They stare at their father, not quick to forgive.)

Ain't ya happy to see me?

(Ermina's leg begins to twitch.)

ERNESTINE: Where you been?

GODFREY: Can I get me a hug or some sugar at least? *(Spreads his arms imploringly)*

ERNESTINE: I don't know.

GODFREY: What about ya, Devout?

(Ermina's leg stops twitching. She quickly approaches her father and throws her arms around his waist.)

ERNESTINE: Ermina!

(Ermina reaches into her father's pocket and retrieves a cookie.)

ERMINA: WELL!

GODFREY: That's my girl . . . Had to clear my head, bring some order to things. I think everything's gonna be all right . . . I got someone for y'all to meet.

(Gerte, wearing a haggard smile, steps into the apartment carrying a suitcase. She clears her throat.)

Darling, Devout, this is Gerte.

(Ernestine and Ermina stare at Gerte.)

My new wife.

(The girls are dumbfounded, caught off guard by the declaration. Gerte gracefully extends her hand as if practiced.)

GERTE *(By rote)*: I'm very pleased to meet you. I'm sure we will get on fondly. I've heard charming stories about you both. Devout, you are as pretty as your father said, and Darling, congratulations are in order for completing your studies this coming summer.

(Both girls gasp. Gerte turns to Godfrey to ensure that she has produced the correct information; he nods affectionately.)

ERMINA: She white!

(Awkward silence.)

GODFREY: Well, should we all sit?
ERMINA: Why? She won't be white if we sit down?

(Godfrey clumsily fumbles for Gerte's hand. The gesture is mechanical, the mark of unfamiliarity.)

GERTE: It is a lovely apartment.
GODFREY: She won't bite. Will ya?

(Gerte lets out a deep belly laugh. The girls continue to stare contemptuously at Gerte, who slaps Godfrey's hand.)

GERTE: I told you not to make me laugh.

(Gerte continues to laugh heartily, without taking a breath for air. Ernestine and Ermina stare at her.)

ERNESTINE *(To audience)*: Oh God, did she have to be German? If he had to have a white lady, why not a French lady or an English lady like the demure Olivia de Havilland with her modest downward glance. But there she is like Marlene Dietrich, a cold bitter whore laughing in our doorway. She might as well be wearing a satin tuxedo and blowing smoke in our faces.

GODFREY: Ain't you going to say anything?

ERMINA: Ya drunk? Ya all right?

GODFREY: Don't stand there looking foolish, say something.

ERMINA: Huh?

GODFREY: Darling.

(Gerte extends her hand a second time.)

Take her hand.

(Ernestine reluctantly seizes Gerte's hand, giving it a hard shake.)

ERNESTINE: Mommy wouldn't like this one bit. Oh no! Mommy ain't even dead a year.

(Gerte ceases to be amused.)

GERTE: I'm sorry. I lost my mother when I was young.

(Lily stands in the doorway.)

ERNESTINE: I don't want you here!

GODFREY: Don't say that, Darling.

(Ermina's leg begins to jerk uncontrollably.)

LILY: What's this all about, Godfrey?

GODFREY *(Defensive)*: We met, we fell in love, we married.

(Blackout.)

❆ Act Two

Scene 1

Limbo. Ernestine, dressed in her finest clothing, stands in a circle of light. She wears a huge black "V" sewn above her bosom.
   Lily, in the living room, gathers some of her personal objects, including her suit.

ERNESTINE *(To audience)*: The revolution still hadn't come even though I peered out the window each day in anticipation. Gerte swept the stoop every day at four, Mrs. Levy turned on the television at five, Daddy went to work at six and Aunt Lily prepared to go uptown to commune with "possibility and the future" at seven.

LILY: How I look?

(Lily, dressed up, peers in a compact mirror and applies lipstick.)

ERNESTINE *(To audience)*: Not a word, not a whisper of Daddy's "Divine" inspiration. Sister was the portrait of calm.

(Lily fixes her hat.)

LILY *(Suddenly nostalgic)*: The scent of the ocean used to travel up to our porch on the back of a nice summer breeze, your mama and I would stand patiently for hours, courting. The boys had to take a number just to knock on the front door, and they'd bring us withered hibiscus. Everyone always said I would be the one to marry early, 'cause I was considered the better looking of the two. Ain't it funny how things work out. Well, hell, I didn't like standing still, and you gotta stand still long enough to attract yourself a man, I suppose. *(Laughs)* Never been interested, outgrew the notion of a family back in '47. How I look? Like an agitator? You ain't listening to me nohow. I'm talking to myself. *(Takes out a flask and takes a quick drink)* You go on to your Peace Mission, I'm not sure Father Divine will understand the mystique of this pretty face. I don't think he'll appreciate that I'd rather spend his dollar on a bottle of bourbon. It's a small price to pay for salvation. *(A moment)* She going?

ERNESTINE *(To audience)*: Whenever a good dose of reality is about to set in, Father Divine descends. Why have conflict when you can feast?

(Lights rise on the Peace Mission. An immense, elaborately set banquet table adorns the stage. The Crump family, including Gerte, are dressed in their finest clothing. Like Ernestine, Ermina also wears a huge "V." The family is dwarfed by the table crowded with prodigious portions of food concealed in silver dishes. Godfrey reads over his list of questions for Father Divine.)

GODFREY: I don't know what question to ask Sweet Father first. I've planned this so long, I'm shaking.

ERNESTINE *(To audience)*: So it is. Awaiting Sweet Father's arrival. Searching for salvation in the tender juices of a mutton chop layered in our favorite mint jelly, God speaks the language of our stomachs.

GODFREY: Amen!

ERNESTINE: Any doubt of Sweet Father's power is allayed by the rapture incited by the lemon tarts at the end of the table.

(Ernestine greedily eyes the platter at the end of the table. The Crump family sits, patiently preparing to feast. Gerte peeks into the containers.)

GERTE: Relish, brisket—

GODFREY: Haven't seen a meal like this since my Uncle Milan passed away and don't you know none of his lady friends would be outdone at the wake. But didn't we find a touch of bliss in his wife's sorrow. *(Beaming)* Isn't this wonderful?

ERNESTINE *(To audience)*: The porcelain dish of butter is now the sacred vessel of salvation.

GERTE: Is so much food necessary? There are starving children in Europe. *(Lifts the lids of containers)* Pudding, dumplings—

ERNESTINE *(To audience)*: We're eating for all mankind.

GODFREY: A communion.

GERTE *(Overwhelmed by the abundance)*: Gravy, peas—

ERNESTINE *(To audience)*: Then, suddenly, in the middle of the feast—

(Gerte rises from behind the table and sheds her dress to reveal a slinky white cocktail dress. She climbs onto the table as music swells. A bright spotlight hits Gerte as she slowly traipses across the table singing "Falling in Love Again." Godfrey, aghast, ceases to eat. Gerte completes the song. All fall silent.)

(To audience) Well, at least I wish she had, but there she sat, eagerly awaiting Sweet Father's arrival and making Daddy proud.

(Gerte returns to her seat.)

We probably would've eaten ourselves into oblivion, but Sweet Father's Duesenberg took a flat outside of Trenton.

ERMINA *(Whispered)*: If he God, why don't he sprout wings and fly here.

ERNESTINE: You tell him!

GODFREY: Don't worry, Sweet Father'll find a way to join us. He knows how long we've been awaiting his arrival. Trust me, he won't let us down.

ERNESTINE *(To audience)*: But he did.

(Godfrey sits, frozen. The others dutifully clear the banquet table around him.)

GODFREY: Wait! I . . . I still got all of these questions I wanted to ask Sweet Father. My pockets are stuffed full of paper.

(The banquet table is removed, leaving Godfrey sitting alone. Godfrey pulls handfuls of paper from his pocket. Ermina exits.)

But he promised and now I got to wait another year before I get the answers. Oh no! If he is the God he proclaims to be, I need his answers now, I need him to help me move on.

ERNESTINE *(To audience)*: He'd followed an address on a bottle of something that soothed him and supposed that potion would be in abundance up North.

GODFREY: Back home, everything was played according to a plan. Right? I knew just how my life would be. I knew everything I needed to know. And now I got me a new pair of shoes worthy of the finest angel and a handful of misgivings.

GERTE *(Comforting Godfrey)*: We came together because of Sweet Father, there is power in that.

(Godfrey slowly exits. Gerte turns to Ernestine.)

(Thinking aloud) But I've been to speakers' corner, there are a half-dozen messiahs waiting to replace him.
ERNESTINE *(To audience)*: Not God, imagine.

(Lights rise on a smirking, laughing Lily. She stops abruptly and lights a cigarette in the shadow of the three gold balls of a pawn shop. She rips off her wristwatch and earrings.)

Lily said God was given to us by a government bent on pacifying the masses with religion. And now Gerte had gone one step further and threatened to take our God completely away.

Scene 2

Brower park. Ermina stands in a pool of light.

ERMINA *(Without a breath)*: Scat cat, hip, jive, cool baby, dip dive. Be bop, shoo bop, de dap, de dop. Give me some skin, babe. Far out, sweet daddy. Hang tight, hang loose, dig this, out of sight, take it easy, you're blowing my mind, everything is copacetic, the most, gonest, funky!

(Lights rise on Ernestine.)

ERNESTINE *(To audience)*: Ermina is discovering the language of the city.
ERMINA: Back off, Ernie, your vibe ain't happening.
ERNESTINE *(To audience)*: Gerte has driven her to hopeless popularity. James Watson, Simon Richards, Lawrence Alleyne and even that Chinese fella. Victory and Virtue.

The third "V" got lost somewhere near Trenton along with Father Divine's Duesenberg.

(Ermina pulls her sweater tight.)

ERMINA: Hush now, I don't want the boys to think we too chummy.

ERNESTINE *(To audience)*: It's finally green like down home. We're supposed to be at the market, but we're in Brower Park. All the teenagers are gathered in clusters arranged by blocks. Near the water fountain is Bergen Street, Kingston Avenue is huddled by the park entrance and it's just me and Ermina from Dean, being we're the only colored people on that block. *(To Ermina)* Don't run off, you hear. Ain't supposed to be talking to no boys.

ERMINA: . . . Oh Ernie, leave me alone, if ya wasn't so prissy maybe a boy might give ya a smile or something. Why don't you go off to the pictures, you're cramping my space.

(Ermina flicks her fingers and turns up her dress. An upbeat Louis Jordan tune plays. Ermina snaps her fingers to the beat.)

ERNESTINE *(To audience)*: I can see the gals whispering about us, "They communist, she father married a white lady."

ERMINA: "What it like living up there with a white lady?" "She make you scrub the floors?" "She really blonde?" "Hear they smell like a wet dog when their hair gets wet?" "She a Nazi like Adolph Hitler?"

ERNESTINE *(To audience)*: The only reason they bother to talk to me is to ask about Gerte.

ERMINA: LEAVE US ALONE, IT AIN'T OUR FAULT SHE WHITE!

(Ernestine smiles. Music continues to play in the distance.)

ERNESTINE *(To audience)*: Well, it's a warm day at least, perfect for a celebration. Somebody got a car radio, can listen to new, hip songs for a change.

(Ermina approaches Ernestine. They dance together. Ermina breaks away.)

ERMINA: I got me four invitations to the dance. I don't know which to choose. It so hard.
ERNESTINE: Daddy ain't gonna let you go nohow.
ERMINA: Maybe that boy over there. He father run a funeral home up on St. John's.
ERNESTINE: He don't look like nothing.
ERMINA: He look like money, plenty good enough for me. *(Smiles gloriously)*
ERNESTINE: Oh, go on, he ain't even looking over here.
ERMINA: Shucks. He looking. *(Gives a "Lily" wave)*
ERNESTINE: Oooo, I'm telling Daddy. He told me to watch you.
ERMINA: Watch what? Who was watching he when he run off and married he-self a white lady. Shhhhh.
ERNESTINE: What?
ERMINA: I do believe Mommy's scratching to get out of her grave. I can hear her nails breaking away at the pine. I wouldn't blame her half a bit if she started a good old-fashion haunting.
ERNESTINE: Ooooo. You taking Mommy's name in vain.

(A moment.)

ERMINA: I ain't listening to ya nohow.
ERNESTINE: Little Miss Sassy. What's wrong with ya?
ERMINA: Nothing. *(A moment)* I'll tell ya something, though, if I had me twenty dollars I'd get Randall's cousin who was in prison to break you-know-who's kneecaps like they done that boy over on Park Place. That way she'd get scared and go away.

ERNESTINE: They done what?

ERMINA: See, if you didn't sit in the house on your behind all day you'd know. Whack! Whack! Yup!

ERNESTINE: Nah!

ERMINA: I hate it up here! Nothing seem like it should be. Nothing! It ain't normal for a white lady to be living in a house with colored folks. She don't even cook right.

(Lights rise on the living room. Gerte stands over the table chopping cabbage. Potted plants and colorful rugs decorate the room in a feeble attempt to brighten the otherwise bleak apartment. The dressmaker's dummy prominently displays Ernestine's graduation dress, which is beginning to take shape. Ernestine pins the hem on her dress. Ermina sits at the table, intensely watching Gerte. She studies the woman with a scientist's scrutiny.)

GERTE: Such a pretty girl shouldn't wear a sour face. You must like complaining very much.

ERMINA: Maybe . . . Was you one of them Jew-hating Germans, them Nazis?

(Gerte stops what she is doing. Ernestine shoots Ermina a cautionary glance.)

GERTE: What sort of question is that?

ERMINA: I don't know, it seem direct.

GERTE: That's ridiculous. What do you think? Who put those thoughts in your head?

ERMINA: Mrs. Levy says—

GERTE: She's an old woman. You think I can bear Mrs. Levy's whispering? The grinder is from the same town as my father. He married a Jewess. Mrs. Levy trusts him with her finest cutlery.

ERMINA: She say—

GERTE: As long as there is rent in the envelope my business is not hers!

ERMINA: Well. (*Snatches up a magazine from the couch and heads toward the front door*)

ERNESTINE: Where are you going?

ERMINA: I'm gonna sit on the stoop and git some fresh air. Someone's a little too persnickety.

(*Ermina flips up the back of her dress and exits. Ernestine continues to work on her dress, periodically glancing up at Gerte. Silence.*)

GERTE: "Persnickety," what is this word?

ERNESTINE: It mean . . . persnickety.

(*Gerte returns to her task.*)

GERTE: Ernie?

ERNESTINE: Yes, ma'am.

GERTE: Why don't you ever speak to me?

ERNESTINE: I don't know.

GERTE: It makes me uncomfortable for both of us . . . to be here and no one says anything. Why don't you go outside with Ermina then? (*A moment*) Don't you have friends, Ernie?

ERNESTINE: No, ma'am.

(*A moment.*)

GERTE: What do you like to do?

ERNESTINE: I like going to the pictures.

GERTE: Me too.

ERNESTINE: I like going with Sister 'cause she always got something wise to say.

GERTE: Maybe we can go together. Your father thinks we are
similar. We both like the pictures. Yes?

ERNESTINE: I don't think so.

GERTE: Why not?

ERNESTINE: The kids in school would talk.

GERTE: I see . . . Ah . . . Your dress is coming along very nicely.
I was looking at the lace you bought and I think it's quite
nice around the collar where the stitching is crooked.

ERNESTINE *(To audience)*: Crooked? My mother could make
the most perfect seams. Almost like a machine.

GERTE: If you want me to help you . . . well . . . I'm not much
of a seamstress . . . I . . . *(Fumbles with the cabbage)*

ERNESTINE *(To audience)*: In the newsreels, the Germans
always wore the ragged faces of our enemy.

(Gerte smiles uncomfortably.)

GERTE: Are you scared of me, Ernie?

ERNESTINE: Yes, ma'am.

GERTE: What do you think? . . . I'm not horrible, really.

ERNESTINE: No, ma'am.

GERTE: I'm just not used to so much silence.

*(Gerte walks over to the radio and turns it on. Swing music
fills the room.)*

ERNESTINE: Daddy don't like music in the house on Sunday.

GERTE: What a shame, it's a lovely radio.

(Ernestine switches off the radio.)

It is so like him to buy something he doesn't use. *(She
chuckles)*

ERNESTINE: He didn't buy it.

GERTE: When I was young there was always music in the
house. My brother played the piano. My father the viola

and I . . . I . . . (*A moment. She returns to chopping cabbage and accidentally nicks her finger*) Damn!

(*Lily, hungover and in her bathrobe, enters and sits down, letting her head rest against the table.*)

Ahh! Late night. We've missed you today. How goes we?

LILY: What do you mean?

GERTE: Are you feeling well?

LILY: Copacetic. And I thought you were asking some deep German question.

GERTE: I'm glad to see you are feeling better.

(*She pours Lily a glass of water from a pitcher. She sets it in front of Lily. Lily quickly drinks down the water.*)

Would you like some coffee?

(*Gerte returns to cutting cabbage. When Ernestine isn't looking, Gerte periodically shoves cabbage into her mouth. Lily turns on the radio, flipping through the stations until she finds bebop. She does a few steps.*)

LILY: Smooth. Huh?

(*Gerte and Ernestine exchange glances.*)

Yeah, bebop. Dig. Listen to that, he takes a melody we've heard a hundred of times and makes it familiar in an entirely different way.

(*Gerte stops to listen.*)

GERTE: Yes. It is wonderful. I like this music very much. I used to hear this colored musician play jazz in Berlin, when I was

a teenager, before the war. Have you ever heard of Pierre
Boussard?

LILY: No.

GERTE: He said he was quite famous in the United States, but
they all say this to German girls. *(Laughs at the memory)* He
played the saxophone beautifully. He was a colored man.

LILY: Yeah, you said that.

GERTE: When I arrived in America, I thought all colored people either played jazz or were laborers. I didn't know. I grew
up in a small town about seventy kilometers from Berlin.
I could tell you the name of every person, man, woman
and child who lived there. Ask me and I could tell you
exactly. I was seventeen, *(To Ernestine)* your age, when
I went to the city and first used a proper toilet. Ya. And in
Berlin, I tasted tobacco and whiskey. Ya. And danced to
"insane" music, as my father called it. "Caution abandoned." And imagine hearing the Negro voice for the first
time on a recording, oh, it was . . . brilliant. *(Groping for
words)* It was freeing to know that someone so far away
could give a musical shape to my feelings. I wanted to visit
America, see the people who create this music. Go West.
The pictures. Same dreams everyone has.

ERNESTINE: Yeah?

GERTE: I thought I was as pretty as the girls in the pictures.
Stupid. *(A moment. She savors the music)* It was wonderful, at least for a while. Then it got difficult, the Nazis, the
war, and things happen just as you're finding yourself. *(A
moment. She turns off the radio. To Ernestine:)* But Godfrey doesn't like.

(Silence.)

LILY: Godfrey don't like the sound of the rainfall. Godfrey
don't like nothing he can't control. Don't you ever want to
scratch up his shoes, crumple his hat?

(Gerte begins to laugh.)

GERTE: I like that he comes home every day at the same time with cookies in his pocket and smelling of sweets. I like that he dresses so finely to go and bake bread.

LILY: Well, I'm glad somebody does. *(Giggles as she retrieves a glass and a bottle of whiskey)* I'm just taking a nip to make my headache go away. You want some, Gertie?

GERTE: Gerte. No thank you, I refrain out of respect for the time of day.

LILY: What are ya talking about? It's three o'clock in the afternoon, bar's been open going on three hours.

(Gerte and Ernestine watch Lily self-consciously wipe the glass and pour herself a generous glass of whiskey.)

What? I don't generally do this, but I've been nervous as of late.

GERTE *(Sarcastically)*: Just how is your . . . "revolution"? Working hard? You're spending a lot of time up at the headquarters in Harlem. Where is it exactly?

LILY: Lenox Avenue.

GERTE: That's right, Lenox Avenue. I haven't heard you mention it in quite some time.

(Lily stands.)

ERNESTINE: Yeah, you ain't said much.

LILY: 'Cause it's liable to end up in one of your essays. You got too much imagination to keep a simple secret. You gotta cigarette, Gertie?

(Gerte glances over at Ernestine, then reluctantly reaches into her apron and produces a cigarette. Gerte returns to chopping.)

A light?

(Gerte tosses Lily a pack of matches.)

GERTE: Godfrey mentioned that you were searching for work? I saw a sign for an agency on Nostrand. If you want I will write down the address when I pass.

LILY: That's very helpful of you. But nobody wants to hire a smart colored woman. And I ain't gonna be nobody's maid. Too many generations have sacrificed their souls in pursuit of the perfect shine.

(Gerte busies herself with cutting again.)

GERTE: My mother used to get dressed every day, no matter whether she had someplace to go or not. Even after she fell ill she'd dress each morning as though the ritual could ward off the inevitable.

LILY: I'll note that. Anyway, my suit's in the cleaners. A nightgown, a Fifth Avenue outfit, it don't matter what I wear. The only thing people see is the brown of my skin. You hear, baby. *(Laughs)* So why even bother to get dressed.

GERTE: Must we always do this?

LILY: What are we doing?

GERTE: Can't you forget our differences behind this closed door. When I see you I see no color. I see Lily. *(She lights a cigarette)*

LILY: Well, when I see ya, I see a white woman, and when I look in the mirror, I see a Negro woman. All that in the confines of this here room. How about that? What do you see, Ernie? You see any differences between us?

ERNESTINE: Yeah.

LILY: There you go.

GERTE: May I say to you both, I have seen what happens when we permit our differences—

LILY *(Enraged)*: Don't lecture me about race. You are the last person on earth I'd look to for guidance. *(Pours another drink)*

GERTE: You are some philosopher, you get strong after a few sips from that bottle.

LILY: What do you know?

GERTE: I nearly starved to death after the war, I know quite a bit about pain.

LILY: Oh, do you?

GERTE: Please, Lily I don't want to have to do this . . . Ernestine, darling, would you fetch me a bowl?

(Ernestine stands up and heads toward the kitchen. Lily grabs Ernestine's arm.)

LILY: You're not a servant and I didn't hear her say "please."

(A moment.)

GERTE: Please.

(Lily smiles triumphantly and releases Ernestine's arm.)

Why do you always rearrange my . . . my intentions?

LILY: You mean reinterpret?

GERTE: Yes.

LILY: These girls must never be made to feel like servants in their own house.

GERTE: I am their stepmother. It is from that authority that my request came. Your imagination gives me more credit than I deserve. *(Whispered)* How long can you slip coins out of Godfrey's trousers or sell off bits of your clothing? I know how much that suit meant to you. I know, because I've sold off things of my own.

LILY *(Suggestively)*: Tell me this, what passes through the mind of a man that won't even touch his wife? What's he running from?

GERTE: We've asked each other no questions. And if his Sweet Father does not permit us to lie as man and wife, then I accept that. I love Godfrey.

LILY: Love, a man like him, shine his shoes more than he talks to his own family.

GERTE: Yes . . . *(Laughs)*

LILY: Well, I . . . know . . . Godfrey.

GERTE: And I know Godfrey.

(Ernestine returns with the bowl. Lily stops herself from commenting. Gerte lifts the cabbage into the bowl.)

Did I offend you, Ernie?

ERNESTINE: No, ma'am.

GERTE *(Snaps)*: Don't call me "ma'am." It makes me uncomfortable.

ERNESTINE: Yes, ma'am.

(Gerte lifts the bowl and exits into the kitchen. Ernestine returns to working on her dress.)

LILY: She don't fool me with her throw rugs and casseroles. She don't know the half of it. *(Impulsively flips on the radio. She stands, holding the bottle in her hand)* Listen to it, Ernie, that's ours. We used to live communally in African villages. That's the truth. And when conflict arose we'd settle our differences through music. Each village had its own particular timeline, a simple rhythm building outward towards something extraordinary, like bebop. And folks would meet at the crossroads with drums, to resolve their problems, creating intricate riffs off of their timelines, improvising their survival. It's a beautiful notion, ain't it? It's more than beautiful, it's practical.

ERNESTINE *(To audience)*: At least I wish she had said that, if the past evening hadn't got the better of her senses.

(Music stops abruptly and Lily takes a drink.)

LILY: My ideas are "premium" in some circles. *(Leans against the dress dummy, watching Ernestine work)* You're fussing with that thing like it was a baby. Ain't you got bored of it yet? *(A moment. She plops on the couch)* Could you get me an ashtray?

ERNESTINE *(Sucking her teeth)*: You need to be moving about, been sleep all day.

LILY: Never mind what I need to be doing. I got big plans tonight. I'm resting up. I'm not just sitting here. I'm thinking.

(Ernestine finds Lily an ashtray, then returns to her task; she's excited to share her work with Lily.)

ERNESTINE *(Ventures)*: Psst, Sister . . . Don't you think Mommy would love this dress? She picked the pattern, you know.

LILY: Why don't you tell me again.

(Lily mouths the next sentence along with Ernestine:)

ERNESTINE: I bet you it's gonna be the prettiest dress at graduation . . . And look here, I nearly got everything right. Except around the neck, but I've put on this lace and you won't even notice that it's crooked. That's what Gerte says, what do you think?

LILY: White people don't have the same flair for fashion that we do. You give a Negro woman a few dollars, I guarantee you, two out of three times, she'll outdress a white lady who has store credit. Look at Gerte, she dresses like a girl without a figure.

GERTE *(Offstage)*: I HEARD THAT!

(Lily giggles.)

LILY *(Whispered)*: Pierre Boussard.

ERNESTINE *(Whispered)*: You hate her, don't you?

LILY: Who? . . . I don't think about her enough to hate her.

(Gerte reenters with a cloth to wipe the table. Ernestine goes back to fussing with her dress.)

ERNESTINE: Sister, it might be nice to add some lace around the sleeves, so it matches.

GERTE: Lace is a lovely touch.

LILY *(Without looking at the dress)*: Lace makes it look prissy and, quite honestly, a little country. Gals are more sophisticated, you want something smart and to the point.

(Gerte exits into the kitchen.)

ERNESTINE *(To audience)*: The lace was the finest in the Woolworth's sewing section. Expensive. We'd gone by to touch it every day after school for two weeks. Finally, Ermina was the one that stole it, that's how girls do up North.

(Lights rise on Ermina. Her leg shakes.)

ERMINA: Mommy would really want you to have the lace. It will make the dress for sure.

ERNESTINE: So she tucked it under her sweater for me. Daddy had recently bought Gerte a pink cardigan with a satin rose and said he couldn't afford it.

(Ermina's leg shakes violently.)

ERMINA: Leg will stop as soon as we get home. Don't worry.

ERNESTINE: Ermina's leg shook so violently on our bus ride home I thought it was gonna come right off. We soaked it in ice and prayed. That night her leg almost fell off.

ERMINA AND ERNESTINE: Please, Lord, forgive us for our sins, it was only this once that we transgressed, but it was for a very important cause.

ERNESTINE *(To audience)*: But that next day when we looked at the lace in the light of our bedroom it was all worthwhile.

(Ermina fades into the darkness.)

LILY: Lace is a hobby for widows and those convalescing. Frilly clothing makes you look girlish, and that's how white people like to see Negroes. They don't want to think of us as adults. So the neckline's a little crooked, that per-sona-lies it.

ERNESTINE *(Wounded)*: What would you have me do?

LILY: You're only gonna wear it one day in your life and then it's over. Why spend so much time sewing the lace around the neckline. It ain't like you're getting married.

ERNESTINE: How would you know?

LILY: . . . All right, so maybe I don't know. Last time I wore white was to my baptism, and ask me whether I still believe in God.

ERNESTINE: Maybe you need to find that dress.

(Lily laughs.)

LILY: Ernie, I have a suit upon which I pinned many hopes. And now that suit is in the cleaners waiting for me to find the money to retrieve it. You see what I'm saying. You expecting too much from that blanched mess of fabric. What's it gonna get you?

ERNESTINE: I'm gonna graduate in it. I'll be grown.

LILY: Grown. You think 'cause you got a diploma you grown. You'll be ready to step out that door in your white dress and get a job or a husband. Only time you go out this house is if the milk is sour or to see one of them stupid picture shows.

ERNESTINE: They ain't stupid. And I'm no more afraid of walking out that door than you are to get a real job.

LILY: Really? So where you gonna go, Miss Bette? Who is gonna open their door to you? Look at you. Oh, I forgot, you'll be a wearing a white dress. With or without the "V"?

ERNESTINE: You're the one that said that looking good is half the battle.

LILY: Did I?

ERNESTINE: I don't like the way that bottle got you talking. Why you getting on me, Sister? I worked so hard on this dress. You think that the only important thing is your uptown politics. You may have more spirit and heart than I do. But some of us don't have ideas that big. Some of us are struggling for little things, like graduating from high school.

LILY: I'm just saying it won't hurt you to get out a little more.

(Ernestine rips the lace off of the collar.)

ERNESTINE: There, are you happy!

LILY: The world gives nothing, Ernie. It takes.

(Lights fade on Lily. Ernestine stands for a moment staring at her dress.)

Scene 3

The living room. Ernestine is startled as Godfrey and Gerte burst through the front door. Godfrey's clothing is disheveled, his forehead is covered with blood and he holds a cloth over his eye. Gerte's brightly colored dress is stained with blood. Godfrey takes off his spring jacket and throws it on the floor, then searches frantically for a weapon. He finds Ernestine's sewing scissors.

GERTE: Don't! No!

(Gerte stops Godfrey from going back out.)

GODFREY: I'll show those bastards! They don't know who they're messing with! I got something for them!

GERTE: GODFREY! *(Shaken and angry; to Ernestine)* I told him not to speak. "Please do not answer them, Godfrey!"

ERNESTINE: What happened?

(Lily and Ermina enter.)

GODFREY: That bastard's lucky I only caught him with the side of my hand. I was outnumbered, that's all. 'Cause any other time I'd—

LILY: You'd what?

GODFREY: There we go, a colored man and a white lady trying to get from one place to another. Minding our own business—

GERTE: I must have caught their eyes—

LILY: I wonder how that happened?

GERTE: You think I asked them to speak? I forced those vulgarities out of their mouths?

GODFREY: Told 'em not to speak to my wife. "WIFE?" Then "nigger."

GERTE: I did not ask them to speak!

LILY: What did you expect?

GERTE: Stupid men! You're beyond that, Godfrey. What do they know about us.

ERMINA: Who done this to you?

ERNESTINE: You hurt Daddy!

GODFREY: Oh, they had plenty to say. Snickering and carrying on. Outnumbered. Folks on the subway nodding like it's all right for them to crack me in the face with a Coca-Cola bottle.

(Ermina covers her ears as though trying to block out the sound.)

ERMINA *(In one breath)*: Scat cat, hip, jive, cool baby, dip dive.
Be bop, shoo bop, de dap, de dop. Give me some skin,
babe. Far out, sweet daddy. STOP! *(She races out)*

GODFREY *(Flustered)*: If . . . If . . . If . . . I had a . . . *(He paces.
He inadvertently bumps into Ernestine's dressmaker's dummy)*
Does this have to be here?

ERNESTINE: Nah, sir.

GODFREY: Then move it!

(The dressmaker's dummy topples over.)

LILY: Why don't you let the child alone. She ain't done this to
you.

(Gerte lets out a few short cries as if gasping for air.)

ERNESTINE: You want me to get the police?

LILY: What are the police gonna do, take one look and be on
their way.

GERTE: Why not get them. I'll tell them what they should do.

GODFREY: Sister's right.

(Lily tends to Godfrey's eye. Gerte tries to take over from Lily.)

GERTE: So where are the warriors in your revolution now?
Why don't they help us? How are we to lead our lives if we
can't go out for a . . . a picture show on a Saturday night.

LILY: Welcome to our world, Miss Eva. You ain't supposed to,
period! Stop! Thought you knew about all these things,
being from Germany and all.

GODFREY: They messed with the wrong man! This is a thick
head, been rolled half a dozen times. But I have a good
mind to go back out there!

(Gerte goes to comfort Godfrey.)

74

GERTE: Why can't they let us alone? What did we do? We were just sitting there going to the pictures. We were just sitting there.

(Ernestine picks up Godfrey's jacket. She reaches into the pocket and produces a handful of crumbs.)

ERNESTINE *(To Gerte)*: I hate you! You did this! *(Pulls Gerte away from Godfrey)* I hate you!
GODFREY: Don't say that, Darling!

(Gerte backs away from Godfrey.)

GERTE: Your head, you need some ice. I'll get. *(Exits to the kitchen)*
LILY: Jesus, I don't want to have to explain to these children where their daddy gone. Father Divine loaded you with thoughts, but forgot to give you the consequences. These are some big issues.
ERNESTINE: She right, Daddy.
GODFREY: I didn't ask you to git in on this.
ERNESTINE: We didn't have no say to begin with.
GODFREY: Oh, you taking her side?
ERNESTINE: Nah, sir. *(Rests the jacket on the chair)*
LILY: You see, Ernestine, that's your America. Negro sitting on his couch with blood dripping down his face. White woman unscathed and the enemy not more than five years back. You can't bring order to this world. You can't put up curtains and pot plants and have things change. You really thought you could marry a white woman and enter the kingdom of heaven, didn't ya?
GODFREY: I'm sorry I can't meet your high expectations. I'm sorry I can't uplift the race. Perhaps you should find better company.
LILY: Are you asking me to leave?

ERNESTINE: He's not asking that, Sister. Are you? No one wants you to go.

LILY: I'm asking him.

GODFREY: I will not give up my needs for yours.

LILY: What are my needs, Godfrey? They seem so basic I can't imagine you'd ever make the sacrifice.

GODFREY: Sandra left me with a half-dozen undarned socks and two gals that are practically women. Only meaning I had was to bring home jars for jam. When she died . . . Whatcha want from me, Lily?

LILY *(Whispered)*: I ain't good enough for you, Godfrey?

GODFREY: You plenty good.

LILY: Then why ain't I the one in your bed? You'd rather take blows to the head and be a nigger to some simple ass on the subway than lie with me.

(A moment.)

GODFREY: . . . You a communist. You trouble's guide.

LILY: And Miss Eva ain't?

GODFREY: We on different roads, Lily.

LILY: Where are you going?

(She moves closer to Godfrey. Gerte reenters.)

Remember back in Pensacola before—

GERTE: Are you all right, darling?

GODFREY *(To Lily)*: I keep telling you, I ain't that man. You insult my wife, you insult me. All 'cause you got these big ideas about race and the world and we don't fit your picture.

ERNESTINE: Daddy, not now. You're—

GODFREY *(Snaps)*: And now you got my children taking up your lead.

LILY: You say that with such contempt for me. I'm getting tired of you constantly berating me with your sanctified notions. I'm sorry for what happened to you and Gerte, but I will never apologize for who I am. And every day in this apartment you make me and the gals feel like we got to. You'd have these children buried along with Sandra. Shucks, I let a memory carry me this far, but even that memory done run out of fuel. Where is my apology? GODFREY? Where is my apology for all the wrongs done to me? *(Brushes past Gerte and exits out the front door)*

ERNESTINE: Sister! Sister!

(She starts after Lily; Godfrey catches her arm.)

Don't let her go. Daddy, you have no cause to treat Sister that way. She . . . she . . . You gonna let her go, you know where she's gonna go.

GODFREY: What can I do? Ernestine. *(Reluctantly takes out his notepad)* Gerte?

(Gerte lifts the rag from over Godfrey's eye.)

GERTE: I'm sorry, I don't know what to do. *(To Ernestine)* Lily need not be a barrier. She is so full of ideas, but you must decide how you feel about me. *(Takes a deep breath)* And I don't see why she is here anyway? Has anyone thought about how that makes me feel? . . . Well?

ERNESTINE: She's blood.

GODFREY: She's my wife's sister.

GERTE: I am your wife.

GODFREY: What? You want me ask her to leave? You're asking me to cast off everything that came before.

GERTE: I have.

(Godfrey jots something down on his pad.)

GODFREY: I'll make a note to speak to her later.

GERTE: STOP! You've assembled lists that run miles and miles. There's an entire closet crowded with paper and scribbles of things you need to know, things you want to do, questions that must be answered. It would take three lifetimes to get through all of it. (*She retrieves boxes of lists hidden beneath the furniture. She rips up the individual pieces of paper*)

GODFREY: What the . . . the devil are you doing?

GERTE: If you'd pay attention to the world around you, you wouldn't have so many questions to ask.

(*Godfrey tries to stop Gerte; they struggle wildly. She throws the papers into the air like a shower of confetti. Godfrey scrambles to retrieve the pieces of torn paper. In the midst of the struggle, they recognize the absurdity and begin to laugh as they throw the papers in air. Ernestine revels in the shower of paper.*)

ERNESTINE (*To audience*): And upstairs, Mrs. Levy watches television, too loud for this time of night, laughing.

(*Laughter fills the stage. Gerte kisses Godfrey's wound.*)

(*To audience*) Showered in my father's uncertainty, no more questions unanswered.

(*Suddenly, blue, flickering light engulfs Godfrey and Gerte, who kiss passionately, like film stars. A swell of music.*)

(*To audience*) We'd recovered my father from Divine only to lose him to passion. The kiss. The transforming kiss that could solve all of their problems. Their kiss, a movie-time solution.

GERTE: Now make a decision!

(Lights fade on all but Ernestine, who stares down at the fallen dressmaker's dummy. She bends to pick it up amidst the slips of paper.)

Scene 4

The living room. Ernestine cleans up the remains of her father's questions.

ERNESTINE *(Reading)*: Sweet Father, we come North with the idea that things will be better, but we end up doing much the same thing. Why does this happen? And where can I find solace? *(Continues to retrieve slips of paper)* Sweet Father, my daughter has shown a liking for the other sex and I don't know how to speak to her, can you give me some words?

(Lights rise on Godfrey as Ernestine continues to scan the questions.)

GODFREY: Can you give me some words. Sweet Father, the . . . the boss keeps calling me "the country nigger," in front of the other men. They laugh and I want so badly to say something, I want to knock 'em clear across the room, but I need this job. Sweet Father, this city confuse me, but all I know is to keep the door shut. Sweet Father, my wife's sister, she living with us and I don't know how long I'll be able to look away. Sweet Father, sometimes I think about sending my gals back home. Sweet Father, I've wed a white woman like you done, I loves her, but I don't know whether my children ever will? Do I gotta make a choice? Will you help me calm my rage?

(Lights fade on Godfrey.)

ERNESTINE *(Reading)*: Will you help me calm my rage?

(Ernestine continues to gather the questions. Lily enters carrying an unopened bottle of whiskey in a paper bag.)

LILY: What happened here?
ERNESTINE: . . . Daddy's questions.

(A moment. Lily looks around the room.)

I didn't know whether you'd come back.

(Lily finds it hard to look directly at Ernestine. She toys with the bottle in her hand.)

LILY: Well . . . actually Ernie, I . . . I have been invited to a conference in upstate New York, Albany area. I been meaning to tell you. *(Continues to toy with the bottle)* They want me to lecture or something like that. They've recognized that I'm an expert on the plight of the Negro woman. I've been thinking about going.
ERNESTINE: I know you got important things to do.
LILY: Chile, I got too many places to go, that's my problem. You know what I'm talking about. I don't have the luxury of settling down, too much to do!
ERNESTINE: You're lucky, Sister.
LILY: Me? Miss Bette, you're the one who's gonna be graduating in a few days. You'll finally get to wear that white dress. I can't wait to see you grab that diploma and march on down the aisle.
ERNESTINE: I'm scared, Sister.
LILY: You can't sit here waiting on the world to happen for you, picking up your father's questions. Let him clean up his own mess. *(Sets the whiskey bottle on the table)*
ERNESTINE: May I have a taste?

LILY: Your daddy wouldn't like—

ERNESTINE: Daddy ain't here.

(Lily pours herself and Ernestine a drink. Ernestine reluctantly lifts the glass, takes a sip and cringes. Ernestine and Lily share a laugh.)

Mommy used to sit with us every evening. We'd get excited about what we had done during the day. Even the simple things became miraculous in the retelling . . . We'd laugh so much, Sister, like now . . . It ain't gonna be like that anymore, is it? I want to go someplace where folks don't come home sullied by anger.

LILY: Nobody likes for things to change, Miss Crump.

ERNESTINE *(Ventures)*: I think I'm a communist.

LILY: Why do you say that?

ERNESTINE: 'Cause don't nobody want to be my friend in school. Can't I be part of your revolution, so folks heed when I walk into the room?

(Lily laughs long and hard.)

LILY: Ernie, I came up here just like you, clothing so worn and shiny folks wouldn't even give me the time of day. I came with so much country in my bags folks got teary-eyed and reminiscent as I'd pass. It was the year white folk had burned out old Johnston, and we'd gathered at Reverend Duckett's church, listening to him preach on the evils of Jim Crow for the umpteenth time, speaking the words as though they alone could purge the demon. He whipped us into a terrible frenzy that wore us out. I'd like to say I caught the spirit, but instead I spoke my mind . . . A few miscalculated words, not knowing I was intended to remain silent. You know what a miscalculation is? It's saying, "If y'all peasy-head Negroes ain't happy, why don't you go up to city hall and demand some respect. I'm tired of praying, goddamnit!" Mind ya, I always wanted to leave. And mind ya, I might not have said "goddamn." But those words spoken by a poor colored gal in a small cracker town meant you're morally corrupt. A communist, Ernie. Whole town stared me down, nobody would give me a word. It was finally the stares that drove me North. Stares from folks of our very persuasion, not just the crackers. You want to be part of my revolution? You know what I say to that, get yourself a profession like a nurse or something so no matter where you are or what they say, you can always walk into a room with your head held high, 'cause you'll always be essential. Period. Stop! But you gotta find your own "root" to the truth. That's what I do. Was true, is true, can be true, will be true. You ain't a communist, Ernie!

ERNESTINE: No?

LILY: Not yet! You just thinking, chile. A movie star can't have politics.

(Lily laughs. A moment. Gerte enters from the bedroom, flustered.)

GERTE: Excuse me. I heard the noise. I thought Godfrey was home. Sometimes I get scared in the dark when he is at work. I fix myself something to eat and I feel better. *(Gives Ernestine an imploring smile, then heads toward the kitchen)*

LILY: Do you want a drink?

(Gerte stops short.)

GERTE *(Surprised)*: Thank you.

(Lily passes her glass to Gerte. Gerte knocks the drink back.)

LILY: Easy does it.

(Gerte refrains from making eye contact with Lily.)

It's a little quiet, ain't it? Wouldn't mind some music.

(Ernestine turns on the radio. Mambo music plays. Lily pours Gerte another drink. The women stand awkwardly for a moment. Lily offers Gerte her hand. Gerte accepts it. The music swells as they are swathed in the brilliant, flickering glow of the cinema. Lily and Gerte do an elaborate mambo.)

ERNESTINE *(To audience)*: At least I wish they had. But there they stood.

(The music stops abruptly. The women stand silently, facing each other.)

LILY: Are you sure you don't want a drink?
GERTE: I should go to sleep, really. *(She begins to leave)* Good night. *(As she leaves, she touches Lily's shoulder)* I wish—
LILY: Please don't embarrass me with your articulation of regrets.

(Gerte smiles and exits.)

(To Ernestine) You're looking a little tired yourself.
ERNESTINE: Will you turn out the light?

(Lily gives Ernestine a hug. Ernestine exits. Lily makes her way over to Ernestine's graduation dress. She rips the lace off of the bottom of her slip and begins to sew it around the collar.)

 # Epilogue

SUMMER

Ernestine stands in a spotlight wearing her white graduation gown, with the ragged lace border around the collar. She holds a diploma in her hand.

ERNESTINE *(To audience)*: The principal says the world is to be approached like a newborn, "handled with care." What he didn't say was what happens when the world doesn't care for you.

(Lights rise on the living room, which is decorated for a graduation celebration. A huge white cake sits on the table.)

GODFREY, GERTE AND ERMINA: Surprise!
GODFREY: I hope you don't mind if I take that diploma down to the job with me, I want to show it off to the boys.
ERNESTINE: Just don't get anything on it.
ERMINA: Better not!
GODFREY: Look! Your favorite cake, three layers, custard filling.
ERMINA: But you gotta open the gifts before anything.

(Ernestine lifts one of her presents.)

GODFREY: Oooo, and I got a surprise for ya also.

GERTE: Not yet, Godfrey.

GODFREY: I can't wait . . . Down at the bakery they need another gal. One word from me and you're as good as in.

ERNESTINE *(To audience)*: Bakery? Imagine a life in the bakery by his side with no greater expectation than for the bread to rise.

(A moment. Godfrey smiles gloriously.)

(To Godfrey) I don't know that that's what I want to do.

GERTE: It's a good job, Ernie, steady.

GODFREY: I . . . I already told the folks at the bakery that you'd be working for them.

ERNESTINE: You should have asked me, Daddy.

GODFREY *(Wounded)*: I don't see what the problem is. You have no job promised and nobody's knocking down this door to ask for your hand in marriage. I'm offering you something wonderful, Ernie.

(Ernestine turns away from her father.)

ERNESTINE: But Daddy, I'm going to Harlem.

GODFREY: Forget about Lily, you follow her you know what you'll be taking on. Don't be this way, it's a happy day. Gerte cooked up a meal and ya got a whole room full of presents.

ERNESTINE: I ain't following Lily.

GODFREY: Then why else would you want to go?

ERNESTINE: Why are you always blaming somebody else? Maybe this doesn't have anything to do with anybody but you and me. You're always making the right choice for yourself, but you never think about how I may feel.

GODFREY: That ain't true. I came North for you gals, please, Darling—

ERNESTINE: I'm not Darling Angel, I'm Ernestine Crump, it says so on my diploma.

GODFREY: I didn't mean it that way.

ERNESTINE: But you did!

GODFREY: Look at you, Ernie. You're my little gal, you really don't know what's out there.

ERMINA: Why ya gonna go?

(Lights slowly begin to fade on all but Ernestine.)

ERNESTINE *(To audience, smiling)*: Poor Ermina. She'll carry my memory in her leg now, a limp that will never quite heal.

(Ermina limps across the room to Ernestine.)

(To audience) The room in the basement. The mourning. The prayers. The dinner table. The television upstairs. The sweets.

GODFREY: You're old enough to make up your own mind. I fed you for years, I took up where your mother left off. If you ain't happy, you've gotten what I can give.

GERTE: Godfrey, she'll be all right.

ERMINA: Let's go outside and sit on the stoop, watch all the white gals in their graduation dresses. Let's go to a movie, forget about all this until tomorrow. Let's go down to Coney Island and pretend to ride the Cyclone. Let's get some ice cream.

(Lights continue to fade on all but Ernestine, who is swathed in the blue, flickering glow of the movies. Gerte sings a few lines from "Falling in Love Again.")

GODFREY *(Singsong)*: I got something in my pocket for my baby.

ERNESTINE *(To audience)*: In the movies the darkness precedes everything. In the darkness, the theatre whispers with anticipation . . .

(She stands, lost and confused on a noisy, crowded street corner in Harlem.)

Finally, Harlem . . . Lost . . . *(To invisible crowd)* Does anybody know how I get to Lenox Avenue? Lenox Avenue? The Party headquarters! You know, Lily Ann Green. Lily Ann Green. Lily . . . *(Holds out a sheet of paper)* Nothing's there but an empty bar, "Chester's." Blue flashing neon, sorta nice. I order a sloe gin fizz and chat with the bartender about the weather. It looks like rain. It's only men. They make me nervous. But they remember Lily. Everyone does. So I tell them, "I've come to enlist, in the revolution, of course. To fight the good fight. I got a high-school diploma. I'll do anything. I'll scrub floors if need be. You see, I care very much about the status of the Negro in this country. We can't just sit idly by, right? Lily said we used to live communally in Africa and solve our differences through music by creating riffs off of a simple time-line building out toward something extraordinary, like . . . bebop." The bartender tells me he knows just the place I'm looking for, address 137th Street between Convent and Amsterdam. And here I find myself, standing before this great Gothic city rising out of Harlem. Black, gray stone awash. At the corner store they tell me it's . . . City College. *(A moment)* In the movies . . . well . . . Years from now I'll ride the subway back to Brooklyn. I'll visit Daddy and Gerte and we'll eat a huge meal of bratwurst and sweet potatoes and realize that we all escape somewhere and take comfort sometimes in things we don't understand. And before I graduate, Ermina will give birth to her first child, lovely Sandra. She'll move home with Nana for a few years and she'll be the one to identify Lily's cold body poked full of holes, her misery finally borne out. Years from now I'll read the *Communist Manifesto*, *The Souls of Black Folk* and *Black Skin, White Masks* and find my dear Lily amongst the pages. Still years from now I'll remember my mother and the sweet-smelling humid afternoons by the Florida waters, and then years from now I'll ride the Freedom Bus back down home, enraged and vigilant, years from now I'll marry a civil servant and argue about the Vietnam war, integration and the Black Panther movement. Years from now I'll send off one son to college in New England and I'll lose the other to drugs and sing loudly in the church choir. *(Lifts her suitcase, beaming)* But today I'm just riffing and walking as far as these feet will take me. Walking . . . riffing . . . riffing . . . riffing.

(Lights slowly fade as Ernestine continues to repeat the line over and over again. A traditional version of "Some Enchanted Evening" plays, then gives way to a bebop version of the song. Blackout.)

END OF PLAY

POOF!

Production History

POOF! premiered at Actors Theatre of Louisville (Jon Jory, Producing Director; Alexander Speer, Executive Director) on March 20, 1993, as part of the Humana Festival of New American Plays under the direction of Seret Scott. The set design was by Paul Owen, the lights by Karl E. Haas and the costumes by Kevin R. McLeod. The stage manager was Julie A. Richardson and the production dramaturg was Michael Bigelow Dixon. The cast was as follows:

LOUREEN   Elain Graham
FLORENCE   Yvette Hawkins

Characters

SAMUEL, Loureen's husband
LOUREEN, a demure housewife, early thirties
FLORENCE, Loureen's best friend, early thirties

Time

The present

Place

Kitchen

A Note

Nearly half the women on death row in the United States were convicted of killing abusive husbands. Spontaneous combustion is not recognized as a capital crime.

Darkness.

SAMUEL *(In the darkness)*: WHEN I COUNT TO TEN
I DON' WANT TO SEE YA! I DON' WANT TO HEAR
YA! ONE, TWO, THREE, FOUR—
LOUREEN *(In the darkness)*: DAMN YOU TO HELL, SAM-
UEL!

(A bright flash.
Lights rise. A huge pile of smoking ashes rests in the mid-
dle of the kitchen. Loureen, a demure housewife in her early
thirties, stares down at the ashes incredulously. She bends
and lifts a pair of spectacles from the remains. She ever so
slowly backs away.)

Samuel? Uh! *(Places the spectacles on the kitchen table)*
Uh! . . . Samuel? *(Looks around)* Don't fool with me now.
I'm not in the mood. *(Whispers)* Samuel? I didn't mean it
really. I'll be good if you come back . . . Come on now,
dinner's waiting. *(Chuckles, then stops abruptly)* Now stop
your foolishness . . . And let's sit down. *(Examines the spec-*
tacles) Uh! *(Softly)* Don't be cross with me. Sure I forgot

93

to pick up your shirt for tomorrow. I can wash another, I'll do it right now. Right now! Sam? . . . *(Cautiously)* You hear me! *(Awaits a response)* Maybe I didn't ever intend to wash your shirt. *(Pulls back as though about to receive a blow; a moment)* Uh! *(Sits down and dials the telephone)* Florence, honey, could you come on down for a moment. There's been a . . . little . . . accident . . . Quickly please. Uh!

(Loureen hangs up the phone. She gets a broom and a dust pan. She hesitantly approaches the pile of ashes. She gets down on her hands and knees and takes a closer look. A fatuous grin spreads across her face. She is startled by a sudden knock on the door. She slowly walks across the room like a possessed child. Loureen lets in Florence, her best friend and upstairs neighbor. Florence, also a housewife in her early thirties, wears a floral housecoat and a pair of oversized slippers. Without acknowledgment Loureen proceeds to saunter back across the room.)

FLORENCE: HEY!

LOUREEN *(Pointing at the ashes)*: Uh! . . . *(She struggles to formulate words, which press at the inside of her mouth, not quite realized)* Uh! . . .

FLORENCE: You all right? What happened? *(Sniffs the air)* Smells like you burned something? *(Stares at the huge pile of ashes)* What the devil is that?

LOUREEN *(Hushed)*: Samuel . . . It's Samuel, I think.

FLORENCE: What's he done now?

LOUREEN: It's him. It's him. *(Nods her head repeatedly)*

FLORENCE: Chile, what's wrong with you? Did he finally drive you out your mind? I knew something was going to happen sooner or later.

LOUREEN: Dial 911, Florence!

FLORENCE: Why? You're scaring me!

LOUREEN: Dial 911!

(Florence picks up the telephone and quickly dials.)

I think I killed him.

(Florence hangs up the telephone.)

FLORENCE: What?
LOUREEN *(Whimpers)*: I killed him! I killed Samuel!
FLORENCE: Come again? . . . He's dead dead?

(Loureen wrings her hands and nods her head twice, mouthing "dead dead." Florence backs away.)

No, stop it, I don't have time for this. I'm going back upstairs. You know how Samuel hates to find me here when he gets home. You're not going to get me this time. *(Louder)* Y'all can have your little joke, I'm not part of it! *(A moment. She takes a hard look into Loureen's eyes; she squints)* Did you really do it this time?
LOUREEN *(Hushed)*: I don't know how or why it happened, it just did.
FLORENCE: Why are you whispering?
LOUREEN: I don't want to talk too loud—something else is liable to disappear.
FLORENCE: Where's his body?
LOUREEN *(Points to the pile of ashes)*: There! . . .
FLORENCE: You burned him?
LOUREEN: I DON'T KNOW! *(Covers her mouth as if to muffle her words; hushed)* I think so.
FLORENCE: Either you did or you didn't, what you mean you don't know? We're talking murder, Loureen, not oven settings.
LOUREEN: You think I'm playing?

FLORENCE: How many times have I heard you talk about
being rid of him. How many times have we sat at this very
table and laughed about the many ways we could do it
and how many times have you done it? None.

LOUREEN (*Lifting the spectacles*): A pair of cheap spectacles,
that's all that's left. And you know how much I hate these.
You ever seen him without them, no! . . . He counted to
four and disappeared. I swear to God!

FLORENCE: Don't bring the Lord into this just yet! Sit down
now . . . What you got to sip on?

LOUREEN: I don't know whether to have a stiff shot of scotch
or a glass of champagne.

(*Florence takes a bottle of sherry out of the cupboard and
pours them each a glass. Loureen downs hers, then holds
out her glass for more.*)

He was . . .

FLORENCE: Take your time.

LOUREEN: Standing there.

FLORENCE: And?

LOUREEN: He exploded.

FLORENCE: Did that muthafucka hit you again?

LOUREEN: No . . . he exploded. Boom! Right in front of me.
He was shouting like he does, being all colored, then he
raised up that big crusty hand to hit me, and poof, he was
gone . . . I barely got words out and I'm looking down at a
pile of ash.

(*Florence belts back her sherry. She wipes her forehead and
pours them both another.*)

FLORENCE: Chile, I'll give you this, in terms of color you've
matched my husband Edgar, the story king. He came in at
six Sunday morning, talking about he'd hit someone with

his car, and had spent all night trying to outrun the police. I felt sorry for him. It turns out he was playing poker with his paycheck no less. You don't want to know how I found out . . . But I did.

LOUREEN: You think I'm lying?

FLORENCE: I certainly hope so, Loureen. For your sake and my heart's.

LOUREEN: Samuel always said if I raised my voice something horrible would happen. And it did. I'm a witch . . . the devil spawn!

FLORENCE: You've been watching too much television.

LOUREEN: Never seen anything like this on television. Wish I had, then I'd know what to do . . . There's no question, I'm a witch. (Looks at her hands with disgust)

FLORENCE: Chile, don't tell me you've been messing with them mojo women again? What did I tell ya.

(Loureen, agitated, stands and sits back down.)

LOUREEN: He's not coming back. Oh no, how could he? It would be a miracle! Two in one day . . . I could be canonized. Worse yet, he could be . . . All that needs to happen now is for my palms to bleed and I'll be eternally remembered as Saint Loureen, the patron of battered wives. Women from across the country will make pilgrimages to me, laying pies and pot roast at my feet and asking the good saint to make their husbands turn to dust. How often does a man like Samuel get damned to hell, and go?

(She breaks down. Florence moves to console her friend, then realizes that Loureen is actually laughing hysterically.)

FLORENCE: You smoking crack?

LOUREEN: Do I look like I am?

FLORENCE: Hell, I've seen old biddies creeping out of crack houses, talking about they were doing church work.

LOUREEN: Florence, please be helpful, I'm very close to the edge! . . . I don't know what to do next! Do I sweep him up? Do I call the police? Do I . . .

(The phone rings.)

Oh God.

FLORENCE: You gonna let it ring?

(Loureen reaches for the telephone slowly.)

LOUREEN: NO! *(Holds the receiver without picking it up, paralyzed)* What if it's his mother? . . . She knows!

(The phone continues to ring. They sit until it stops. They both breathe a sigh of relief.)

I should be mourning, I should be praying, I should be thinking of the burial, but all that keeps popping into my mind is what will I wear on television when I share my horrible and wonderful story with a studio audience . . . *(Whimpers)* He's made me a killer, Florence, and you remember what a gentle child I was. *(Whispers)* I'm a killer, I'm a killer, I'm a killer.

FLORENCE: I wouldn't throw that word about too lightly even in jest. Talk like that gets around.

LOUREEN: You think they'll lock me up? A few misplaced words and I'll probably get the death penalty, isn't that what they do with women like me, murderesses?

FLORENCE: Folks have done time for less.

LOUREEN: Thank you, just what I needed to hear!

FLORENCE: What did you expect, that I was going to throw up my arms and congratulate you? Why'd you have to go and lose your mind at this time of day, while I got a pot of rice on the stove and Edgar's about to walk in the door and wonder where his goddamn food is. *(Losing her cool)* And he's going to start in on me about all the nothing I've been doing during the day and why I can't work and then he'll mention how clean you keep your home. And I don't know how I'm going to look him in the eye without . . .

LOUREEN: I'm sorry, Florence. Really. It's out of my hands now.

(She takes Florence's hand and squeezes it.)

FLORENCE *(Regaining her composure)*: You swear on your right tit?

LOUREEN *(Clutching both breasts)*: I swear on both of them!

FLORENCE: Both your breasts, Loureen! You know what will happen if you're lying. *(Loureen nods; hushed)* Both your breasts Loureen?

LOUREEN: Yeah!

FLORENCE *(Examines the pile of ashes, then shakes her head)*: Oh sweet, sweet Jesus. He must have done something truly terrible.

LOUREEN: No more than usual. I just couldn't take being hit one more time.

FLORENCE: You've taken a thousand blows from that man, couldn't you've turned the cheek and waited. I'd have helped you pack. Like we talked about.

(A moment.)

LOUREEN: Uh! . . . I could blow on him and he'd disappear across the linoleum. *(Snaps her fingers)* Just like that. Should I be feeling remorse or regret or some other "R" word? I'm strangely jubilant, like on prom night when Samuel and I first made love. That's the feeling! *(The women lock eyes)* Uh!

FLORENCE: Is it . . .

LOUREEN: Like a ton of bricks been lifted from my shoulders, yeah.

FLORENCE: Really?

LOUREEN: Yeah!

(Florence walks to the other side of the room.)

FLORENCE: You bitch!

LOUREEN: What?

FLORENCE: We made a pact.

LOUREEN: I know.

FLORENCE: You've broken it . . . We agreed that when things got real bad for both of us we'd . . . you know . . . together . . . Do I have to go back upstairs to that? . . . What next?

LOUREEN: I thought you'd tell me! . . . I don't know!

FLORENCE: I don't know!

LOUREEN: I don't know!

(Florence begins to walk around the room, nervously touching objects. Loureen sits, wringing her hands and mumbling softly to herself.)

FLORENCE: Now you got me, Loureen, I'm truly at a loss for words.

LOUREEN: Everybody always told me, "Keep your place, Loureen." My place, the silent spot on the couch with a wine cooler in my hand and a pleasant smile that warmed the heart. All this time I didn't know why he was so afraid for me to say anything, to speak up. Poof! . . . I've never been by myself, except for them two weeks when he won the office pool and went to Reno with his cousin Mitchell. He wouldn't tell me where he was going until I got that postcard with the cowboy smoking a hundred cigarettes . . . Didn't Sonny Larkin look good last week at Caroline's? He looked good, didn't he . . .

(Florence nods. She nervously picks up Samuel's jacket, which is hanging on the back of the chair. She clutches it unconsciously.)

NO! No! Don't wrinkle that, that's his favorite jacket. He'll kill me. Put it back!

(Florence returns the jacket to its perch. Loureen begins to quiver.)

I'm sorry. *(She grabs the jacket and wrinkles it up)* There! *(She then digs into the coat pockets and pulls out his wallet and a movie stub)* Look at that, he said he didn't go to the movies last night. Working late. *(Frantically thumbs through his wallet)* Picture of his motorcycle, Social Security card, driver's license, and look at that from our wedding. *(Smiling)* I looked good, didn't I? *(She puts the pictures back in the wallet and holds the jacket up to her face)* There were some good things. *(She then sweeps her hand over the jacket to remove the wrinkles, and folds it ever so carefully, and finally throws it in the garbage)* And out of my mouth those words made him disappear. All these years and just words, Florence. That's all they were.

FLORENCE: I'm afraid I won't ever get those words out. I'll start resenting you, honey. I'm afraid won't anything change for me.

LOUREEN: I been to that place.

FLORENCE: Yeah? But now I wish I could relax these old lines *(Touches her forehead)* for a minute maybe. Edgar has never done me the way Samuel did you, but he sure did take the better part of my life.

LOUREEN: Not yet, Florence.

FLORENCE *(Nods)*: I have the children to think of . . . right?

LOUREEN: You can think up a hundred things before . . .

FLORENCE: Then come upstairs with me . . . we'll wait together for Edgar and then you can spit out your words and . . .

LOUREEN: I can't do that.

FLORENCE: Yes you can. Come on now.

(Loureen shakes her head no.)

Well, I guess my mornings are not going to be any different.

LOUREEN: If you can say for certain, then I guess they won't be. I couldn't say that.

FLORENCE: But you got a broom and a dust pan, you don't need anything more than that . . . He was a bastard and nobody will care that he's gone.

LOUREEN: Phone's gonna start ringing soon, people are gonna start asking soon, and they'll care.

FLORENCE: What's your crime? Speaking your mind?

LOUREEN: Maybe I should mail him to his mother. I owe her that. I feel bad for her, she didn't understand how it was. I can't just throw him away and pretend like it didn't happen. Can I?

FLORENCE: I didn't see anything but a pile of ash. As far as I know you got a little careless and burned a chicken.

LOUREEN: He was always threatening not to come back.

FLORENCE: I heard him.

LOUREEN: It would've been me eventually.

FLORENCE: Yes.

LOUREEN: I should call the police, or someone.

FLORENCE: Why? What are you gonna tell them? About all those times they refused to help, about all those nights you slept in my bed 'cause you were afraid to stay down here? About the time he nearly took out your eye 'cause you flipped the television channel?

LOUREEN: No.

FLORENCE: You've got it, girl!

LOUREEN: Good-bye to the fatty meats and the salty food. Good-bye to the bourbon and the bologna sandwiches. Good-bye to the smell of his feet, his breath and his bowel movements . . . (*A moment. She closes her eyes and, reliving a horrible memory, she shudders*) Good-bye. (*Walks over to the pile of ashes*) Samuel? . . . Just checking.

FLORENCE: Good-bye Samuel.

(*They both smile.*)

LOUREEN: I'll let the police know that he's missing tomorrow . . .

FLORENCE: Why not the next day?

LOUREEN: Chicken's warming in the oven, you're welcome to stay.

FLORENCE: Chile, I got a pot of rice on the stove, kids are probably acting out . . . and Edgar, well . . . Listen, I'll stop in tomorrow.

LOUREEN: For dinner?

FLORENCE: Edgar wouldn't stand for that. Cards maybe.

LOUREEN: Cards.

(*The women hug for a long moment. Florence exits. Loureen stands over the ashes for a few moments contemplating what to do. She finally decides to sweep them under the carpet, and then proceeds to set the table and sit down to eat her dinner.*)

END OF PLAY

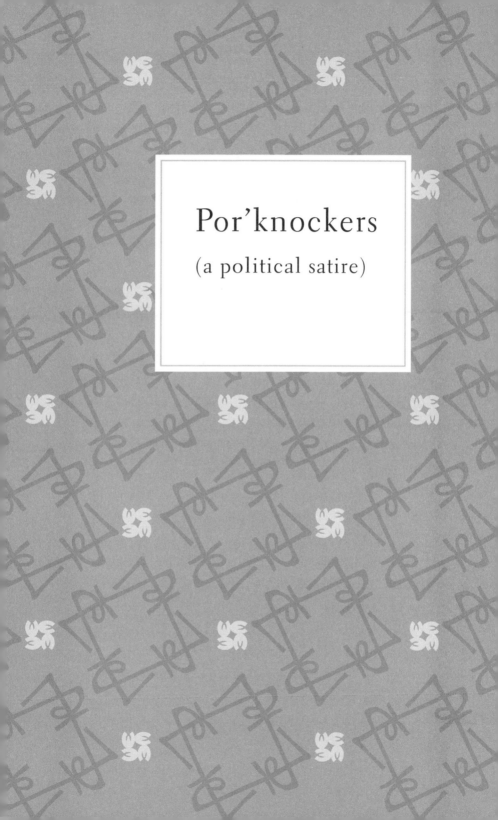

Por'knockers

(a political satire)

Pork-knockers or por'knockers are associated with legends of endurance and the capacity to absorb the fear of terrifying elements to which they are exposed. They are now on the verge of extinction in the rain forests of Guyana and South America where, for generations, they "panned" the creeks and riverbanks for gold.

Their time ceases with the arrival of machineries and great mining companies.

When game was scarce or rations at a low ebb, the por'-knocker literally hammered on every barrel in his campsite for remaining vestiges of pork or meat. He knocked or drummed on the barrel as if it were the deck of a ship.

Ships are symbolic to por'knockers who are often of mixed heritage and blood. Their antecedents were both slaves through the Middle Passage and great navigators in the mold of Magellan.

The vanishing por'knocker is a paradox as the twentieth century draws to a close.

He is a father figure of new wildernesses in great cities.

He asserts his kinship with the poor of all races and with great navigators of olden times who were driven to "pork-knock" the high seas for shrimp or fish when their vessels were becalmed and hunger stared them in the face.

—*Wilson Harris*

Wilson Harris is a celebrated author of Caribbean fiction and non-fiction, focusing on his native Guyana.

This note was written for the accompanying program to DTW's 1994 production.

Production History

Por'knockers received a workshop production at Dance Theater Workshop in New York City (David White, Artistic Director) as a part of DTW's First Light program, curated by Chiori Miyagawa and George Emilio Sanchez, in September 1994 under the direction of Michael Rogers. The design concept was by Terry Chandler and the sound by Chris Todd. The cast was as follows:

LANCE	Byron Utley
KWAMI	Lou Ferguson
AHMED	Earl Nash
TAMARA	Kelly Taffe
JAMES	Ramon Moses
LEWIS	Richard Topol

Por'knockers received its world premiere at the Vineyard Theatre in New York City (Douglas Aibel, Artistic Director; Jon Nakagawa, Managing Director) in November 1995 under the direction of Michael Rogers. The set design was by G.W. Mercier, the lights by Phil Monat, the sound by Aural Fixation and the costumes by Candice Donnelly. The production stage manager was Robin C. Gillette and the production manager was Mark Lorenzen. The cast was as follows:

LANCE	Ray Ford
KWAMI	Afemo Omilami

AHMED	Earl Nash
TAMARA	Sanaa Lathan
JAMES	Ramon Melindez Moses
LEWIS	Daniel Zelman

Characters

LANCE, coal-black Guyanese gold miner, twenties

KWAMI, Guyanese-American man, early forties

AHMED, African-American man, early twenties

TAMARA, African-American woman, late twenties/early thirties

JAMES, African-American man, early thirties

LEWIS, Jewish-American man, early thirties

Time

1995

Place

The play's action moves between the Guyana rain forest and a
stark apartment in East New York.

A Note

Por'knockers is a political satire, written prior to Oklahoma
City and 9/11.

Prologue

A tropical rain forest in Guyana, the not so distant past.

The sounds of the forest and rushing water.

Lance, a coal-black man in ragged Fruit of the Loom underwear, goes through the elaborate motions of panning for gold in a muddy riverbed. He moves with the highly ritualized motions of a man overly familiar with the terrain. He never looks up from his work, from his dance.

KWAMI *(Amplified voiceover)*: Wading knee-deep in muddy water, shaking a rusty tin pan in an eternal rhythm, he feared he'd never find the end. How had he come to be standing there?

(Lance stands erect, contemplating his situation.)

LANCE: Uh?

KWAMI *(Amplified voiceover)*: He'd stood in the very same posture every day since the rains ended. He'd moved tons of mud and let gallons of water slip between his fingers, all for that tiny speckle of fortune. Would the forest ever quiet long enough for him to think?

(Lance dips his pan into the water and shakes it, swirls it around. A moment.
   Darkness. Silence.)

Scene 1

Brooklyn, New York. 1995.
Darkness. Silence.

KWAMI *(In the darkness)*: One Mississippi, two Mississippi, three Mississippi, four Mississippi, five Mississippi, six Mississippi, seven Mississippi, eight Mississippi, nine Mississippi, ten Mississippi, eleven Mississippi, twelve Mississippi, thirteen Mississippi, fourteen Mississippi, fifteen Mississippi, sixteen Mississippi, seventeen Mississippi, eighteen Mississippi, nineteen Mississippi, twenty Mississippi . . . *(Continues)* . . . thirty Mississippi, thirty-one . . .

(Lights up: a dangling light bulb.
   It is a stark, dimly-lit room with a table, several chairs and venetian blinds stained yellow. On the table is a rotary telephone, practically an antique. In the corner of the room is a refrigerator. Nothing hangs on the walls except a Chinese bank calendar from 1991.
   A weed, unnoticed, pushes through the floorboards.
   Kwami, a middle-aged man in a dark blue suit, sits facing Ahmed, a young man with a bald head wearing an ill-fitting dark blue suit, who sits holding his breath. The suit, in fact, looks as though it might belong to Kwami.
   Ahmed lets go of his breath and gasps for air.)

Told ya, brother! No way you'd survive.
AHMED: Come on man, you counted too slowly. That was at least a minute.

KWAMI: Thirty-one seconds . . . you'd be dead.

AHMED: Yeah? And you wouldn't?

KWAMI: I've prepared myself for disaster. This is a fortified body, 'tain't just pretty.

(Kwami displays his muscular chest. Ahmed fidgets in his chair.)

AHMED: Fuck that shit. Ain't never gonna hafta hold my breath for more than a few seconds.

(Kwami makes quick flicks of his tongue. Then slurps and winks. Ahmed sucks his teeth and dismisses the action with a wave of his hand.)

KWAMI: A warrior leaves nothing to chance.

AHMED: Not the warrior speech today! I'm tired of that shit!

KWAMI: You can't shut out your ancestors.

(An elaborate coded knock sounds. Kwami opens the door. Tamara enters carrying two six packs of beer and a briefcase. Tamara wears a well-tailored blue business suit with a red Gucci scarf around her neck.)

TAMARA: Beer.

AHMED: You're just in time, he's about to give his warrior speech.

TAMARA *(Expressionless)*: Hooray. Gather women and children.

(Ahmed breaks into laughter. Kwami gives Ahmed a blank stare and Ahmed abruptly stops laughing. He turns his focus to Tamara. She places the beer in the refrigerator.)

AHMED: What's up with that?

TAMARA: For after. I thought maybe we might want to celebrate.

(A moment. Silence.)

AHMED: Yo, why I gotta to hold my breath for more than thirty-one seconds? Ain't no rhyme or reason: ain't no river to be crossed, ain't no ocean in East New York. Tell 'em Tam—

TAMARA: No names. Because you might. You never know when you'll find yourself in deep water.

(Ahmed flicks his wrist at Tamara and moves to the other side of the room to sulk.
Kwami does not respond. He lights a cigarette.)

AHMED: Where the fuck are they?

TAMARA: It's a holiday.

KWAMI: Patience, they'll get here.

(Tamara checks her watch and sits down.)

TAMARA: The subway. Pen. Paper. If you'd written a quick note to your assemblyman last November, maybe they'd have been here already.

(Tamara smiles. The loud coded knock sounds again.
Hesitation.
Kwami opens the door, and James bursts in with frenetic energy. He carries a tattered briefcase, which he abruptly drops to the ground near the door. He is stylishly dressed in a double-breasted dark blue suit, a burgundy tie and a leather cap cocked to the side. He launches into speaking without acknowledging anyone in the room.)

JAMES: Jesus, I think someone's following me. Can you believe it? *(Peeks through the blinds)* Since this morning at the coffee shop. White guy with a Redskins jacket, a fucking Redskins jacket in East New York. I didn't notice him until I got to the Utica Avenue stop. He kept peering up at me from his newspaper, *The New York Times. The New*

York fucking *Times*, very conspicuous once you pass the
Grand Army Plaza station. Ain't no white folks this deep
in the hood.

TAMARA *(Jokingly)*: Maybe he found you attractive.

JAMES: Oh no, I recognized his type . . . Redskins jacket . . .
Washington, D.C. Keep up with me, folks.

(Ahmed peaks through the blinds again.)

AHMED: There's no one out there. Why you always got to enter
a room like that? You always got to raise the level of anxi-
ety. Why can't you ever just enter, say hello and then shut
the fuck up!

JAMES: And hello to you.

(James nods hello to each person.)

KWAMI: Thirty-one seconds . . .

AHMED: Don't start!

KWAMI: Baby brother's mad 'cause he can't hold his breath for
more than thirty-one seconds.

AHMED *(Angered)*: I ain't mad! Now! Why you startin' with me?

TAMARA: Don't let them take you there, baby! You know they
will if you let them.

AHMED: That's right. I ain't mad.

*(James sits down at the table and nervously digs into his
pocket for a nail file.)*

JAMES: I could have been followed. Might as well have been if
I think that I was, right? Remember when I was collecting
disability from the city? You remember when I strained
my back, remember that? They had a private eye up my
ass every time I stepped out of my front door: at the bodega, at the laundromat, at the muthafucking supermarket,

watching me like a hawk to make sure I wasn't lifting any-thing heavy, like I'm damn fool. Man, they watching every penny. Make a working man a criminal. I'd peek over my shoulder and a dude would be down the aisle salivating over Chips Ahoy! cookies. I'd spend hours in the super-market just to mess with him. I wouldn't buy nothing, just wander aimlessly down the aisles looking at shit! Just to get him angry. *(Cracks open a beer)* Just what I needed. *(Knocks it back in one swallow)*

TAMARA: That was for after.

(A moment.)

JAMES *(Apologetically)*: I didn't realize. *(Sets the empty beer down)* So I do a little celebrating now. Hell, I—

(Tamara stares down at her watch.)

KWAMI: It's almost time to go.
TAMARA: Do you really think you should be drinking?

(James wipes his mouth.)

JAMES: Sorry.
TAMARA: Always.
JAMES: Where's—
KWAMI: He'll be here soon.
AHMED: How come we always got to wait on him?
KWAMI: He's coming from Manhattan.
TAMARA: Holiday!

(The coded knock sounds on the door. Kwami opens the door.
Lewis, a white man in his early twenties, steps in. He wears a dark blue tailored suit and carries an expensive briefcase. He is clearly out of breath.)

LEWIS: I had to run from the train station. Who chose to meet here? I thought we were going to meet in the city. East New York, do you know what it's like for a white guy wearing a suit in East New York? Everybody kept looking at me like I was a cop on the take or the landlord coming to collect . . . I'm sorry, it's probably me projecting. I don't know why I felt that way. Hell, they probably didn't give me a second thought. I have to put that in check, that's the white man in me, I mean, I am a white man, so it's not the white man in me, it's just me. But you know what I mean? I thought we were going to meet in Manhattan. *(Takes out a handkerchief and dabs his forehead)*

KWAMI: I changed my mind.

LEWIS: Is there a bathroom here?

(Kwami points to the side door. Lewis rushes in. They all stand and straighten their clothing.)

AHMED: You see the way he just walked in, didn't acknowledge nobody? Didn't throw out any respect. I told you about him. No apology or nothing like he expects that we'd be waiting on him. I'm gonna teach that boy a lesson one of these days.

KWAMI: Calm! We don't need that energy now!

AHMED: Yeah, but you'll see . . . Don't come to me if something happen. I'm watching him!

(He continues to mumble beneath his breath. He walks up to the bathroom door.)

We gotta wait on you some more?

(Lewis reemerges. He stands face to face with Ahmed. Lewis smiles.)

LEWIS: Ready?

AHMED: We been ready.

KWAMI: We have everything?

(*They all nod and lift their briefcases. Blackout. The sound of the forest.*)

Scene 2

The tropical rain forest.

A blast of thunder, followed by a streak of lightning.

Lights rise on Lance knee-deep in muddy water, digging, frenzied.

He stops for a moment to wipe his brow. He's frightened.

Another crash of thunder is followed by the sound of a heavy downpour.

LANCE: NOOO! NOOOO! Not yet!

(*Blackout. Silence.*)

Scene 3

The room. Crickets. Distant thunder can be heard from outside.

Ahmed, Kwami, Lewis and Tamara are scattered about the room. They are wet. Ahmed fiddles with a portable radio with clumsy anticipatory fingers, excited.

AHMED: Did you see that shit? Did you hear it? Glass shattered everywhere, rained down like confetti. It was the joint.

(*He looks to Kwami, who nods approvingly. Ahmed bursts into joyous laughter. Kwami joins in, they laugh long and hard.*)

LEWIS: It was pretty awesome, man. No way I thought the building would go up like that.

(Lewis slaps Ahmed's hand.)

TAMARA: I thought it was a bit showy, myself.

AHMED: Showy? It was art.

LEWIS: It burned and crumbled into the nothing that it stood for.

TAMARA: I still think it was a bit showy. A little Hollywood for my taste.

KWAMI: That building was an insult, an affront. We took it down, and nobody got hurt. That was the point. *(Sings)* "These magic moments . . ." *(Continues to sing as the others speak)*

(Tamara manages a smile.)

AHMED: CAN'T MESS WITH US! We showed those mutha-fuckers who's in control. *(Slaps his chest)*

KWAMI: That's right!

(He retrieves a couple of beers from the refrigerator. They each take one and ceremoniously proceed to drink.)

TO LIFE, LIBERTY AND THE PURSUIT OF HAPPI-NESS!

(They all raise their beers.)

TAMARA: It seems so—

LEWIS: Back home, no one would believe it. What do you think, Dad? Respect. Discipline. Fear. Oh no, we've joined the ranks. We'll be right up there in the pantheon, don't you think?

TAMARA: Let's not get too giddy.

(A *moment. They all look at her.*)

Standing there. Being there. Watching, I thought the heavens would open and shower down some good grace. The rain threw me. I'd expected for a moment there would be some clarity, a vision through the broken glass and kerosene haze. I expected to hear some triumphal chorus arise. Not really, but you know what I'm saying. I guess I feel queasy.

(A *moment.*)

But, we succeeded. I suppose.

(*Tamara awkwardly raises her beer and drinks it down. They don't respond.*)

KWAMI: So, when our "you know who" gets here we'll make the phone call.
LEWIS: Let's just make it now, you know while the adrenaline is still flowing. It's getting late. He may not show.
KWAMI: We should all be here for the moment.
AHMED: Everybody else managed to be back here on time, where's his punk ass? Bitch is always holding us up. He's probably talking to the authorities. What you know about him?
KWAMI: He's blood. Thick. A-one. Ace boon coon. HOME! What do I know about any of you? Until three months ago we all had separate paths, separate agendas.
AHMED: BOOM! We all one!
LEWIS: Hey man, see if it's on the radio yet.
AHMED: And you know it!

(*Ahmed fiddles with the radio.*)

TAMARA: You can level an entire building with wires and explo-
sives, but you can't get a simple portable radio to work?

AHMED: Ha ha. It's probably these cheap-ass batteries. I bought
them today off a brother on the corner. *(Opens the back of
the radio to examine the batteries)* You see that shit, look at
these joints! Ain't even in English.

TAMARA: Should everything be in English? Would that make
the world a better place? Would those batteries be any
more effective?

AHMED: It probably say "they ain't no good."

TAMARA: They are not any good.

AHMED *(Imitating Tamara)*: They are not any good.

KWAMI: Enough!

*(Ahmed curls his upper lip and pretends as if he is going to
hit Tamara, then strokes his bald head. The coded knock
sounds on the door. It is rapidly repeated over and over
again, growing with intensity. They all freeze. Uncertain,
tense. Kwami finally opens the door.*
A moment.
James walks in.)

Why are you rapping like some goddamn por'knocker?
Scare us half to death.

(Kwami raps out the correct code.)

JAMES: Sorry. Have you heard? I rode to the end of the line
and back. Do you know, in the middle of the day for the
last few stops on the IRT, practically nobody gets on or off?
I looked out the window, I could see people on the street
corners, sitting on their stoops, rapping as though nothing
was going on in the world 'cept for their conversations.
They were active, but not going anyplace, standing, sitting, waiting . . . And there I was, just me, traveling to the

121

end of the line . . . You see, I wanted to make sure I wasn't followed. It was just me at the final stop and I thought, God, not that I believe in God I was using the term parenthetically, who are these people who make this trip to the end each day? Who are these people on the fringe of the world as I know it? It was deep. You know, like a fucking revelation. And ya know I ride the subway every day and don't give a thought to where anybody's going, 'cause you know if I did I'd be afraid. I'd be afraid of who I was sitting across from. Was I sitting across from a man who was gonna go home and rape his daughter? Was I sitting across from the stockbroker that embezzled my pension? Or God forbid a terrorist who'd just killed some children.

KWAMI: Please, give us a rest. I thought something happened to you, man. We agreed to meet an hour ago and you're out there "riding" the subway like it's some deep existential experience. You were supposed to be here, that was part of the plan.

JAMES: But it seems the plan has been thrown off a bit. That we're improvising now, that we're feeling our way through unexplored terrain.

KWAMI: What are you talking about?

JAMES: Did you hear?

TAMARA: Hear what?

JAMES: You don't know? You don't know?

LEWIS: What are you talking about, man?

JAMES: You don't know?

KWAMI: No, we don't know.

JAMES *(Whispered)*: There were people in the building . . . children.

KWAMI *(Aside to Kwami)*: Where'd you hear that bullshit? The building was empty. It's a bold face lie! This was planned like clockwork.

(A moment.)

TAMARA: What's up?

(No response.)

Am I speaking out loud?

JAMES: I stayed behind and watched. The fire traveled like a terrible wind, without any consideration. I stood there, unable to move, to shout for help. I didn't know.

TAMARA: What happened?

JAMES: It was on the radio in the bodega. There were . . .

AHMED: Yeah, and?

JAMES: A group of children, black kids, broke through the fence and were playing in the building . . . They said—

KWAMI: Nobody was supposed to be in the area.

JAMES: I know. I checked it out a hundred times. I went over this, man. I didn't know. I swear to you.

TAMARA: Wait a minute. What are you saying? Are you saying that we killed some . . . children?

JAMES: That's what they say.

LEWIS: He's lying.

JAMES: I'm lying. I'm gonna lie about something like that?

LEWIS: You can't believe everything that you hear, fundamental rule. It's what they want people to believe.

TAMARA: How many?

JAMES: I don't know. Twelve maybe.

TAMARA: Are you telling us the truth Ja—

KWAMI: No names.

JAMES: I was there. I wanted to see that new building burn to the ground, all that arrogance swept away in one swoop . . . . I thought good riddance. Good-bye. It was finished. Then the firemen brought . . . the first . . . the first—
(Stops himself, he can't say the words)

(Ahmed nervously begins to pound out a hip-hop rhythm on the floor. Kwami gives him a cold hard stare. Ahmed stops.

Silence.
The sound of the rain.
Kwami lights a cigarette then takes a slowly paced circle
around the room. They all watch in anticipation. Tamara
begins to say something, then reconsiders.)

LEWIS: Jesus! *(Shakes his head)*
TAMARA: Are we going to talk about it?

(Kwami nods, still in thought.)

JAMES: Did you call?
TAMARA *(Snaps)*: We were waiting for you.
JAMES: Don't let me stop you.
LEWIS: Should we? What do you think?
JAMES: I think it's all fucked up. I think it's been set up, that
    THEY got wind of our shit and made this happen. They're
    probably listening to everything we're saying. I got that
    vibe, man.
KWAMI: You always got that vibe.
JAMES: This, the "vibe." It don't feel right. I ain't feeling good
    about this.
KWAMI: This is what it's about, my friend. Ain't supposed to
    feel good.
JAMES: I need a beer, where the beers at?

(They all point to the refrigerator. James retrieves a beer from
the refrigerator and knocks it back in practically one sip.)

KWAMI: It happened. There is no way anyone could have known.
TAMARA: Happened? No! You don't plan something for
    months and then say "it happened." No—something went
    very wrong. Something broke down. *(To James)* Someone
    didn't—
KWAMI: Please don't go there. No one in this room would
    willing—

JAMES: I didn't know, I swear.

AHMED: Where you been? You talking with somebody? You didn't know! Where you been?

JAMES: Get out my face. *(To Kwami)* Tell this punk to back off, 'cause he may get hurt.

AHMED: Yeah?

KWAMI: Sit down!

(Ahmed reluctantly acquiesces.)

JAMES: Why is everybody looking at me? *(To Lewis, singing the Sesame Street song)* "One of these things is not like the others, one of these things don't fit in."

LEWIS: Don't pull that on me. We been through this, I'm as down as everybody else in this room. Tell 'em . . . Kw—

KWAMI: No names.

LEWIS: Tell 'em.

AHMED: Yeah, I don't trust his ass. From the city.

KWAMI: Calm please. I can't think, we need no further obstacles. The gloom is thick enough.

(Kwami picks up the telephone and begins to dial.)

TAMARA *(Nervously)*: You're still gonna call?

KWAMI: Yes. We should. *(Thinks. Reconsiders. Decides)* It was our intention. Am I correct?

TAMARA: Not yet. Let's wait.

(Kwami sets the receiver down.)

I think we need to talk about it. Re-evaluate, you see what I'm saying.

(Ahmed surprisingly nods in agreement.)

LEWIS: Then what? Get into a pedagogical discussion about the mechanics, get lost in the nature of power, violence, authority, truth and society, like some introductory college course on civil unrest? We did it! Let's just make the damn phone call and get out of here. I'm tired! I gotta travel back to the city. The longer we discuss it, the more difficult it's going to be.

AHMED: Yeah, no sweat off your back. Right, white boy? Mr. Chomsky!

LEWIS: Righteous brother number one speaks again! I ain't sweating, my man.

(Ahmed gets in Lewis's face.)

Can we make a decision? I want to get out of here!

(Lewis sits down. Ahmed backs off triumphantly.)

JAMES: Yeah, he's right. The sooner the better.

TAMARA: Those were children in that building. You said it yourself. They died. And we . . . killed them. You're tired, want to go home. I'm sorry about that. Who can sleep?

(Silence.)

AHMED: Man this suit is hot. I don't even know why we had to wear them.

KWAMI: High tops and cut offs just don't speak the same language. Buziness be buziness.

(A moment. Ahmed returns to fiddling with the radio. It whines.)

LEWIS: Was it too difficult for you to get batteries that worked?

AHMED: In my neighborhood, yeah. That's the way shit is, right? That's what this bullshit is about! Brothers gotta fight for every little piece of nothing.

(Ahmed slides the radio over to Lewis.)

TAMARA *(To herself)*: So much for our symbolic act. No one hurt. No real harm done, not yet. "A demonstration of our rage, our disaffection, a signpost of what was to come."

(Kwami lights a cigarette, and lets the match drop to the ground. He's forgotten that he has already lit one. Tamara extinguishes his other cigarette in the ashtray. Lewis begins shaking his head as though he's fighting a thought; he fusses with the radio.)

LEWIS: I'm an organized person by nature. The minutest things throw off my entire rhythm. When I agreed to this all I agreed based upon the assumption, the precept, that nothing would go wrong.

AHMED: What world you rocking with?

KWAMI: Can we bring this down one notch? We're all excited. Remember why we are here. Think. We haven't failed. It's over! We did it! Our mission is complete, brothers! Sister! Please.

JAMES: Yeah, we didn't do this, *they* did. They knew. I mean, they were reckless in their decision-making, they constructed the building.

LEWIS: True. They never should have erected that government building on a sacred site, someplace where chil—

AHMED: I don't like this.

KWAMI: We proceed as planned.

AHMED: That your decision?

(Kwami nods.)

You're right. Cool. Those kids shouldn't have been there. They got caught in the middle, sometimes it's like that. Ain't our fault. It's fate and shit. God willed them in that building. It's God's will not ours, God decided the moment they'd die, not us.

KWAMI *(Convincing himself)*: That's right!

TAMARA: Wait a minute. Just like that!

KWAMI: Listen . . . There is always the probability that something will go wrong. We're book sustained, educated by theories. What I know, I know because I've been told. What I don't know, I learn as I do. The unknown after all is where death lurks. Confronting the unknown on a mission like this is an inevitability, and therefore syllogistically speaking, death was an inevitability, we knew that.

TAMARA: I didn't know that. We discussed the hypothetical possibility of death, but we didn't discuss it as an inevitability. That word wasn't brought up. I'm sure nobody used it. I'm searching my memory right now.

(A moment. She thinks it through.)

No! I'm sure inevitability was not a word introduced at any of our meetings. We were shaping a dialogue, yeah? Actualizing concerns, politicizing the agenda. But this was not appropriate. *(Panicked)* This was not appropriate. This was not appropriate. This was not appropriate—

AHMED: Do you want to say it one more time?

TAMARA: THIS WAS NOT APPROPRIATE! We're playing for keeps now, my friends.

(Ahmed shakes his head.)

AHMED: We are warriors, remember?

JAMES: Warriors!

KWAMI *(Preaching)*: Chango and Ogun rules! In battle it is inevitable that someone must die.

(The men nod in agreement, seduced by the words.)

TAMARA: But children. Isn't that what this was supposed to be about?

(*A moment. She looks from face to face.*)

ANSWER ME! Were their deaths an inevitability?

KWAMI: Regrettably so.

JAMES: We are warriors!

KWAMI: Warriors!

AHMED: Warriors!

LEWIS: Warriors!

TAMARA: I am not a warrior. I'm not a *(Whispered)* killer. I will not take responsibility. In fact, I refuse. Excuse me. I'd like to get some air.

(*Tamara turns to exit.*)

KWAMI: This is not a lecture you can walk out of.

(*Tamara returns to her seat.*
   A moment. Ahmed goes into the refrigerator and takes out another beer.)

AHMED: You gonna cry?

TAMARA: Yes, if you don't mind?

(*She fights back tears. Ahmed goes to comfort her.*)

Get away from me.

LEWIS: What's wrong? Your little book of rhetoric doesn't have a remedy today? You should be feeling relieved that you've left the land of myth for reality.

TAMARA: That's very white male of you, to tell me how I should be feeling.

KWAMI: Pain is pain is pain. It does not go out of style like a double-knit suit. You have to take responsibility, otherwise the act has no meaning and those children will have died for no reason, merely becoming statistics in a white man's book.

(Kwami lifts the receiver and dials some numbers. He listens to the person on the other end then hangs up.)

TAMARA: Because you have the power to destroy, it does not make you powerful. You can't fight a river with a pile of sticks unless you know just where to place those sticks.

KWAMI: We're on the battlefield darling, rhetoric does not stop bullets.

(The room falls silent. Kwami takes out a pack of cigarettes. He ceremoniously offers one to each person. They, however, decline. He proceeds to light his cigarette. He takes several puffs.)

TAMARA: What if one of those children was destined to lead the revolution?

AHMED: I guess they wasn't. Bang!

(A moment.)

TAMARA: You're cold-blooded.

AHMED *(Whispered)*: Warrior.

TAMARA *(Taunting him)*: Thirty-one seconds.

(Sounds of the forest. The whoosh of water in a pan. They sit for a moment.)

LEWIS: You see, we should have made the phone call. I want to get out of here. This is already eating too deep into my life. Where's the phone? *(Lifts up the telephone and dials. He hears a voice on the other end)* Uh! Uh!

KWAMI: Tell them we are—

(Lewis hangs up the receiver.)

LEWIS: Don't get on me! I couldn't think of what to say. I couldn't think of what to say . . . I didn't want to take responsibility. All that history rushed in man, I was fucking George Washington, J. Edgar Hoover. I was that fat southern pig blowing hate out my nose crying "hee haw" and shit as the church blew and those children died. It was suddenly too resonant for me. Too rich. Too deep, too . . . too . . . too damn real. There's something very Middle East about this. When the woman on the other line said "hello . . . hello, hello." I couldn't bring myself to say the words. I couldn't think of the phrasing suddenly, whether I should sound angry or sorry, or impertinent or indifferent. Whether I should draw my words out so that she's anticipating each syllable. I wanted it to be my mother there saying it's all right darling, it's all right! Come home! I should have kicked it to her and let that fucking establishment bitch know that I . . . We . . . We—

AHMED: Boom! There it goes!

(Sounds of the rain forest envelop them. The lights fade on all but Kwami.
Blackout.)

Scene 4

Rain forest. The sound of flies and mosquitoes.
Lance shakes his tin in a circular pattern. He stops to swat flies, then returns to his ritual singing as his story is being told.

LANCE *(Sings):*
When our life's brief story here shall end forever
When the storms shall beat no more; (beat no more)

Without Pilot we shall cross the mystic river,
To a fairer brighter shore.
Then our truest dearest Friend the King eternal,
Face to face we shall behold . . .
Yes, from Him we shall receive the crown supernal
    when our story has been told . . . When our story
    has been told . . .
When we reach the gates of gold!
We shall meet Him face to face, when our story has
    been told . . .

KWAMI *(Amplified voiceover)*: Swarms of vicious flies and mosquitoes pestered him, dipping and diving at his blackened
skin for sustenance. It had been a long time since he
could remember life without their infernal whisper. He'd
feared their return after the rains, knowing that these next
few months would be the worst. Yes, because the forest
would turn mean this season. This was the time of year
that he always contemplated leaving behind his pit for the
cane liquor and the cordial indifference of a prostitute; the
time of year when he'd become Cortés and dream of a
metropolis of gold and lapis lazuli. He'd daydream . . . of
the forest and its vast offering. Moving, searching, closely
watching his steps, which meant too often he was looking
downward. He'd masturbate incessantly with thoughts of
no one in particular. It was too difficult to conjure the face
of someone without them transforming into some dread-
ful creature of the forest. It was the time of year that he'd
question his quixotic mission. Then . . .

LANCE *(Singing)*:
    When our life's brief story here shall end forever
    When the storms shall beat no more; (beat no more)
    Without Pilot we shall cross the mystic river,
    To a fairer brighter shore.

(Lance stops swirling his pan and examines the contents more thoroughly.
Kwami takes out a handkerchief and dabs his forehead.)

KWAMI *(Amplified voiceover)*: On the frontiers of insanity, he'd find a speck of gold: tiny, precious and glorious. The flies and mosquitoes would retreat from his consciousness and the forest would become home again.

(Silence.)

Scene 5

The room. A few new weeds have sprouted through the floorboards.
They have all removed their suit jackets.
James finishes off a beer and crushes the can.

JAMES: Sun's down. We got a decision?

(They all look to Kwami.)

KWAMI: Why are you looking at me?
AHMED: Well?
KWAMI: I don't want to make the decision for all of us.
LEWIS: I'll stand by whatever you decide.

(They all nod.)

KWAMI: Please don't put me in that position. All right?
AHMED: Who else is gonna do it? Man, you in control. You the one brought us together. *(Beats out a rhythm on the table)*
KWAMI: Stop!
AHMED: Just trying to liven things up.
LEWIS: Must you always be heard?

AHMED: You got a problem with that?

LEWIS: Yeah I do.

AHMED: Whatcha gonna do about it?

LEWIS: I'm going to tell you I have a problem. I have a problem with you constantly making little noises. We're all here trying to fight for a little peace of mind and you insist on making it difficult. Tapping, talking, yapping. Silence is sometimes more of a statement.

AHMED: How you gonna back that up, white boy?

LEWIS: Fine—beat me unconscious! At least then I won't have to hear your incessant tapping.

(Ahmed stands, Lewis stands. A brief staring match ensues. They press their chests up against each other.)

KWAMI: Sit down!

LEWIS: I'm tired of him getting in my face. I don't have to be here. I'm here because I want to be.

JAMES: We're all here 'cause we want to be.

LEWIS: You know what I'm saying.

AHMED: Yeah, FBI got to be in everything.

LEWIS: Oh that again. FBI, CIA. Yeah, I'm drawing a check from all of them. Yeah guy, I'm wearing a wiretap. Can you speak up? I can't hear what you're saying? You don't really believe that. Keep at it guy, but unless you got proof I suggest you back off and find another place to direct that indicting stare of yours.

(They both sit. James goes into the refrigerator and retrieves two beers, one for himself and another for Lewis.)

AHMED: What about me?

JAMES: You're too lightweight.

(Ahmed goes to the refrigerator himself.)

TAMARA: And I suppose I'm invisible?

JAMES: I'm sorry baby, you want a beer?

TAMARA: No thank you sweetheart, I don't have anything to celebrate now that I'm one of America's most wanted.

AHMED: I like being wanted. It's like, ah shit there ya go, picture of you in high school splashed across the screen.

(Ahmed poses.)

TAMARA: You're so stupid.

AHMED *(Wounded)*: Why you call me stupid?

TAMARA: It was the first word that came to mind. I apologize.

(Ahmed walks across the stage.)

AHMED: Fuck you, how you like them words?

TAMARA: The imagination. The language.

AHMED: Yeah well, I'm a street rebel baby, I'm a revolutionary through and through, I'm carrying on the folk tradition. I'm the real thing, baby.

TAMARA: And I'm suffering in this heat.

JAMES: Suffering. When I face the cameras outside this door: "Why'd you do it?" I had no choice. I'm angry. "Why are you angry?" Because of the circumstances. "Can you give us more detail?" You see, for years I've been wearing these shackles around my feet and—

AHMED: Yeah, yeah.

JAMES: I listen to you go on about nothing . . . Come on man, what are we gonna do?

(A moment.)

Hell, might as well toss a coin.

KWAMI: Those were children. We're not gonna toss their fate up in the air.

JAMES: Their fate is sealed, it's ours we're deciding.

TAMARA: Yes, I think we should—

JAMES: Do you have a better idea?

KWAMI: I don't know, brothers . . . and sister. I'm in a quandary. I've done plenty of bold things in my lifetime, but here *(Points to his head)* in my head. Y'all keep turning to me, but we already decided to reject traditional paradigms of leadership. Therefore, I will not make the decision, it would make me a hypocrite. And I can't bear the thought of taking that journey twice in one day.

JAMES: Well, someone's gonna have to dig us up out this quandary. You always got that thoughtful look. *(James listens, then peeks through the blinds)* Shhhh. Shhhh.

LEWIS: This paranoia of yours is beginning to scare me. Excuse me, but could we find our way back to East New York.

(Tamara nods emphatically.
Kwami slowly reaches into his pocket.)

KWAMI: Yes . . . I don't want to do this, but what are our options? If we are going to be impartial, and we . . . let the spirits . . . All right . . . heads we make the phone call, tails we go home and meet in a month to assess the damage and re-strategize.

(Kwami pulls out a nickel.)

TAMARA: A nickel?

KWAMI: What are you suggesting?

TAMARA: I'm superstitious, the biggest decision of our lives is going to hinge on a nickel. I think it should be a quarter.

(They all dig into their pockets.)

JAMES *(To Ahmed)*: I don't even know why you're pretending.

(Ahmed sucks his teeth.)

Flipping George Washington, the irony is too ripe.

LEWIS: I got a dime.

AHMED: I have some pennies.

TAMARA: Maybe the pennies will bring us good luck.

JAMES: The little brown coin . . . Lincoln . . . I hate this country, man—even the fucking change reflects the hierarchical social breakdown of society. You see what I'm talking about now.

KWAMI: Does anyone have a problem with flipping a dime?

(They think.)

TAMARA: As long as we're comfortable with the fact that it's the smallest of the coins.

JAMES: I'm personally comfortable with that.

(They all nod.)

AHMED: Who . . . who is gonna flip it?

(A moment.)

KWAMI: I'll do it.

(Lewis hands Kwami the dime. He tosses it up in the air and allows it to fall.)

Heads.

LEWIS: Best of three—

AHMED: Five.

JAMES: Seven.

(The sound of rainfall. Kwami closes his eyes and drops the coin.
    Blackout.)

Scene 6

The rain forest.
  Lance lies flat, bewildered. He wails.
  Kwami conjures, his eyes closed.

KWAMI: The forest had covered over his path and his rusted
  machete was no competition for the seasonal captivity.
  He'd have to wait. Wait some more. Wait until the forest
  gave way, gave reason to move through.

  (Silence.
    Lights fade in the forest.)

Scene 7

Silence. The room.
  They sit staring blankly.
  Tamara stands, suddenly possessed by a good idea.

TAMARA: We are going at this entirely wrong. We've been
  struggling with whether we should make the phone call,
  and the question now is "why?"

  (A moment.)

KWAMI: We know why. Don't we? *(The others nod in agreement)*
  There you go!

  (Tamara returns to her spot.)

TAMARA: Why? *(Silence)* No, there *you* go. Why?
LEWIS: We've spent the last few months going over this.

TAMARA: Humor me. We made that list when we were in the theoretical stage of planning, when the intent was different, now we're dealing in absolutes.

KWAMI: Why should anything change?

(Ahmed sucks his teeth.)

AHMED: Why we always gotta talk shit to death? We know what we want. We want emancipation, bang! We want freedom, boom! We want equality, bam! That ain't no secret! Goddamn! Can we just move on.

TAMARA: Then you make the call and tell that woman those children died because we want emancipation, bang! We want freedom, boom! We want equality, bam! Can we be any more general than that? And she'll say, "Sure thing, coming right up. I understand completely. I didn't know. Let me just program your request into the computer, Mr. Nubian Warrior and please hold for a moment. It may take a few minutes to delete the hundreds of years of history and oppression. We're backed up today, technology. Geez I wish you'd called sooner. Ah now, that was easy . . ."

(A moment.)

Sorry parents, your children died for a special prosecutor paid for by the government. An ad hoc committee to evaluate the situation, to draw conclusions, to make recommendations and administer tokenism. A community liaison or even better, a program that services the hundreds of sad and impoverished "youths."

(A moment.)

We have done something bold . . . unexpected, and I think we should ask for something bold . . . unexpected.

KWAMI: Now what are you suggesting?

AHMED *(Sardonically)*: Yeah?

TAMARA: What do you want?

AHMED: A lot of things.

LEWIS: I want to free the political prisoners. Leonard Peltier, Elmore Geronimo Pratt, Mumia!

TAMARA: Wish granted, but the prison's still crowded.

LEWIS: I want reform—

KWAMI: Equal educational opportunities for African-American children.

TAMARA: Wish granted, bachelors bestowed. Where's your job?

JAMES: I want reciprocity for the years of servitude, a monument across from the White House, and forty acres and a mule.

TAMARA: You got that. What next, brother, if you can't pay your taxes to keep your land.

KWAMI: I want the judicial system overhauled. Cultural awareness! The truth!

AHMED: I want the white man to get off my back. The antidote to racism.

TAMARA: Let's keep digging, delving, brothers. Get to the source. If you had to have one thing that would set things right. UNO! What would you ask for?

JAMES: I want to know whether man really did go to the moon. And if so, how come that shit ain't colonized yet. You're wondering the same thing. I want to know whether sugar is more addictive than crack, and how come it's only in black communities that you can buy candy for a nickel: Now and Laters, Sour puss, Mary Janes, Super Bubble, Laffy Taffy. MMMmmm. Anyone have a stick of gum?

(Ahmed reaches into his pocket.)

Driving the point, right? They get us hooked and wired on that shit, desiring a little sugar before school, it's only a nickel right? Then as we get older we desire a little sugar after work, but it ain't cool to be sucking on a lollipop, so you get a forty of Colt, kick it back with the boys, yeah buddy. Then they wonder why we're so angry. It's because our teeth are rotting and we don't have access to personal physicians named Larry or Bobby. So we have to turn to gold to hide the discoloration of our teeth and discover that we actually like gold 'cause it looks so fine against our brown skin, then we want to wear it around our necks and then our lovers and our wives want to wear it. But hell, we don't have enough money. Please, please baby more sugar, more gold. *(Peeks out the blinds, whispering)* So we sell things. Little things at first, right? And that ain't enough. Then we sell big things, which become crimes . . . Then our sugar is taken from us. Don't take my sugar. By the very folks that gave it to us in the first place.

LEWIS: Point being?

JAMES: Point being! I want basic things, God damnit. I want cable television on my block, I want leisure time. That's what I'm talking about. I want to have a lawn that I nurture and cultivate over the years.

AHMED: Yeah, yeah . . . I want my friends to be alive when I call them.

(A moment.)

Yeah, yeah . . . You know what I want, one of those jeep joints. Up there chilling with the sunglasses and a honey, and that's the truth. Give me the phone. I'm gonna call 'em, tell 'em park that jeep in front of City Hall or else shit's gonna blow up bang, bang, bang.

(Ahmed rushes frantically around the room shouting "bang" at the top of his lungs. He breaks into laughter.)

TAMARA: Moral bankruptcy, poverty, human decay. Folks have always been poor, folks have been poor before there was a word to describe "poverty." It's only in this century that it's become a crime. *(Begins to laugh)*

LEWIS *(Excited)*: I want to shut down the stock exchange for one day. No, no . . . I want to take a hostage. *(Nods emphatically)* One of those establishment bigots. No, the media people, those manipulative fucks that are really in control. Let's take someone big, right at the source of the news like Dan Rather or fucking Bryant Gumbel.

AHMED: Nah, not the brother. Nah, the guy on ABC with the big head.

TAMARA: Take 'em all, keep 'em in your basement, but it still doesn't solve the problem at hand.

KWAMI: The problem is we shouldn't want so many things. We want too much, which leads to wanting too little. There was a time when we were all in sync with nature. I could share with you all that I had, because I knew the forest could always provide me with everything that I needed. You see, no man was richer than another because we all possessed the same guidebook to nature. What did the Western world do besides rob us of our wealth? It robbed us of our faith that no matter what, we'd be able to survive. The West took from us the will to survive on the bounty of the land. The faith that nature would provide.

AHMED: What you want?

KWAMI: My faith restored. How am I gonna pick up the telephone and ask for that to be delivered. Why are we getting caught up in what we want? What about what we don't want.

JAMES: I don't want sugar: donuts, cinnamon buns, macaroons, candied yams, sweet potato pie, coconut cream pie, key lime pie, pie period, pie, pie. I don't want lemon tarts, chocolate ice cream, strawberry ice cream, grape soda, grape icies, grape Now and Laters, wine, sherry, port, cognac, whiskey, beer, malt liquor . . .

TAMARA: Let's get back to the point.

JAMES: Which was?

TAMARA: The phone call.

LEWIS: Let's just do it, let's just say we're a group of—

AHMED: Black.

JAMES: African-American—

KWAMI: Diasporatic peoples—

LEWIS: Acting on the desire—

AHMED: Conviction.

TAMARA: Need.

JAMES: Necessity.

LEWIS: . . . to awaken this country to the persuasiveness of disaffection and alienation. It was—

AHMED: is—

KWAMI: Was . . .

LEWIS: . . . essential to grab the attention of the population by means of a bold and unfortunate act, but this is a society—

TAMARA: Patriarchy.

JAMES: Country.

KWAMI: Eurocentric hegemony.

AHMED: Place.

LEWIS: "Culture" that responds to violence and therefore a violent act provides the path of least resistance to the psyche of this nation . . . How's that?

AHMED: Why he gotta be the one to shape our demands? Ain't that what we're talking about? See how insidious their shit is, white folks creep in to take control even when they don't have it. "Psyche!" What kind of bullshit is that? I'll call.

(He picks up the telephone and begins to dial.)

Hello. Yeah, I'm calling 'cause . . . 'cause . . . This is a . . . *(Slams down the receiver)* I couldn't remember. I'm nervous. Tell me again.

TAMARA: If you can't remember, then it isn't right.

AHMED: Let me try again.

KWAMI: You're too young to remember how we struggled, how we plotted and planned. How inspired we were by the words of leaders. How our pride bloomed into a movement. You're too young to remember the era of optimism.

AHMED: I remember seeing Martin Luther King die on television, all the family was all gathered round. My moms was all curled up a crying and shit on the couch.

JAMES: You are lying, muthafucker.

AHMED: I remember that shit as though it was yesterday. Niggers—

TAMARA: The word.

AHMED: Went out their minds, burning and looting, chanting shit like "Burn baby burn" "Hell no we won't go!" Stokely and Huey. "Power to the People!" "Freedom whitey" "*Pig.*" I was like give me a match 'cause I'm angry. Little fingers struggling to light up a book of matches. Set fire to the G.I. Joe doll and watch his plastic head melt in the muthafucking schoolyard against the black tar. "Burn baby burn." "Attica! Attica!"

JAMES: You are the lyingest muthafucker.

AHMED: I seen King take a bullet, fall back like this. *(Demonstrates)* Right on TV, just plain as day.

TAMARA: You saw Martin Luther King get shot on television?

(Ahmed nods.)

KWAMI: It wasn't televised.

AHMED: Yes it was. I seent it.

(They all shake their heads.)

I seent it on television.

KWAMI: You saw Paul Winfield as Martin Luther King in the miniseries "King."

(A moment. Ahmed processes the information.)

AHMED: But that ain't the point! WHAT I'M SAYING IS THAT TO A CHILD'S MIND IT AIN'T DIFFERENT. Still wanted to burn shit. Yeah so, I wasn't part of the movement. I didn't fucking march to Selma or hold up armored cars with baby rifles and pose for pictures with them damn afros and Woolworth dashikis.

(He goes through a series of famous Black Panther poses.)

You can tell who the serious niggers were from the pictures 'cause their afros were all tatty and they had that look in their eye like "That's right, I didn't have time to buy the blowout kit, I'm on fire . . . I'm a revolutionary, baby." *(Walks around the room with a demonstrative menacing swagger)* Problem was, niggers—

TAMARA: I've told you about using that word.

AHMED: The problem with folks then was they couldn't get that shit straight, kept running up on the FBI. I'm tired of being told about the good ole days. You the only one that was there, Kwa. Ain't mean shit to me! This is my generation, we in control, we don't let nobody walk over our backs. It ain't about what we want it's about how we get it. That's right! Allah be praised!

TAMARA: Oh now you're the black Muslim warrior? Make the call, brother man.

(Ahmed approaches the phone as though it were a kung fu opponent. He does an elaborate display, ending with the crane stance. He lifts the receiver and dials the numbers.)

AHMED: Hello, this is a brother and I'm calling on behalf of *(Without a breath)* The Diasporatic Folks Revolutionary Collaborative for Justice and Equality. I . . . We . . . *(Looks at the others, who nod him on)* We are calling to take responsibility for the . . . *(A moment. Confusion. He listens to the voice on the other end)* This is an emergency! *(Slams down the receiver)*

LEWIS: What happened?

AHMED: "I'm sorry Mr. Brother of the Diasporatic Folks Revolutionary Collaborative for Justice and Equality, this service is taking messages for Doctor Mehta. If it's an emergency I CAN GIVE YOU HIS DIRECT LINE!" *(Looks to each person)* Wrong number.

KWAMI: Couldn't be.

AHMED: Wrong number, I'm telling you like it is. I don't think any of y'all want to make this phone call. That's what I think. I think y'all just like the other wannabedown revolutionary notgetanythingbedones, like to make speeches and raise eyebrows and talk about the devil be doing this and the devil be doing that, but when it comes to backing up with some real heat y'all ain't there. Y'all playing like you got FBinformantcointelprolike syndrome. Let a brother fall to the wayside in the midst of battle. That ain't right! In my neighborhood 'fore you run into battle you need to know who got your back. You see what I'm saying, I'm talking for real now, I'm talking from the heart. *(Slaps the right side of his chest)*

LEWIS: Your heart's on your other side man, for future reference. *(Demonstrates with a pat on the chest)* That's where the heart is. So if you feel chest pains on that side, it's gas. The other side, well it's the heart. The heart. *(Winks)*

AHMED *(Sarcastically)*: Thanks for the tip.

LEWIS: I got your back. You got mine.

AHMED: That gives me confidence to run blindly into battle.

TAMARA: Why does everything come down to war analogies. Revolution has as much to do with giving birth as taking life. That's what we have to keep remembering. We're not taking anything, we're giving, giving African-Americans the opportunity to live that "Horatio Alger's constitutional I love America thang." It's a gift of hope, of life.

LEWIS: A little inspirational moment from the professor.

(Tamara bows.)

TAMARA: Yes, I'm an academic. My apologies to all for knowing a little something more than how to turn the television
on and off.

KWAMI: What's the problem? I'll call information and get the
right number.

JAMES: Excuse me, seventy-five cents? That's what it cost to
call information. Do you really want to pump anything
more into the system than necessary? I suggest we find the
white pages.

*(They search the room for the white pages. James goes to the
refrigerator to get himself another beer.
Lights fade. For a moment the room is the rain forest.
Lance sleeps with one eye open.)*

Scene 8

*The room.
The sound of the rain forest.*

LEWIS: It's getting late.

JAMES: We know.

AHMED: Probably thought this would be a game.

JAMES: Man, back off. It's too hot for conflict. We're all in this
pit together.

TAMARA: I'm sick of this. What the fuck are we doing?

AHMED: Fuck?

TAMARA: Yeah, what the fuck? I've been in this room too long
with you people. You're wearing me down. I'm losing my
individuality.

JAMES: Poor thing.

TAMARA: Don't you think you've had enough beer?

JAMES: What, you wanna be my mother now?

TAMARA: Oh please, I'm counting my blessings that I'm not.

(A moment.)

KWAMI: Will you all just shut the fuck up! If you don't have anything constructive to say, QUIET!

(A moment.)

TAMARA: Don't tell me to shut up, I've been in this room listening to you *men*. Talk your bullshit, whine, cry. Play at being warriors. Now I feel like speaking freely, like purging my feelings. PLEASE!

JAMES: You see what's happening, we're addicted to our misery. We lift the veil and we have nothing. That's a terrifying prospect my Afrodescent muses, isn't it? We are junkies trying to meet our quota of pain and pleasure.

(Ahmed gives him the finger.)

You see now, we're bonded by our hopelessness.

TAMARA: Speak for yourself.

JAMES: Isn't it my prerogative to speak for us all, isn't that what we have chosen to do. Correct me if I'm wrong. Stop me when I violate the perimeters.

KWAMI: Take it easy.

JAMES: This culture thrives on misery. Look at the news. Look at poor Ahmed, whoops I'm sorry I said your name. Misery quota rises in this room.

(Ahmed scowls.)

Do you want to hurt me now *Ahmed*? PAIN! Look at us, the more miserable we are, the more we have in common.

I'm feeling very close to you all. *(Perks up at the thought)* Remove our misery, we will have nothing left to unify us.

KWAMI: You've had too much to drink.

JAMES: Our complaints are our mantra, it's what keeps us close to God and our God intact. Us African peoples know God and misery. *(Sings emphatically, almost manic)*

We are climbing Jacob's Ladder,
We are climbing Jacob's ladder . . . *(Continues song till end)*

(Staggers across the stage) We can trace this conspiracy of misery all the way back to the "founding fathers." They knew. These men were no ordinary men, these were visionaries, seers. They knew that one day banks would exist, interest rates, mortgages and bankruptcy court. They knew about polyester and other miracle-wash fabrics that would be bought on 125th Street for a pittance. They knew that a glorious history would be woven to hide their diabolical schemes behind. They passed down recipes for segregation, Jim Crow and television sitcoms about family life to taunt others. For God's sake, they introduced the laugh track to make our misery more palatable. They coined phrases like "nigger," "malt liquor" and "projects" to erect barriers. They knew that a few men, white men like themselves, would have homes in the suburbs and eat steak au poivre with their mistresses on Friday evenings before the last metroliner back home, where they'd beat their wives for asking questions. And nevertheless be envied for their prosperity. They knew Vietnam would happen, they knew that L.A. would burn, they knew about crack long before we were tempted to take our first puff. *(Feigns smoking a crack pipe)* Ah! Our mistake is we've chosen an act of terror. A diabolical act! That's no longer a revolutionary notion in this society. Acts of terror are welcome, an adage for this decade. If we wanted to be sub-

versive, counter, we should in fact be committing random acts of goodwill. Cleaning up neighborhoods overnight, eradicating corruption, distributing medicine, educating young people. Imagine the horror that would set in, the frenzy of the politicos struggling to restore the status quo, authorizing random deaths to elevate the misery quotient, introducing disease and discontent as part of the welfare package to keep people wanting more and more. We have made a rather serious tactical error in our strategy, my brothers and sister. I didn't realize it until this very moment. *(Heads for the door)* I'm off now to commit acts of goodwill. You can't stop me, damnit, I'm determined to bring the system to a halt. Jefferson said that every twenty years a society must undergo a revolution. And I, now, am off to lead! Revolution, but we're using primitive weapons, weapons of our forefathers, weapons of destruction. What we need is a new vocabulary. SMILE! You can't stop me. I'm determined to shower this culture with happiness. Spread goodwill to all mankind. I love you. *(Kisses Ahmed on the mouth)* I love you all. I'm off. Have a nice day!

(Lights fade on all but James.)

Oh yeah, this plot was woven centuries before you or I were born. The thread is delicate like silk. They mined this territory clean.

(Lights fade on James, as they rise on Lance panning for gold.)

LANCE: Huh? *(Resumes panning)*

(Crossfade to room. James picks up the receiver.)

JAMES: And you say we shouldn't make this phone call? That's where you're wrong, we were meant to make this phone call, not to do so would be disturbing the balance, the web, destiny . . . Give me the phone. I'm not strong enough to resist fate's forearm. Please, I want to take responsibility for you, my comrades. I'm the captain of this shipwreck. I am destined to die in service of the cause, 'cause my life was given to causes. I need this further burden to bear. I love you all. Random acts of goodwill. Random! Good! Acts! Good! Good! Good! GOOD! Will! WILL!

(James sinks down to the floor with the receiver in his hand. He passes out.
    Tamara takes the phone out of his hand and hangs it up. Kwami lights another cigarette.)

KWAMI: He's out for the evening.

(Lights slowly fade.
    Rain forest.)

LANCE: Huh?

(Lance bangs the barrel, struggling to free a piece of salted meat.
    Crossfade to room.)

Scene 9

They stand over James. Ahmed bends down and shakes him.

AHMED: I think he's dead.
KWAMI: Leave him. He's not dead.
TAMARA: Not yet.

(A moment.)

AHMED: Y'all just gonna leave the brother there?

KWAMI: Yes. Nobody told him to go get drunk.

LEWIS: Ah, to have no worries in the world. And to think this time last night I was hanging out with friends drinking shots of Jägermeister in one of those detestable yuppie watering pits, debating the merits of Scientology and reduction of the English language to politically expedient sound bites, infuriating the bartender by speaking much too loud about *religion* and *politics*. Something he clearly did not want to hear. "Do you mind?" he said. And everyone around him nodded all at once. And he repeated himself, "Do you mind?" Ah, I recognized the cautionary tone. And asked, "Do I mind what?" *(Calmly)* Do I mind that in this day and age in America if I want to talk about political issues other than those sanctioned by the news media and the self appointed pundits, I have to whisper it behind closed doors like some fucking crack junkie. Do I mind that, guy?

AHMED: I bet he kicked your ass.

LEWIS: Oh no no no. I pointed the finger at him, man. The finger. Which, mind you, is not used as much as it used to be. We've lost all of our great finger pointers, everyone is much too interested in being polite, just in case.

(Lewis demonstrates how he pointed his finger.)

TAMARA: Very artful. That's finger pointing at its all time best.

LEWIS: You jest, but . . . I pointed it, then dipped into my arsenal to conjure the most incisive word to use against his narrow-mindedness. And the word *pimp* rolled off my tongue before I even had a chance to really think about it. Pimp! And it disarmed him in the most incredibly satisfying way. I could see him searching for an appropriately

demeaning retort. But before he could respond I left that
establishment knowing that I was more powerful than
him. And yes I did mind. And by God he'd see. *(Stops
short, lies down next to James. He cuddles up next to him)*
I hope he's dreaming of sweets. Ah, yes.

AHMED: Damn, you are always so dramatic.

(Lewis lies flat.)

I swear to God y'all always gots to convolute things.
Enough, I have other things that gots to get done.

LEWIS: Ah, to have no worries in the world.

*(Ahmed begins to tap out a rhythm. He catches himself.
They all smile at his demonstration of restraint. Kwami is
silent, introspective.)*

TAMARA *(To Kwami)*: Would you please say something?

KWAMI: I'm trying.

TAMARA: I move that we choose a leader. And I move that person be you.

(Lewis points to Kwami.)

AHMED: Yeah!

KWAMI: I see. When there's something valuable at stake everyone wants a voice, everyone wants a share. But when it
comes to the difficult tasks, down to the nitty gritty, bare
bones, the shit, if I may say so, you all absolve yourselves
of the responsibility. Point the finger.

TAMARA: That's ridiculous. You have history. That's all.

KWAMI: Too much. You think I relish the thought of picking
up that telephone? You think I have words? My silence is
my confusion.

(A moment. Silence. They all stare at Kwami.)

But I guess it must be done. And I have history.

(He walks over to the telephone. He glances at the slip of paper with the telephone number. He begins to light a cigarette, reconsiders.)

Whoa!

(He dials and places the receiver to his ear. His hand shakes ever so slightly.)

Hello.

(A moment. Lights fade on all but Kwami.
He is suddenly in the rain forest. In the distance, Lance is hunched over with his tin in hand. There is a moment of recognition. The phone rings in the jungle.
Lance stands erect. He grabs his machete.
A moment.)

Hello? Hello?

(Lance laughs heartily, deep and robust. He smiles, revealing a mouthful of gold teeth.)

(Amplified) Hello?

(He turns his head; he is now in the jungle facing Lance, who is willing to defend his gold to the death.)

Daddy?

(Lance raises his machete.)

LANCE: You can't have it. It's mine.

KWAMI: Daddy.

LANCE: It's mine!

KWAMI: Daddy?

LANCE *(Shouts)*: It's you that made me clever, made me noble, made me stay here!

(Lights rise in the room. Lance returns to digging for gold. The rain forest retreats.)

TAMARA: Are you all right?

(Kwami stands in a daze. Tamara takes the receiver from Kwami's hand.)

LEWIS: Hello . . . Daddy?

(Ahmed snaps his fingers.)

KWAMI: I . . . I . . . it was my father.

AHMED: Ah man don't talk to me about your father, we're tired of that warrior speech. Black man in the Guyana rain forest hunting for gold. Like it suppose to make us feel better. Your father probably just ran off, and forgot to tell y'all. He's gone man, he ain't never coming back from the jungle.

(Kwami lunges for Ahmed and grabs him around the neck, choking him.)

KWAMI: Let me tell you something about my father. He was a good man. He worked hard. Harder than you ever will. I know what kind of man my mother would have married. Because your father wasn't there, does not mean mine wasn't, he was always there.

(A moment.)

AHMED: We ain't talking about my father. *(Clearly shaken)* I don't even think about my father.

TAMARA: Don't go there!

KWAMI: There is strength in the tales of ancestors. That's how they live and breathe.

AHMED: Why don't you give us all a rest. Let go.

(Kwami lets go of Ahmed.
He hugs Ahmed. The two men stand that way for a moment.)

KWAMI: I'm sorry.

TAMARA: You all right?

LEWIS: We agreed we wouldn't bring family into this. You know, we don't want to know anything about each other. It's easier. We'll just disappear back into the world without any connection.

TAMARA: Yes. I agree. But with all due respect it is a wee bit easier for you to disassociate.

LEWIS: Keep pushing me further away. I'll go.

(Kwami sits down almost in a trance.)

Hey . . . are you there?

AHMED: Looks like we lost another one.

(Tamara hangs up the phone. Lights fade.)

Scene 10

Lewis stands over the inebriated James.
  James awakens. The room is beginning to take on attributes of the rain forest.

JAMES: I had the most horrifying dream.

LEWIS: You can't run, you can't hide from the grim reaper.

KWAMI: I'm afraid death is still with us.

(A moment.)

AHMED: Afraid? Nah, that's not what this is about.

KWAMI: Isn't that what revolution is about? Fears you won't get, can't have.

AHMED: Maybe y'all. Not me. I ain't afraid.

TAMARA: Perhaps you're a more evolved creature than us. But we are merely mortals, we have emotions.

AHMED: You think I'm not capable of deep feelings? I can cry as readily as the next brother.

LEWIS: Are we actually discussing whether or not he has feelings? Has it come to this point? If we had to distill this moment down to its very essence, place it in a centrifuge . . . *(Whips his hand around in a circular motion)* Would it all come down to whether or not he has feelings?

(A moment.)

I mean you feel, he feels, we all fucking feel . . . We're all afraid.

AHMED: I'm not afraid . . . of death . . . I'm just afraid of having no one there to witness it. I want to die in glory. In slow motion like a John Woo flick jammie. *(Moves in slow motion. He simulates the sounds of bullets hitting him)* Paper flying and shit. I want people to remember my death as a defining event, a death that will be passed down for generations. "Oh you remember how he died?" I want the myth to grow larger and larger, so when folks walk by the spot they'll say, "Oh shit, that's where it happened. BANG!" The story will bring folks together. "Were you there when it happened?" The national news, the lead story, me in a graduation picture, junior high school wearing that red bow tie my moms fished out of a bargain bin at McCrory's. It will be news not because of who I was, but because of how it happened. I don't want people to say oh what a pity, what a waste, I want my death to blow their minds—bet! In fact, my death may be the best thing to happen to me peoples.

TAMARA: That's the most depressing thing I've ever heard. You're not serious.

AHMED: Why not?

TAMARA: Number one, no one should live life as a preamble to death. It practically nullifies the entire notion of living. It's sort of like some primitive belief that by sacrificing the young the village will thrive. It all strikes me as a bit . . . peculiar.

AHMED: You're the smart one, tell me how what we did is any different from that. You see what I'm saying. You really don't understand this brother's communication. Talking like you know. Tomorrow you'll be back at your university sitting crossed leg behind a mahogany desk. You really don't understand what's out there. What I'm fighting for.

TAMARA: I'm struggling the same as you, despite the appearance of calm and this fabulous suit.

(Tamara twirls to show off the suit and sits down.)

KWAMI: Can we just give it a rest?

TAMARA: I have given him a break ever since we came together as an alliance. I gave you all a break. Now I'm sick of the indecision, of the arguing, of the general lack of concern for each other. Let me tell you something . . . *(Opens the top button of her shirt and assumes a professorial stance)*

AHMED: Oh no. *(Covers his eyes)*

TAMARA: I'm standing here facing you with the most difficult and wrenching decision of my life. *(To James)* You're drunk, *(To Ahmed)* you're fantasizing your death, *(To Kwami)* you're indecisive, paralyzed by years of struggle and frustration, and *(To Lewis)* you're, you're marginally concerned, it's not your problem, after all you're just here to help . . . I'm tired. I'm confused. I'm angry. We could spend the rest of our lives in this room trying to make a decision. Trying to determine what it is we want. Our impulse was correct, we want something different, we deserve something "better." I can tell you right at this moment the only thing that is going to make things better is for us to make the phone call, take responsibility and move the hell on. And it is now out of love and . . . impatience that I pick up this telephone.

(Tamara picks up the phone and dials information.)

Could I please have the number for the Federal Bureau of Investigations. That's right. Yes. The main office.
KWAMI: We love you.
TAMARA: Hello.

(She glances around the room.
The men stand frozen in anticipation.)

Hello, I'm phoning from the People's Diasporatic Party to take responsibility for this morning's tragic . . . *(Stops)*
KWAMI: What's wrong?
TAMARA: It's voice mail. *(Listens)* Now I'm in voice mail, don't you hate that . . . I don't know what department I want. What department? *(They shrug)* Administration? No. Community Affairs? No. No. No. Public relations? What should I do?
KWAMI: Wait for the operator.

(A moment.)

TAMARA: Oh God. "Holiday," of course, all offices will be closed until tomorrow, 9 A.M. *(Hangs up)* What if I wanted to speak to them today? What if I needed to speak to them today?

(Tamara begins to laugh; they all join.)

JAMES: If that ain't a bitch. You can bank twenty-four hours a day in America, but commit one little act of civil transgression on a public holiday and you can't reach anyone if you want to take responsibility.

LEWIS: Bureaucracy, it was created so no one would have to take responsibility.

KWAMI: Indeed!

AHMED: What are we gonna do?

JAMES: We can still catch the fireworks.

AHMED: Nah, seriously.

KWAMI: Simple, we have no choice, we must go public. We'll call the newspapers—

JAMES: No radio—

LEWIS: No, no, television reaches a wider audience.

AHMED: Definitely television. I want to be remembered.

(The lights slowly fade on all but Kwami.)

Scene 11

The rain forest overtakes the room. Kwami finds himself in its midst.
He smiles.
Lance examines a small gold nugget.

KWAMI: The rain forest grew silent. At the bottom of the tin he found his fortune, all fifty grams of gold rock glistening.

(Silence.)

LANCE *(Sings)*:
> Some morning when our earthly story has been told, comrades,
> And when we all have safely reached the gates of gold!
> We shall meet our blessed Savior face to face, comrades,
> When life's brief story has been told, all been told.

(A moment.)

KWAMI: He'd wade through mud thigh-deep for half his life if he knew the other half would grant something better. No, he imagined a golden city buried beneath the thick layers of the forest and rooted tropical leaves. *(Lance laughs)* No, he wouldn't accept the ration of rice, beans, secondhand education and a pauper's burial. *(Lance holds the chunk of gold out to Kwami)* No, the forest wouldn't beat him.

(Lance does a victory dance. Thunder crashes, lightning illuminates the stage.)

His smile so wide and beautiful that it shamed the forest; yet it had changed for him. It had changed him beyond recognition; his beautiful brown skin was worn like strips of smoked pork. He now resembled his father during those last years of his drunken rage and unprovoked sorrow. The jungle had sculpted him into a dinosaur, hunched and weathered.

(He moves slowly toward the telephone.)

But nothing could take from him the smile on his face when he caught a glimpse at that first speck of gold. His por'knocker dream would return with all its vibrancy.

(*Lance disappears.*

Lights rise in the room. Ahmed, Tamara, James, Lewis and Kwami move toward the telephone.

The light bulb explodes. Blackout.)

END OF PLAY

Mud, River,
Stone

I was thumbing through the international section of the newspaper in the casual way many of us do each morning, when I came across an article that captured my imagination. It was filed out of Maputo, Mozambique but bore no byline: it recounted a bizarre incident in a remote African village, which would warrant no more than a paragraph on a heavy news day. I read it first with the moral indignation of an armchair activist, outraged enough to gasp aloud, but moved onto the next page by the end of the paragraph.

Later I found myself rereading the article. It was a reminder of a vicious war that raged for nearly two decades (more than half my life) in one of the poorest countries in the world, a war fueled by the cold war and the legacy of colonialism; a war that conscripted children, robbing them of an education and a future; a war that ceased to have meaning for many soldiers fighting in it. The article could have been the narrative of any number of African nations in the process of shedding the vestiges of armed conflict. As I read on, what struck me most were the terrible scars left by the struggle, which would now take more than a generation to heal, for the people of Mozambique had been at war so long they did not know how to cope with peace

The article (*New York Times*, October 14, 1994) had the strangest effect on me. And out of that came *Mud, River, Stone.*

The following is a fragment of the article:

Maputo, Mozambique: for four days in July any traveler who had the bad luck to drive through the village of Dombe was ordered off the road at gunpoint

and taken hostage, becoming a prisoner not of war
but of fractious peace.

The captors, demobilized guerillas sent home
after a sixteen-year civil war, demanded food and
blankets from the United Nations, and when the
offering proved inadequate, the United National officials were added to the crowd of captives.

—Lynn Nottage
1997

Production History

Mud, River, Stone was commissioned by the Acting Company in New York City (Margot Harley, Producing Director; Daryl Samuel, General Manager). It received its world premiere at Studio Arena Theatre in Buffalo, New York (Gavin Cameron-Webb, Artistic Director; Brian J. Wyatt, Executive Director) in November 1996 under the direction of Seret Scott. The set design was by Hugh Landwehr, the lights by Dennis Parichy, the sound by Rick Menke and the costumes by Martha Hally. The dramaturg was Victoria Abrash and the stage managers were Eve Clulow and David S. Stewart. The cast was as follows:

SARAH BRADLEY	Cheryl Turner
DAVID BRADLEY	Marc Damon Johnson
JOAQUIM	Marcel Braithwaite
MR. BLAKE	Ross Bickell
AMA CYLLAH	Mary F. Randle
NEIBERT	Kevin Orton
SIMONE FRICK	Drew Richardson

Mud, River, Stone received its New York City premiere at Playwrights Horizons (Tim Sanford, Artistic Director; Leslie Marcus, Managing Director) in December 1997 under the direction of Roger Rees. The set design was by Neil Patel, the lights by Frances Aronson, the sound by Red Ramona and the costumes by Kaye Voyce. The production stage manager was Laurie Goldfeder. The cast was as follows:

SARAH BRADLEY	Paula Newsome
DAVID BRADLEY	Michael Potts
JOAQUIM	Maduka Steady
MR. BLAKE	Brian Murray
AMA CYLLAH	Oni Faida Lampley
NEIBERT	John McAdams
SIMONE FRICK	Mirjana Jokovic

Characters

SARAH BRADLEY: a well-put-together African-American business woman, early thirties

DAVID BRADLEY: a hip African-American journalist, early thirties

JOAQUIM: an African man, a former soldier, now serving as the hotel bell boy, early twenties

MR. BLAKE: a white African business man of English descent, late fifties

AMA CYLLAH: a West African aid worker, educated in England, late twenties

NEIBERT: a Belgian tourist and adventurer, late twenties

SIMONE FRICK: a European U.N. negotiator, an overeager often patronizing official, thirties

Time

The present

Place

Briefly Manhattan; South East Africa

ꆦ Act One

Scene 1

David, an athletically fit, African-American man, sits at a dinner party clutching a stone in his hand. His wife, Sarah, sits expressionless next to him. She's a stylish African-American woman with a scarf tied around her neck and Armani sunglasses propped on her head. They are surrounded by party guests.

DAVID: This is the stone.
SARAH: A reminder.

(A moment.)

DAVID: You see, we were told it would be cheaper to buy a secondhand jeep. I didn't know Sarah couldn't drive standard until I twisted my wrist wrestling with a fallen tree limb. We were also told to buy basic backpacking gear at the sporting goods outlet—
SARAH: Apparently not basic enough. Thank God the first aid kit contained pain killers.
DAVID: Yeah, well, I'd expected the terrain to be a little kinder. The tour book made it sound simple and just a tiny bit adventurous.

169

SARAH: I'd never been camping. I'm from Harlem. The out-
doors, it scares me. Nature makes me think of white men
in fatigues, you understand.

DAVID: One of my friends had been to Africa a few years back,
raved. He said it would change our lives. *(A moment)* He
said, If *he* had to do it all over again *he'd* go it alone, sans
tour. See the continent without the filter. I thought it
would be easier. You know, on us.

(The lights begin to focus in on David and Sarah.)

SARAH: So we selected our destination. No conflict in years, well
paved roads, signs in English, courteous civil servants—

DAVID: Tour buses, shops with quaint carved animals—

SARAH: And folklore shows that made us sentimental. We're
beginners, a few trips to the Caribbean and a time share
on the Vineyard. Martha's Vineyard during off season,
that's adventure. *(Takes off her glasses and tries to clean the
lenses)* But he wanted to really see the continent, like the
naturalists on the "Discovery Channel."

DAVID: And why not? The splendid savanna speckled with
trees and high grass. The sun melting into a distant mountain range covered in a perpetual mist. *(Imitates the cry of
a bird)*

SARAH: He wanted to see the mud and stone ruins of our
ancestors.

DAVID: I'd always imagined our trip accompanied by a sound
track. A perfect blend of rhythms by Africa and orchestra-
tion by Europe. It sounded romantic—

SARAH: If romance is the sound of stripped gears. Two weeks
in Aruba, piña coladas on the beach, my thought. We can
do Africa later.

DAVID: But it was extraordinary: rustic villages, the sweet scent
of burning wood. The children would gather around the
car window and laugh and laugh and laugh.

(They smile at the remembrance.)

SARAH: He let them listen to his Walkman, to rap music. I'd never seen so many beautiful people, the faces, hues of earthen tones.

DAVID: It was like a narcotic. We were finally home. Sarah kept saying, "We'll get pictures on our way back." So I didn't take pictures.

(A moment. As David and Sarah speak the following, the dinner guests slowly strip them out of their party attire and dress them in muddy safari gear.)

SARAH: Then . . . well . . . Ummm . . . the last sign we passed on the road was hand painted, obviously of great importance to someone . . . It was merely a name . . . Bangi or Bansi . . . or . . . I can't remember. Crude and meaningless. But David seemed to think he'd heard the name before. "It's a city on the lake." *(Raps)* "It's a city on the lake. It's a city on the lake. It's a city on lake." After the fourth repetition it sounded . . . cool, like a city on a tranquil lake.

DAVID: I felt the breeze.

SARAH: He insisted that we continue onward.

DAVID: I insisted? That is not how I remember it. I recall you saying, "There is a sign David, it must mean something is ahead. Let's keep going, sweetie."

(Sarah puts her glasses back on.)

SARAH: So we followed that road for two days until it petered out into a stony brook not quite large enough to float down. Then we realized that it wasn't a road at all, but a blemish on the landscape etched by a herd of retreating animals. We gave over our common sense to a few words on a map, without a blink of an eye or hesitation.

DAVID: Lost, with nary a clue between us, we ran out of gas.

SARAH: When David emptied that last can of gas into the tank we actually wept like babies. We didn't even notice when the sky darkened.

DAVID: And it began to rain and rain—

SARAH: And rain.

DAVID: Our road became a river. Our passage back . . . was subsumed by nature.

SARAH: And then we were in the forest beneath a dark sullen canopy of trees, filtering through thick rain drops, a virtual ocean. We thought we'd drown in rain water. *(David laughs)* And the forest—

DAVID: Bellowed, a modern jazz ensemble's second encore. Brilliant.

SARAH: Furious. He always sees things in musical terms. We spent the night in the car—

DAVID: Listening to love tunes on the Walkman. Taking turns until the battery faded. Waiting to be rescued. *(Sings)* "Rescue me!"

(The surrounding lights very slowly begin to rise on David and Sarah.)

SARAH: I thought we were going to die.

DAVID: Yes.

SARAH: The trees rustled wildly, and you picked up this stone to defend us, so brave and misguided, not sure from which direction danger might come.

DAVID: It was the only weapon I could find.

SARAH: Understand, we walked for nearly three and a half days.

DAVID: I wanted to abandon the luggage.

SARAH: Thank goodness you didn't, could you imagine being anywhere without a change of clothing? Needless to say the clothing didn't travel very well—

DAVID: Then we saw what looked like a road.

(The beginnings of a hotel lobby appear.)

We were actually sort of surprised to come upon a deserted village. And the hotel, it was—
SARAH *(Half-shouted)*: An oasis.

(The lights rise on the hotel lobby, which has the faded grandeur of the colonial age. It was once quite beautiful, but is now worn from neglect. The front door leads to a veranda crumbling with age. The veranda sags slightly. A huge window, the "fourth wall," overlooks the audience. A grand old staircase twists its way upward like a wandering vine. Overhead, a chandelier serves as a reminder of the past splendor. Sitting on the front desk is a fraying log book and a bell. The pillows on the wicker furniture are well fluffed, but faded from years of exposure to the sun. The bar against the back wall is surprisingly well stocked. The fans moan. In the distance a hand radio plays "Girl From Ipanema" in Portuguese. Mr. Blake, a bombastic white African of English descent, lounges on the couch, drinking a martini and smoking a cigar . . . satisfied. He brushes a fly away from his face. Joaquim, a young African man, wears a bell boy uniform that harkens back to a colonial age. He leans against the wall peering out into space wearing an expression of discomfort and boredom. Outside, a torrential downpour begins. Joaquim shuts the door and returns to his perch. David quickly fumbles through a Swahili phrase book, searching for the appropriate words. Joaquim speaks with a heavy accent.)

JOAQUIM *(Standing at attention)*: Welcome to The Imperial Hotel.
DAVID: He speaks the language!
SARAH: It's a hotel, sweetie.

(They're overwhelmed with excitement.)

We thought we'd get swallowed up by all this rain. We thought we were gonna—

DAVID: Don't say it . . . knock on wood. *(He knocks on the countertop)*

SARAH: I don't want to be wet ever again. I don't even think I can take a shower. *(Laughs)*

JOAQUIM *(Disinterested)*: Yes, yes. I will let the Missus know you are here. *(Exits)*

SARAH: Thank God, is all I have to say. I couldn't walk another step.

DAVID: Well, we're here.

(Joaquim reenters.)

JOAQUIM: Missus wants to know where black people dressed and talk like Europeans come from.

(David laughs at the notion.)

SARAH: We're from the United States. America.

DAVID: *African*-Americans.

SARAH: As if he couldn't guess that?

(Joaquim laughs. A moment.)

DAVID *(Whispered)*: Why do you think he's laughing, Sarah? You think he's laughing at us?

SARAH: Yes. *(A moment)* Well, is there a room available? *(Forces out a smile)*

JOAQUIM: Forgive me, not many people come this time of year. Not since the trouble.

DAVID: Really? Well, we're on vacation, off the beaten path.

SARAH: David likes to brag about his wonderful discoveries. We lost the car and half our cash in the process.

DAVID: We didn't expect it to rain quite so hard.

JOAQUIM *(Disinterested)*: Yes, yes. We do have a room. Please sign the register. *(David signs the register. Joaquim examines the name)* I will show you to your accommodations. *(Gives David and Sarah the once-over)* I'll make sure you're comfortable, you'll be with us for some time then. *(Lifts David and Sarah's bags and ascends the staircase)*

SARAH: What did he mean, we'll be here for some time? *(Whispered)* You think we'll be all right?

DAVID: I don't see that we have a choice.

SARAH: Maybe you should check and see if they accept credit cards.

DAVID: Let's not worry about it now, love. I just want to get some sleep.

(David and Sarah exit. Mr. Blake stands, revealing a gun in a holster around his waist. He checks the register.)

Scene 2

Hotel lobby. Rain continues.

Mr. Blake stares at a fragment of the newspaper. David enters. He is festively dressed, perhaps for dinner. David rings the bell on the front desk. Getting no response, he beats out a rhythm on the bell. Joaquim enters.

JOAQUIM: Yes?

DAVID: Towels? There are no towels in the room.

JOAQUIM: Yes?

DAVID: Would it be possible to have a few towels?

JOAQUIM: The Missus has left, maybe later. *(Turns to leave)*

DAVID: Hey, hey there my friend. And listen, I'm having some difficulty turning on the faucet.

JOAQUIM: I wouldn't worry, there is no water. That's why there is the basin. Let me know if you need me to fetch you more water from outside.

(A moment.)

DAVID: Oh yeah. Wow. Um . . . is there a telephone I could use?
JOAQUIM: It went down. It will be fixed . . . soon.
DAVID: Today? Tomorrow?

(Joaquim remains expressionless.)

JOAQUIM: No.

(A moment.)

DAVID: When?
JOAQUIM: Soon soon.
DAVID: As opposed to soon later?
JOAQUIM: Yes.
DAVID: Thank you, I see.
JOAQUIM: May I help you with something else?

(David spreads a map across the table.)

DAVID: Yeah, one other thing, just where the hell are we?
JOAQUIM *(Standing erect)*: The Imperial Hotel.
DAVID: No, on the map? Um . . . you see . . . we got a little lost.

(Joaquim examines the map. Thinks.)

JOAQUIM *(Pointing)*: There. . . .
DAVID: Really? I thought we were further south.
JOAQUIM *(Pointing to another spot on the map)*: Or maybe there.
DAVID: We can't possibly—okey dokey . . . I can see where this is leading . . . Thank you anyway, man.

(David shakes his head and refolds the map. Sarah enters. She is dressed in colorful resort wear. She straightens her wraparound skirt.)

SARAH: Did you find out what time dinner is served?

JOAQUIM: Supper? I will let the Missus know that you are hungry. I think some bush meat came in this morning.

DAVID: Bush meat?

(He shivers at the thought. Joaquim bows and exits.)

SARAH: I hesitate to ask. *(She gazes out the window, toward the audience)* Sweetie . . . Come look. It's beautiful, even with the rain. *(A moment)* Get the camera!

DAVID: You lost the camera in the gully.

SARAH: This wasn't my idea! Margaret and Harry did Senegal. Got to see the spot from whence their ancestors originated. Their tale of kissing the ground is quite touching.

DAVID: I'm sure. But *we're* determined to have a great time, despite the mad stupid trek here. Tomorrow morning *we're* going to explore the local flora and fauna, we're going to kick back and have *fun*.

SARAH: Promise?

(They gaze out the window together.)

DAVID: Promise! May I?

(Sarah nods. David hugs her from behind.)

SARAH: Sweetie . . . Have you thought about how we're going to get back?

(David starts to answer—)

MR. BLAKE: Excuse me! *(David and Sarah are startled by Mr. Blake's loud, brash Colonial accent)* I'm searching for a five letter prefix with the word "space." Second letter, "Y."

(A moment. David thinks.)

DAVID: Cyber . . . C-Y-B-E-R.

MR. BLAKE: Jesus, you're right! I've been staring at this bloody crossword puzzle for a month, awaiting the solution. I'm not going to ask you what it means, because I'll forget. I have that kind of mind, you know. Thank God it's complete. I can move on to other tasks. Goodness, I think I'll have a cocktail. It was a damn curse to find myself stranded here with only a small fragment of the *Herald Tribune*, with the *Times* crossword puzzle and a 250 word brief on the detention of armed insurgents by the Sultan of Brunei Darussalam. *(Sarah and David shrug)* Where the hell is Brunei? Makes you feel inadequate. The world gets on without ya . . . Hello.

DAVID: Hello.

MR. BLAKE: I take it you're the Bradley's, I'm Blake.

SARAH: Are you waiting for the dining room to open?

MR. BLAKE: The Missus is probably having a nap about this time Actually haven't seen her in days. Our hostess may have fled to the city like anyone else with common sense.

DAVID: But do you know what time the dining room opens?

MR. BLAKE: Time? *(Laughs)* If. If. That's the operative word. Time? My boy, you own the sole watch in this village. And quite a nice one if I may say so. *(David glances down at his watch)* What time do you have?

DAVID: It's close to seven.

MR. BLAKE: Seven o'clock. Ah, I'm savoring the notion. I really should get a new watch, but there is no pleasure in telling time if you're the only one with a regard for it.

(A moment.)

SARAH: Is there a restaurant near by?

(Mr. Blake chuckles to himself.)

MR. BLAKE: No, no. It closed about . . . eighteen years ago, it was a lovely French place, owned by a . . . a Belgian. Charles Bertrand. He moved to the Central Republic during the war. Married. Hear he got the plague. Well, rumors, you didn't hear it from me. Don't worry, Missus is a marvelous cook. You're in for a regional treat if you can stomach grilled Gibbard. *(Re-lights his cigar)*

DAVID: I can't wait.

SARAH: Just who is the Missus?

MR. BLAKE: She owns the place. Proprietress. Would you like to join me for a cocktail, then?

(David looks to Sarah, she nods.)

SARAH: A cocktail? I feel like I'm in the movies.

DAVID *(Amused by the invitation)*: Thanks.

MR. BLAKE *(Bellow)*: JOAQUIM! JOAQUIM! *(Snaps)* Sit down . . . *(Softer)* Please. *(David and Sarah sit on the couch. Joaquim enters)* Where have you been? Didn't you hear me calling?

JOAQUIM: Yes, sir. What may I get you?

MR. BLAKE: Bring me a martini and for my . . . my . . . friends here. *(To David)* Is that your pleasure?

JOAQUIM: Perhaps they may like to have something else?

MR. BLAKE: They'll speak up! *(To David, warmly)* Don't permit me to make assumptions.

DAVID: Martini. Fine.

SARAH: Me too. Why not?

179

(Mr. Blake breaks into a wide self-satisfied grin. He and Joaquim exchange a series of tense glances. Joaquim goes to the bar to mix the drinks. Sarah smiles at Joaquim as he crosses to the bar. Joaquim remains expressionless.)

MR. BLAKE: Never mind him. I'm afraid he lost his sense of humor during the war, now he's perpetually in search of a smile. *(He sniffs the air)* Mmm, you smell sweet. Cologne. That's nice.

SARAH: Excuse me?

MR. BLAKE: Your cologne is lovely. It's a luxury that generally doesn't find its way this far into the bush. Don't let the Missus catch a whiff, things have a way of disappearing and denial is practically a religion out here. *(Laughs heartily)* What brings you to our . . . jungle? We don't generally have the pleasure of American visitors in these parts. I understand the communism thing is a bit frightening to you still.

SARAH: We won, haven't you heard.

MR. BLAKE: Cheers! Yes, I think I . . . I did hear. Well, congratulations. *(Laughs robustly, almost too much so)* Anyway! I'm glad for the conversation. These are the lean years, no one has much to say anymore. Tell me something good. Anything. News. Gossip.

(A moment. Joaquim turns around from the bar, his face hardens into a grimace.)

JOAQUIM: Mr. Blake, do you want it on the rocks?

MR. BLAKE: We've been through this.

JOAQUIM: Tell me again.

MR. BLAKE: No.

SARAH: Is he all right?

MR. BLAKE: Him? Please. Don't be seduced by his theatrics. He'll have you feeling sorry for him. *(Joaquim serves them martinis)* He was a soldier for ten years, you know. *(To Joaquim)* You may go. He probably killed more people than you could imagine.

(Joaquim retreats to the bar.)

DAVID: But he's so young.

MR. BLAKE: Twenty years of civil war you run out of grown men, there's no shame in using boys as long as you win. Anyway, how is your martini?

(Sarah sips her martini.)

SARAH: Strong, but good.

MR. BLAKE: The best. I insist. Top shelf. There is truth in the drink, my father used to say. And he never did business with a man until he'd gotten him blind drunk. Take a look. This may be the finest bar in all the world.

DAVID: Impressive.

MR. BLAKE: Single malt Scotches. Never touch 'em, just like knowing that they're there.

SARAH: Are you on vacation as well?

MR. BLAKE: Business. I . . . I flew in before the rains. Now my runway is a river. And I don't have enough gas to make it back. I must wait.

DAVID: You don't seem bothered.

MR. BLAKE: What else can I do? I choose to do business in the bush, therefore I must surrender to its whims. Supply plane will be in soon?

DAVID: How soon?

MR. BLAKE: Soon . . . soon.

(A moment.)

DAVID: I see. *(Shoots a glance at Sarah)*

SARAH: Just how long is the rain expected to last?

MR. BLAKE: A day, a week, a month. I can't say.

SARAH: You're joking.

MR. BLAKE: Not yet.

DAVID: A month? Come on.

MR. BLAKE: And tomorrow the sun may shine.

SARAH: Please! I'm due back on the job in eight days. There's a board meeting on the first of the month.

MR. BLAKE: We can only hope. *(Shrugs and raises his drink to Joaquim, who sulks at the bar)* But don't let that get you down. Cheers! To a holiday in a beautiful country. Yes?

SARAH: Yes.

DAVID: I'm embarrassed to ask, but just where are we? *(Mr. Blake smiles)*

MR. BLAKE: Let me see your map? *(David unfolds his map across the coffee table. Mr. Blake points to a spot on the map)* We're approximately there.

(David glances over at Joaquim.)

DAVID: No . . . no. We're supposed to be near here. There was a travel advisory in that country.

MR. BLAKE: Is.

DAVID *(Pointing to the map)*: But, we took this road.

MR. BLAKE: No wonder you got lost. That road was never built. It's the way of this country. As though putting it on the map could will it into existence. The World Bank officials come, they . . . they see a map, progress, a huge road cutting across the country. That's the poetry of our existence out here. On paper, we are connected to the rest of the world by a glorious red line, but in reality, we are obscured by the unpredictability of the weather and our government.

DAVID: Come on, you're exaggerating.

MR. BLAKE: Oh no. This country is a bastion of good intentions and ill-fated projects. Every village has a telephone, but few the wires to connect them to the world.

SARAH: Jesus, I've never been truly lost, ever. I always knew eventually I'd find my way to a gas station, a phone booth, a rest stop.

MR. BLAKE: And judging from the map, you crossed the bloody minefields. You're probably the first people to make it down that road with limbs intact since the late eighties. That deserves a fucking toast. Good work! *(Sarah gasps)* Say Joaquim, they crossed the bloody mines to get here! I guess you didn't do your job very well.

(Mr. Blake bursts into laughter. Joaquim is not amused.)

JOAQUIM: We did plenty good job, Mr. Blake. Plenty good.

SARAH: You're just saying that to make me scared.

MR. BLAKE: Not at all. Let me touch both of yous for good luck.

(He touches David on the arm and then Sarah. Sarah laughs at the notion.)

DAVID: There were no signs that said there were mines.

MR. BLAKE: That sort of defeats the purpose I suppose. *(Laughs and knocks back his martini)* Cheers! I'm impressed. I wouldn't have done it. *(Laughs)*

JOAQUIM: Would you care for another cocktail, Mr. Blake?

MR. BLAKE: Of course I would . . . We have the civil war to thank for that. Right, Joaquim? But, the world has probably forgotten. Ah! So, what is it that you do?

DAVID: I'm a journalist.

MR. BLAKE: Journalist, you say? *(Glances over at Joaquim)* Really? On assignment?

DAVID: Well no, I write for a music magazine you've probably never heard of. I mostly cover R&B, hip-hop, urban contemporary. Love. Passion. Crime. Money. You know.

MR. BLAKE: I don't know, but it sounds very interesting. What about your good lady?

SARAH: I'm an investment banker.

MR. BLAKE: Money, money. I like you already. A speculator in these parts is . . . titillating.

(Sarah takes a business card out of her pocket and hands it to Mr. Blake. Joaquim refreshes Mr. Blake's cocktail.)

SARAH: Here is one of my cards. If you're ever in New York and find yourself in need of advice.

MR. BLAKE: Lovely all that color, very nice. I must do that.

DAVID *(To Sarah)*: Sarah, who did you expect to meet?

MR. BLAKE: You never know . . . Thank you. May I keep this? *(Studies the card)* Vice president. A woman with a title. *(Nods in deference, then sticks the card in his breast pocket)*

DAVID: So you're here on . . . business?

(Joaquim refreshes David and Sarah's cocktails.)

MR. BLAKE: Yes, I dabble in this and that, mostly perishables. I cater to the more remote regions of this continent, places most businessmen ain't willing to travel. Shame, quite a fortune to be made in this tangle of trees. Quite a fortune. If you're willing and able.

DAVID: Have you met the other guests?

MR. BLAKE: You and me. Us and we.

DAVID: Really? But it's such a large hotel. I would have thought—

MR. BLAKE: Do you like it?

SARAH: It's fabulous.

MR. BLAKE: My uncle built it in the thirties. *(Strolls through the lobby, proudly)* He had a vision of a railway from the coast cutting across the continent. He built this hotel not even by a river, hoping that he could bribe the officials to have the railway pass through here. But the jungle consumed the railroad before it reached this point. And he lost the hotel in his drunken years, in exchange for the lifting of a spell from his prick. It had gone completely and hopelessly flaccid. In his ignorance, he blamed the spirits. You see, he'd gone native.

SARAH: "Native"?

MR. BLAKE: I meant it in a more descriptive, than pejorative way. This hotel is the final vestige of an age. You wouldn't understand. It's my totem. Besides, Missus has tried to maintain it in all its splendor, don't you think? But I'll tell you though, I hold my prick every time I pass her. *(Nostalgic)* It really was a splendid dream. Can you imagine the insanity that brokered this magnificence? The chandelier was brought up from South Africa. The wood, the finest mahogany, imported from West Africa. The glass, from Cairo. This hotel represents the totality of the Continent. He thought he could bring it all together under one roof. Here now, the embodiment of an idea gone sour.

DAVID: How do the people in the village feel, living in the shadow of this hotel?

MR. BLAKE *(Whispers)*: Can you blame a man for wanting to re-create the lap of luxury in the middle of this beautiful village without a road? There is something seductive about the seclusion. Did you know that everyone in this village was once connected by blood or marriage?

SARAH: It sounds frightening.

(David nudges Sarah.)

MR. BLAKE: Perhaps, but where else could I get a perfect martini in this part of the jungle? My uncle relinquished his dream with the stipulation that the bar always remain stocked. Let the place fall by the wayside. Let the boards rot, but by God let an Englishman always be able to walk in and get a drink. That's . . . vision.

(He laughs robustly. A moment.)

SARAH: So, where is everybody?

MR. BLAKE: Cities. Wickedness, poverty, and twenty years of war have made this village a festival of despair.

SARAH: So much for curiosity. I guess we won't be taking the tour. *(Walks over to the window)*

MR. BLAKE: Another cocktail?

DAVID: Better not . . . What time do you think dinner will be served?

MR. BLAKE: If . . . if . . . that's the operative word at the Imperial. If the rain stops, if the supplies come. If there is peace. If.

(Sarah walks toward the bar to put down her glass. She loses her balance and falls against the bar.)

SARAH: Sorry. I feel a little dizzy.

(The lights begin to flicker.)

DAVID: What's going on?

MR. BLAKE: Oh Jesus, there goes the bloody generator. MISSUS!

(The lights continue to flicker. Joaquim lights a candle. Darkness falls on all but Sarah and Joaquim.)

JOAQUIM: He says his uncle built this hotel, but it is not the truth. Our village did. Look closely at the details throughout the rooms. You will see our history carved into the woodwork. Our stories are all there.

(Blackout.)

Scene 3

Three days later.

The sounds of the forest. Lights rise on Joaquim standing on the veranda. He is watching the rain. Lights fade.

Lights rise on the hotel lobby. The rain continues.

Neibert, a large blond white man wrapped in the bright red cloth worn by a Masai warrior, stands like a statue. He is adorned with colorful African trading beads. He silently puffs on a cigarette.

Ama, a pretty West African woman wearing neat, simple clothing, stands at the front desk frantically ringing the bell. She is soaking wet and carries a knapsack.

Mr. Blake sits in the arm chair with his back to the front desk. Concealed.

AMA: Maximo? Maximo!

MR. BLAKE: I don't think he's here.

AMA *(Startled)*: Oh? You frightened me. *(Mr. Blake stands up, revealing himself. She's disappointed)* Ah, hello Mr. Blake, how goes us today?

MR. BLAKE: Pleasant. Rain. What else can I say? Hello sister.

AMA: What brings you in this weather?

MR. BLAKE: The storm set in over the green sea. Landed. And here I find myself.

AMA: I came to use the telephone and see if there's been any word about supplies for the mission.

MR. BLAKE: Thirty kilometers to use the telephone in the midst of a torrential downpour? It's got that bad? *(He observes Neibert)*

AMA: How do you tell hungry people no?

MR. BLAKE: No. *(Laughs)*

AMA: You seem in good spirits this month.

MR. BLAKE: Do I? Well, we . . . we have guests. It's practically a convention here. One might think we . . . we were planning something. A party. A revolution. *(He studies Neibert)* And it appears, good sister, you've even brought a friend.

AMA: He wandered into the mission a week ago. He was hungry. Lost. *(Whispers)* He's a Belgian.

NEIBERT: You needn't whisper. My ears are quite sensitive from living amongst the Mbuti in the forest. Besides, I'm no longer Belgian, thank you, nor am I lost in the traditional sense.

(Ama rings the bell to the front desk.)

MR. BLAKE: Really? I was unaware that there was more than one way of being lost . . . Are you an anthropologist? Epidemiologist? Entomologist? Or some other over-educated interloper trifling away grant money? I didn't think the government was welcoming your kind quite yet.

NEIBERT: I don't wait for invitations, and naturally I don't recognize artificial boundaries. Government? . . . A tribe, a community, how do you draw lines around that?

MR. BLAKE: My mistake. Are you a hunter then?

(Neibert chuckles to himself.)

NEIBERT: In some people's eyes. But I carry no weapon as you can see.

MR. BLAKE: We have a riddle, sister, a hunter that carries no weapon, no camera. Let me think.

(Ama smiles. Neibert squats down.)

AMA *(Playfully)*: I've learned that a white man always carries a weapon. The most dangerous ones are those you can't see.

(Mr. Blake laughs heartily.)

MR. BLAKE: Propaganda from ancient times.

NEIBERT *(To Mr. Blake)*: Do not tell me, you're a hunter. *(Laughs)* Perhaps not, too smug. You're—

MR. BLAKE: An old drunk. That's the extent of my story. Excuse me.

(He chuckles and returns to his seat. He lights a cigar stub. Neibert mumbles something under his breath. Ama rings the bell again.)

You can let up on the bell. For God sake, you'll wake the dead.

AMA: Maximo is always—

MR. BLAKE: Don't look so worried, sister.

AMA: Oh sorry, do I look worried? *(Looks at the ledger on the desk)* Damnit, I've come up here every other month. *(Reaches out to ring the bell. She stops herself)*

MR. BLAKE: 'Cept the blisters, what else are you expecting? If I were you I'd cut my losses and go home.

AMA: To what? To be married off for a few household items and a motorbike? *(Defensively)* I'm needed here.

(Mr. Blake laughs.)

MR. BLAKE: A pretty girl like you would fetch more than a motorbike. Indeed, I find it a bit odd that you take comfort in other people's miseries.

AMA: Ah, Mr. Blake, there are things you will never understand. *(A moment. She avoids eye contact)* So what's the word? How does the capital look?

MR. BLAKE: It seems peaceful enough. To be honest, I've avoided the capital, too quiet. "It is the calm and silent water that drowns a man."

AMA: Let's hope it's just an old adage.

(Joaquim enters.)

JOAQUIM *(Snaps)*: Who keeps ringing the bell? *(Ama steps forward)* Oh sorry, I thought it was someone else. How goes?

AMA *(Surprised)*: Good . . . Who are you? . . . Where is Maximo?

JOAQUIM: Went to the city.

AMA: Oh?

JOAQUIM: Two months now.

AMA: Oh yes, of course. Gone! I wish I could have said good-bye. He was taking that correspondence course in accounting. Remember, Mr. Blake? He'd wait each month for the plane to bring him the assignments. He'd hurry to complete them so the pilot could carry them back to the city . . . *(Laughs. Then suddenly)* I guess he finally completed that course.

MR. BLAKE: Good ole Maximo!

AMA: So he went to the city?

MR. BLAKE: You sound disappointed.

AMA: Do I? I'm sure he'll write. He said if he left he'd write, let us know what's going on in the world. *(A moment)* But that is not why I'm here . . . Of course. Has anything come for the mission?

(Joaquim shakes his head. Ama's smile disappears. She looks as though she's about to burst into tears, however she miraculously recovers her smile.)

I suppose the phone doesn't work either?

JOAQUIM: It will be fixed soon.

AMA: Soon. We should be so lucky.

JOAQUIM: Do you need anything else?

AMA: Yes . . . I need food for the mission, medicine, books, and a ticket home to Nigeria.

JOAQUIM: I meant—

AMA: I know what you meant, my friend. *(Forces a smile)* I'm Ama and you are?

JOAQUIM: Joaquim . . . I come from the farming village around the bend.

AMA: . . . So when are you going to the city? I'm sorry.

(Neibert peers out the window. He sniffs the air.)

JOAQUIM *(To Neibert)*: May I help you with something, sir?

(Neibert doesn't avert his gaze.)

NEIBERT: The wind is carrying a big storm on its shoulders. Not good. *(Sniffs again)* Not good.

(Neibert lights a cigarette. Joaquim retrieves an ashtray for him.)

MR. BLAKE: You haven't answered the riddle yet. What are you hunting?

NEIBERT: The agogwe.

MR. BLAKE: The agogwe? Nonsense. Don't tell me you're searching for the little red hairy man that dwells in the forest and steals vegetables from farmers.

(Neibert reaches into a leather pouch and produces a tuft of red hair.)

NEIBERT: What is that?

MR. BLAKE: Hair from a baboon.

NEIBERT: Not so.

MR. BLAKE: You're telling me? I have hunted these woods for nearly three decades. If the agogwe exists it does so in myths, folklore and the fantasies of European schoolboys.

(Neibert laughs.)

NEIBERT: The pygmies have seen it and they are the only Africans that truly know these forests. We pretend to know it, but we are afraid of it. Afraid of what we'll find if we disturb the delicate balance between myth and reality.

MR. BLAKE: Indeed, you Europeans remain sentimental for the conquest.

(Ama laughs.)

AMA: True, true. We Africans don't need to capture something to accept its existence. That's why we have many more spirits living amongst us.

JOAQUIM *(Suddenly)*: There is no agogwe. Mr. Blake is right.

(Joaquim returns to his perch against the wall. Neibert approaches him and he stands at attention.)

NEIBERT *(To Joaquim)*: Do you really believe that?

JOAQUIM: Excuse me, I didn't mean to intrude on your conversation.

MR. BLAKE: You're so foolish. You probably went to University and got a degree in something quite useful. Oh no, a bloody working man doesn't have the luxury of exploring the world of mythology. He either accepts or he does not.

NEIBERT: And yet here you are with a martini in your hand as if nothing has happened. Which world do you dwell in, sir?

MR. BLAKE: I've been on this continent far too long to engage in this sort of conversation.

NEIBERT: Do you even care about this forest?

MR. BLAKE: I never let my feelings get in the way of business.

AMA: Shame. A man of your wealth could do much for this region.

MR. BLAKE: Like what? Plant crops to be washed away? Build a factory to be consumed by the jungle in a few years? Mine the mountain sides and poison the rivers? I've done all of that. Come here, my self-righteous hunter of the agogwe. You have the audacity to criticize me for enjoying a martini? Bullshit is what I have to say to that. Bullshit.

(Neibert props one leg against another, as if a Masai warrior.)

AMA: Mr. Blake, let him search for the agogwe. No harm done. I dare not ask your purpose in life.

(David and Sarah enter dressed in resort wear.)

MR. BLAKE: Go on ask me.
AMA: Oh no no no . . . It might make me scared. *(Crosses over to the couch, sits)*
MR. BLAKE: Ah, the charming Americans. They're on holiday.
AMA: Holiday? Travelling in this country, you're very brave. It's encouraging that someone is still interested in our scourge.
SARAH: Good morning.

(David checks his watch.)

DAVID: Actually afternoon. 12:34 P.M.
NEIBERT: Hello.
DAVID: . . . Hello.
AMA: Not much of a holiday? Rain.
SARAH: I've been told it will stop soon . . .
MR. BLAKE: And how are we feeling today?
SARAH: . . . and wish I could say something has changed.
MR. BLAKE: But everything has changed. There is a river where there once was a road. Half of our village has been swept aside.
SARAH: And I was hoping you would tell me the cavalry was outside.
MR. BLAKE: The tsetse fly took care of the cavalry, my dear Mrs. Bradley.

DAVID: Well, the tour book said the region's hot and humid during this season, but three days of pounding rain must be some kind of record.

SARAH: Don't say that, David. That's not comforting.

(David peers down at his watch again. Then stretches his back.)

DAVID: Joaquim, are the phones working yet?

AMA: Queue up.

JOAQUIM: The phones are down.

SARAH: I don't want to be the one to say it, but this is becoming one of those nightmare vacations you read about in *Traveler* magazine. Where is a good concierge when you need one?

DAVID: Sweetie, we agreed that we'd remain positive. This is an adventure.

SARAH: Oh, that's right! I forgot. You, the high adventurer who has never spent more than an hour away from a telephone. You should have heard him screaming last night because he found a beetle between the sheets. "It may bite, it may bite!" "Get it! Get it!"

DAVID: Anyway . . . *(Chipper)* How is everybody doing today?

(A moment. Everyone manages a faint smile.)

SARAH: I'd like a drink.

DAVID: It's a little early.

SARAH: What else am I going to do? Shop?

(Sarah sits at the bar. David stands awkwardly.)

MR. BLAKE: Can I interest anyone in a hand of bridge?

DAVID: Thanks, maybe later, we don't want to have all the fun at once.

(Joaquim goes behind the bar to serve Sarah.)

SARAH: The usual. Leave the bottle out. Leave it there. I'm sure I'll need another.

DAVID: We'll be out of here in a day or two, baby. I promise.

SARAH: You promised yesterday, the day before. "Supply plane's coming, love." Those were your words. Well where is it? *(To Joaquim)* Can you turn on the radio? I can't stand the sound of those fucking crickets.

NEIBERT: They are not crickets, they are the sound of—

SARAH: Thank you, but I don't actually care. I just want them to stop for one minute. One Goddamn minute.

DAVID: This is not the city; you can't turn things on and off.

SARAH: "Where is Sarah?" "Hear she went to Africa." "Interesting. Searching for her roots or something." "Just how much vacation time did she have?" "Well, there was that trip to see her husband's Aunt Aeola in Baton Rouge, seven days."

DAVID: She was dying.

SARAH: But she didn't die, David. She miraculously recovered. And I lost seven vacation days that I need very badly at this moment. *(Gulps down her drink)*

DAVID: Will I hear about poor Aunt Aeola for the rest of my life?

SARAH *(Suddenly)*: I WANT TO GO HOME! I HATE THE SOUND OF THE FUCKING RAIN! I want to hear music and buy colorful fabric. I mean, Margaret and Harry came home from Senegal with all of those fabulous carvings. I'm going to go home with a hangover.

(Joaquim goes behind the front desk and turns on the portable radio. Country-western music sounds. David tries to comfort Sarah. He wraps his arms around her, she breaks away.)

(Calmly) Excuse me . . . excuse me. I'm sorry, I'm being so rude. It's really a pleasure to meet all of you. I'm not the ugly American. *(She grows faint)*

DAVID: Do you want to lie down, love?

SARAH: If I lie down any longer I'll sprout roots.

(She pulls up to the bar. The others watch her.)

DAVID: You sure?

SARAH: Yes. Does everyone need to be looking at me?

(They all turn away.)

NEIBERT: The forest can be deafening.

DAVID: You're telling me. It's like a jam session gone awry.

(Neibert goes to the window and stares out at the rain.)

MR. BLAKE: If you allow me, I have just the remedy for both of you. Something I discovered during a siege in the Congo. It saved my life and the life of a French journalist who oddly enough went on to defame my character. Bastard! *(He goes behind the bar, mixes a drink for David)* Would you care for some cognac, sister?

AMA: No thank you, Mister Blake, but I have been eyeing that bottle of brandy wine.

MR. BLAKE: It would be my pleasure to buy you a drink. A little tithe for the church so to speak.

AMA: Thank you.

(Mr. Blake starts to pour Ama a drink. Joaquim, proprietorial, takes the bottle out of Mr. Blake's hand.)

JOAQUIM: You're a guest here. Let me do that.

(He carefully wipes the dust out of a glass and pours Ama some brandy wine. Neibert reaches into his sack and produces a cigarette.)

AMA: Forgive me for staring, but I've been here two years and I can count on one hand the number of encounters with strangers. It's not that it doesn't happen, it's just that this fractious peace makes you sensitive . . . More cautious.

SARAH: Believe me, we're not here by choice. We took the wrong turn and wandered out of the arms of our idyllic vacation, and into this hotel lobby.

NEIBERT: It's the rain that brought us all together.

DAVID: To be downright honest, I'm glad there are a few more folks. Frankly I was getting worried; I'm a city boy, I'm used to seeing different faces every day. Right? (*He begins to laugh nervously*) Right?

(*A moment.*)

AMA (*Soberly*): Are you with the government?

SARAH: Him? Ask him to name eight African countries?

DAVID: Sarah! (*Sarah laughs and sips her drink*) No, no. I push gangsta rap to young white boys in the suburbs. That practically makes me public enemy number one in the eyes of Capitol Hill. (*Looks over at Sarah; excited*) I cover "the freshest sounds on the air waves."

SARAH: Don't be modest. He's a highly influential journalist, his words sell records. His words are coveted by the top executives in the record industry, they make songs out of a few mumbled lines and an incompetent melody. (*David hums a bass line and demonstrates a little dance with it*) You're talking to a man who has coined phrases, like "Bootie Jam."

DAVID: Bootie Jam.

(*Sarah laughs.*)

SARAH: He's very talented. He could have edited his own magazine, but he permitted someone to talk him out of it. And now *that* someone runs an empire. Right, David?

DAVID: No one cares to hear about my failings. Not all of us can be superstars, Sarah. *(Moves over to the window)* And as you know they wouldn't have given that position to an African-American.

SARAH: That's not true.

DAVID: I'm happy with my job folks . . . I'm happy going to industry parties and cruising the buffet table for goodies and occasionally rubbing elbows with my idols . . . I'm happy that I'm not in some remote region of the world tracking quaint local customs and popping Bactrim. I'm happy!

SARAH: He's very sensitive.

AMA: As is everyone these days.

(A moment. Ama sips her drink.)

SARAH *(Sarcastically)*: Really? Why is that? Is it the time of year? The crickets? The rain?

(Sarah and Ama enjoy a laugh. Ama stops abruptly.)

AMA: Exactly . . . smart dressed lady. Our grain is nearly gone. If the rain continues it will wipe out what subsistence crops the mission has left. And I heard there were soldiers spotted about eighty-five kilometers north. Up country.

SARAH: Sorry I asked.

MR. BLAKE: Ah, it's just talk. You're so serious for someone your age. It's probably nothing.

AMA: I don't want to get caught in the middle.

MR. BLAKE: It's a little soon to run, don't you think?

AMA: Young men are disappearing again. A forest that has supported the same people for years is teeming with new faces. And even you are back, Mr. Blake. Why?

(Joaquim's mask of indifference slackens. He moves closer to hear the conversation.)

MR. BLAKE: As I said, I got caught in the rain.

AMA: Isn't that how it always begins. *(Snickers)*

NEIBERT *(Suddenly)*: I saw them.

AMA: You see!

NEIBERT: She's right! Some seventy kilometers north. I kept well out of their way. They were drunk. Up country. Drunk soldiers gathered people in the village center. It might have been nothing. I left the village before I could ask questions. I don't ask questions. I know not to stay, not to be seen.

SARAH: Intrigue. Please. What's the big deal? He sees a couple of drunken soldiers and suddenly you're all wearing long faces.

MR. BLAKE: Peace is a general's worst nightmare. That's why the long faces, Mrs. Bradley.

DAVID: Oh come on. We're in the middle of the jungle. What's the problem?

JOAQUIM *(Suddenly)*: Soldiers? How many? You think they come for me, sister?

AMA: . . . I don't know.

JOAQUIM: Why soldiers? Mr. Blake say there is peace in the city. You know something, Mr. Blake?

MR. BLAKE: This is not business to trouble yourself with, Joaquim. Look at that, my glass. Empty.

(Neibert abandons his stance. Joaquim fidgets, growing increasingly agitated.)

NEIBERT: Why are you lying to him? *(Mr. Blake gets up)* They may come. May fight. It is inevitable, no?

MR. BLAKE: Oh go on.

JOAQUIM: Do you think there will be trouble again? War?

MR. BLAKE: What I think is irrelevant. I was removed from this equation. Don't you remember that stinky little skirmish about ten years back? It was the last suggestion I was to make. And my friend, it ended badly. Unfortunately, I sided with the loser. But these things happen. I've retired to a more practical trade.

NEIBERT: Elephants, rhino, tropical birds. What other rarity are you exploiting this month?

MR. BLAKE: I live a clean life. I'm a . . . businessman, my Belgian oddity. I provide a service to the good people of this wounded forest. Who else is going to bring goods in and out of this chaos? You? I think not. But I forgive you, and to show you my good faith, I'll buy you a cocktail.

NEIBERT: You'll poison me as well. No, thank you.

MR. BLAKE: How gauche. Have a drink. Talk to me in twenty years, talk to me about the poison.

(Mr. Blake crosses to the bar. Joaquim leans against the wall, clearly shaken.)

AMA: You can see what this region has done to us. It hasn't always been this way, but I probably don't need to explain the history to you. It is a magnificent country. When I came here there was great promise.

SARAH: Are we in danger, sister?

AMA: Mrs. Bradley, sorry to disappoint you, but I'm not a nun.

SARAH: Oh really? Then why does he call you sister?

AMA: He's a member of the backwhen tribe . . . who still yearn for back when the colonies served Leopold, Elizabeth . . . so on. He can't imagine an African woman in a position of power if it's not ordained by the Lord.

NEIBERT: He's a pig.

MR. BLAKE: I'm here, you needn't refer to me in the third person. Mrs. Bradley, the Imperial Hotel is probably the safest place in this entire country. I don't know why everyone is getting excited. A few soldiers up country. If we jumped to attention every time that happened we'd be on our feet all of the time.

(Joaquim grows increasingly agitated.)

JOAQUIM: Stop talking about this! No! I don't want to hear. I listen to the voices on the radio, they say a new nation is born. No more fighting, put down your guns. Peace! They tell the truth. How could such a handsome voice lie to so many people? No? But maybe they do lie. *(Turns off the radio)*

SARAH: Come on people, you're scaring me. No trouble, right? *(Silence)* We're gonna get out of here soon?

MR. BLAKE: When the rain stops.

SARAH *(Spooked)*: What about your plane, don't you have a radio? Couldn't we call for assistance? Find out what's going on?

MR. BLAKE: Sure, but quite frankly a scared tourist and a deserted village don't constitute an emergency in this region. You really should make yourself comfortable. There is conversation, wine and food. Relax!

SARAH: Relax? Do something, David!

DAVID: Like what?

SARAH: That's typical. Well, we're not staying here another night. This adventure is over. We're leaving, sweetie.

DAVID: Be my guest.

JOAQUIM *(Snaps)*: Nothing has happened, everything is okay. No soldiers!

(Silence. Ama goes over to the bar. A moment.)

DAVID: Hey, what was the war about?

(Mr. Blake laughs heartily.)

MR. BLAKE: Power. Control. Money.

JOAQUIM: Land. Food. Culture.

MR. BLAKE: That's what I meant. Mr. Bradley, these soldiers were the worst of the scavengers. It hardly matters what side they're on anymore. They shift allegiance at will, but their appetites remain the same. At any rate, nothing has changed.

JOAQUIM: How can you say that?

MR. BLAKE: Simple, nothing has changed. Look at you, you still take orders. And I don't know why you're frightened. For God's sake, you created this situation. You in these little backwater villages that put that monster in his place.

(Joaquim walks over to Mr. Blake.)

JOAQUIM: Why do you insult me? Take it back.

MR. BLAKE: They're just words. So I take them back, that changes nothing. Enough! Go back to work!

JOAQUIM: *Ewe Lizungu lichafu sana!*

MR. BLAKE: *Lichafu! Kweli!* How dare you speak to me like that!

JOAQUIM: You are not my commander. I don't have to take your orders!

MR. BLAKE: My uncle built this hotel, don't forget. And it's my investments that keep it open for business. How else would your pitiful salary be paid? I know, I know you don't want to hear it.

JOAQUIM: No, my village built this hotel. They carved these designs, they tore through the forest and carried these fine things on their backs. It is the smell of their sweat that sweetens this lobby.

MR. BLAKE: But it was my uncle's inspiration.

JOAQUIM: You will take everything from us, even credit.

MR. BLAKE: I don't have to, you don't deserve any.

(This comment strikes Joaquim like a blow.)

JOAQUIM: I have given you no cause to strike your tongue at me.

(He walks toward Mr. Blake. Mr. Blake, uncomfortable, straightens his posture.)

MR. BLAKE: This game is over, you can go back to work. NOW!

(Joaquim takes another step toward Mr. Blake. The men stand face to face. They play a game of chicken, waiting for the other to be the first to concede.)

DAVID: Gentlemen. Gentlemen.

(David and Neibert, sensing the growing tension, stand alert. Mr. Blake reaches for the gun in his holster. Joaquim grabs Mr. Blake's arm and takes the gun from his holster.)

MR. BLAKE: Don't be foolish, merely going for a cigar. *(Joaquim points the gun at Mr. Blake)* That's right—shoot me, that's the only thing you know how to do.
NEIBERT: It would be self defense. I will testify.
MR. BLAKE: Shut up!
AMA: Please.
JOAQUIM: I take no more insults. I take no more orders. From you, Mr. Blake, or any other man who walks through that door and asks me to bow to his desires.
MR. BLAKE: What are you gonna do now that you've drawn my gun on me? You need this job, Joaquim. You need this roof, this bed, this food.
JOAQUIM: I don't like your tongue. Talk is how it started before. Soldiers talk to my family. You don't like so much, now that Joaquim has control, that Joaquim's tongue is powerful.

(Joaquim places the gun to the back of Mr. Blake's head. There is a collective gasp.)

AMA: Really. He's an old man, close your ears to his nonsense.
JOAQUIM: And have him insult me with his spiteful eyes? All of you against the wall! No. Over there. *(Points to the couch)* Sit down.

(David, Ama and Sarah scramble to sit on the couch. Joaquim pulls Mr. Blake over to the couch and sits him down.)

NEIBERT: I refuse to sit. I prefer to adopt a traditional resting
position. *(He squats)*

JOAQUIM: Sit down, white man.

NEIBERT: Are you talking to me?

JOAQUIM: Yes, stupid!

NEIBERT: But I am with you, my brother.

JOAQUIM: You are not with me. Now sit down, next to him.
(Points to Mr. Blake) Do not try me. Now quiet.

(Neibert sits down next to Mr. Blake.)

MR. BLAKE *(To Ama)*: Sister, you see what you started with
your paranoia. This is ridiculous.

JOAQUIM: Now you understand that I am in control here.
There will be no talking unless I authorize it. When you
address me, it is to be as Mr. Joaquim or Lieutenant Sir.

MR. BLAKE: Which do you prefer?

JOAQUIM: You may call me Lieutenant Sir.

MR. BLAKE: Look at that, he's given himself rank. We better be
careful, he'll be a general in no time.

JOAQUIM: Shut up! *(Mr. Blake gets up and walks over to the
bar)* What are you doing?

MR. BLAKE: I'm making myself a martini . . . Lieutenant Sir.

JOAQUIM: No!

MR. BLAKE: Yes.

(He continues to fix himself a drink.)

DAVID: Hey, has it occurred to you that we're being taken
hostage.

SARAH: "Taken hostage," isn't that redundant?

MR. BLAKE: I'll tell you this much, he'll have a much more
agreeable hostage if I'm plastered.

AMA: You really should sit down. Don't upset him Mr. Blake,
it will make it easier.

MR. BLAKE: Nonsense, he can deny me my freedom, but by God he can't deny me my obstinacy. The truth is, I've sat through half a dozen of these in my lifetime. I have no problem with him, after my martini I might quite like this disagreeable fellow. Within a month it will all be a memory. A story. Right Lieutenant Sir? He will barely remember how he ran amok of your holiday, my dear Bradleys. *(He stirs his martini)*

AMA: If you're smart, you'd sit down.

MR. BLAKE: I've been on this continent all of my life. I forged a life here, a good life, a gentleman's life with barely an education. I have survived war, famine, attacks by wild beasts and disease. I'm still standing here with a martini in my hand and a fan overhead to keep me cool. I'm part of this country, I'm an African. *(To Joaquim)* For God's sake, this isn't what your mama would want. She brought you up here when you were a boy, a little naked thing running about the grounds, begging for peanuts. You probably don't remember. She came during the epidemic to fetch water from the white man's well. Smart lady. Survivor. *Lieutenant Sir* put a bullet through my head, do it now while you still can, but ask yourself before you do, so why did *he* survive? How can *I* survive? Now may I have my martini?

(Joaquim nods. Mr. Blake lifts the glass.)

JOAQUIM: And for me?

(Mr. Blake mixes another martini.)

SARAH: Three cheers for the amateur pop psychologist.

MR. BLAKE: Mumbo jumbo.

NEIBERT: You're a parasite! Why don't you shut up.

MR. BLAKE: You shut up!

JOAQUIM: SHUT UP ALL OF YOU! *(He takes the martini. He drinks it with difficulty, as though tasting liquor for the first time)*

AMA: Mr. Joaquim?

(Joaquim paces, keeping the gun positioned at the hostages gathered on the couch.)

JOAQUIM: Quiet. *(Decides)* Yes?

AMA: If you have a complaint with Mr. Blake I wish you'd settle it between yourselves. What do you hope to accomplish?

JOAQUIM *(Thinks)*: I want food for my village: grain, and a wool blanket for my mother. No matter what happens nothing changes for us here. A new leader comes, promises a better life, we fight along his side, we go home hungry, we die. No more. It is my turn to take. No more soldiering for someone else.

(Sarah clears her throat.)

DAVID: Listen brother, I am with you. If I was hungry . . . well . . . I understand completely. "Power to the people," but—

JOAQUIM: Now you are with me. When I was serving you martinis you forget you are a black man. Don't say thank you with the same ease as an Englishman or a Frenchman. I don't want you with me, son of slave.

DAVID: But I am with you. And to set the record straight, my father was a salesman in midtown Manhattan, okay?

SARAH: Don't agitate him, David.

DAVID: Agitate him? *(Sings)* "I'm on vacation. I saved for two years to get here."

JOAQUIM: Holiday? When was the last time I took holiday? *(Points to Mr. Blake)* You are going to take me to your radio in the plane.

MR. BLAKE: It doesn't work.

(Joaquim cocks the gun.)

JOAQUIM: NO?

(Mr. Blake straightens his posture and begins to move.)

AMA: This isn't necessary. The supply plane will be in soon and the mission will gladly share its grain.

JOAQUIM: I won't wait any longer.

NEIBERT *(Frantically)*: I must be able to smoke a cigarette otherwise I will go crazy!

SARAH: I vote that we make this a non-smoking room.

(Joaquim reaches into Neibert's pouch, lights a cigarette and places it in Neibert's mouth.)

Oh, I see how this is going to be.

JOAQUIM: Sit still. *(To Mr. Blake)* You come with me. *(He shoves Mr. Blake toward the door)* This forest has eyes and ears. Run and I'll hunt you down like an animal.

(Joaquim pushes Mr. Blake out the door and exits. They all breathe a tremendous sigh of relief.)

NEIBERT: I will go back to the mission. Get help!

AMA: Who? The elderly? The infirm? He won't hold us very long. He's young. He doesn't want us! He'll hold us for a day, get scared and then run into the bush.

DAVID: And if he doesn't?

(David races to the doorway and peers out.)

AMA: We wait.

SARAH: I'm sick of playing this waiting game. We wait for the rain to stop. We wait for the phone to be repaired. We wait for dinner. We wait for a plane to appear.

AMA: As we say in Nigeria, "no matter how long the night, the day will surely follow."

SARAH: Why don't I just write him a check and he can buy some grain for the village. And I will personally mail his mother a wool blanket from the United States.

AMA: Mrs. Bradley, this is not about grain and a blanket.

SARAH: Are we actually being held hostage by the bellboy?

DAVID: It seems that way.

SARAH: Welcome home, David.

(The lights slowly fade on all but David and Sarah. Blackout.)

✨ Act Two

Scene 1

Hotel lobby. Rain continues.

Joaquim marches David, Sarah, Ama, Mr. Blake and Neibert into the lobby. They are thoroughly exhausted and ready to drop.

Joaquim wears Sarah's sunglasses and her Gucci scarf around his neck. He smokes one of Mr. Blake's cigars.

JOAQUIM: Attention! Hands up! SHOES! *(Snaps)* Shoes! Off! Place them there!

DAVID: Here we go again.

(Joaquim frantically rushes around, giving orders.)

MR. BLAKE: Shoes now.

(They take off their shoes.)

SARAH: I will not! Not these shoes. No, no, no. Not these, Lieutenant Sir. *(Defiantly)* And what if I say no, what if we all say no!

(Joaquim grabs Sarah roughly by the arm.)

DAVID: Hey there! You watch how you handle her. *(He moves toward Joaquim)*
SARAH: David, don't.

(Sarah reluctantly removes her shoes and adds them to the pile.)

JOAQUIM: Line up! Hands up!
SARAH: I don't understand why we're doing this.
JOAQUIM *(In Sarah's face)*: BECAUSE, when the authorities arrive, Mrs. Bradley, I want them to see order! It is how things are to be done.
MR. BLAKE: If they come.
JOAQUIM: They will come!
AMA *(Taunts)*: Let's hope before your soldiers.

(They line up at attention, a ritual they've obviously performed before. Joaquim, with the haughty self-importance of a five-star general, walks down the line inspecting their stances. Joaquim then carefully surveys the shoes. He removes his old worn boots and measures his feet against Neibert's.)

JOAQUIM: Neibert!
NEIBERT: Yes sir.
JOAQUIM: No shoes?
NEIBERT: I own none, sir. It against my belief.

(Joaquim pretends to play target practice with the pile of shoes. He picks through the pile and chooses the best pair.)

SARAH *(Thinking aloud)*: What's wrong, you don't like mine? Well, tell whoever wears them to take care of them. They were very expensive.

JOAQUIM: Fit good. We wear the same size, Mr. Blake.

MR. BLAKE: How about that. Now that you have our shoes and a bit of our dignity, may we be dismissed, Lieutenant Sir?

JOAQUIM: No, not yet!

(He gives Mr. Blake the once-over.)

AMA: I'm afraid no one's coming, Mr. Joaquim. Your demands are like so many other prayers swept away by the rain.

JOAQUIM: We will see! No, we will celebrate! And they'll say, "Mr. Joaquim, sorry it took us so long." "Mr. Joaquim, do you need something else?" "Mr. Joaquim, may I call you Mr. Joaquim? Mr. Joaquim your presence is requested in the city, his honor wishes to commend you!" *(He enjoys his new shoes. He marches back and forth across the lobby)*

MR. BLAKE: Comfortable, Lieutenant Sir?

(Joaquim nods.)

JOAQUIM: Yes! Most! Like! These must cost you plenty money. Oh yes, take me many years to save for these. Now they're mine. Stand at ease. Stand easy. *(Continues his march before them, like a soldier standing guard)*

NEIBERT *(To Ama)*: Cigarette?

AMA: No, thank you.

NEIBERT *(To David)*: My brother?

DAVID: No.

AMA: May I sit?

JOAQUIM: No.

SARAH: This is ridiculous.

(Sarah impulsively organizes the pile of shoes into two neat rows. Then returns to attention. Joaquim, amused, returns to his march. Ama breaks her stance.)

AMA *(Under her breath)*: Maximo would never have done this.

JOAQUIM: What did you say? What is your problem now?

AMA: I said, Maximo would never have done this. No! He was a decent and good fellow. *(Joaquim ignores Ama)* I miss him. He used to sit at the desk and jot down notes. He liked to write down what I said, that way when the hotel was empty he'd read our conversation and wouldn't feel alone. No, this wouldn't have happened if he had stayed put.

JOAQUIM: Is that so? *(Teasingly)* Sounds like you were in love with Maximo.

AMA: I loved that he was here . . . That when I'd walked the long distance, there'd be someone happy to see me. And we would sit on the veranda and dream together. He'd be a businessman and I . . . a saint. If the crops failed or one of the nuns took ill, I'd come here and there was always Maximo . . . He'd put on his portable radio and we would dance. *(She laughs at the remembrance and hums)* I'd walk all this way for a dance.

NEIBERT: We can dance.

AMA: It's not the same. Sorry.

JOAQUIM: You! Dance for me.

AMA: No.

(Joaquim stomps out a rhythm. Ama does not move at first. Joaquim dances playfully.)

JOAQUIM: Dance. Dance. Dance!

(Ama gives in, self-consciously dancing. The rhythm grows faster and faster, until she can barely keep up. Neibert, in a trance-like state, joins in.)

Stop! No more dancing, it is foolish and borgeoit!

MR. BLAKE: You mean bourgeois.

JOAQUIM: Don't tell me what I mean!

(He grabs Ama and shoves her back into place. They all stand silently watching Joaquim enjoy his new pair of shoes.)

Sister, sister, what if I told you Maximo got married. *(Taunts)* A city girl, pretty too.

AMA: Did he? There you have it.

(On the verge of tears, Ama turns away from Joaquim. Joaquim strokes the back of her neck flirtatiously.)

JOAQUIM: You don't need to think of him anymore. What did he do for you? Talk sweet words of nonsense and love.

AMA: Don't touch me!

JOAQUIM: Who is crueler now? I, who stay and keep you company, or he who abandons you for the city?

(Ama raises her hand to strike Joaquim, but stops herself.)

AMA: This is what you call company? I am a captive, standing here like a piece of livestock. I won't! I hope to God the authorities come "Mr. Joaquim," so they can see how miserably you're treating us. Then they'll give you nothing!

(Ama sucks her teeth and defiantly marches away. Joaquim does not know how to react to this blow to his power.)

JOAQUIM: You are all dismissed!

(Ama races to the front desk and bangs on the bell.)

AMA: Missus! Missus! MISSUS! *(Joaquim laughs.)*

JOAQUIM: I don't think she can hear you. Maybe Mr. Blake is right. She has gone to the city also.

(Mr. Blake immediately goes to the bar and pours himself a shot of vodka. Sarah, ever belligerent, stares out the window. Joaquim goes to Ama; she moves away.)

NEIBERT *(Dreamily)*: We are not captives. As long as we can breathe in and out, we are free. Captivity is a state of mind. Right, my brother? *(Turns to David)*
DAVID: I'm happy you can find comfort, but you've already fled the real world.
JOAQUIM: David, I am thirsty.

(David goes to the bar and fixes Joaquim a drink.)

NEIBERT: My brother, if you relaxed, let down some of that soul brother pride, we might find a common ground, even manage a conversation, my brother.
DAVID: I am not your brother. I can't explain, but it's like you've forced your way into a private club.
JOAQUIM: Enough, I'm thirsty.
NEIBERT *(Innocently)*: Excuse me?
DAVID: Don't take offense, but you are a white man. *(Sings)* "You're not black, you're not an African." WHITE! When you say "my brother" you're assuming a bond that does not exist.
NEIBERT: Really? And you are an African by virtue of your color?
DAVID: And ancestry. Yes.

(David sets Joaquim's drink on the table and he belts it back.)

JOAQUIM: More!
MR. BLAKE: Ah, but there is one thing wrong with your supposition. *(He digs into his shirt pocket)*
JOAQUIM: What are you doing?

(Joaquim grabs what Mr. Blake is reaching for and produces a passport. He throws it on the ground.)

MR. BLAKE: That. There is my passport. It's the one thing Joaquim and I have in common. And you see how much respect he has for it. If he'll permit you to look, you'll see I was born in this country. That makes me an African. *(Picks up the passport and leafs through it)* David Bradley, would you give up your eagle for this passport? Would you become an African? Ah, you have to think, don't you?

JOAQUIM: ANSWER!!

DAVID: I'm proud of being an African-American.

SARAH: Wasn't it you, the non-tax-paying, this country can kiss my black ass, David Bradley, who refused to vote in the last primary because you were angry?

DAVID: Yeah and? I complain about fried food, but I'd die right now for a bucket of fried chicken.

(Joaquim sips his drink. He enjoys watching the others bicker.)

SARAH: Oh come on David, you did not just say that.

NEIBERT: How can you talk of poison!

DAVID *(To Neibert)*: I'm tired of your holier than thou attitude.

JOAQUIM: That's right! Look at him.

DAVID: I've put up with people putting me down for my entire life, for not being black enough, for acting like a white boy 'cause I like the Rolling Stones. Yes, I happen to like the Rolling Stones. But I'll be damned if I'm gonna have a white man challenge my legitimacy as an African person. Oh no, we fought too long and hard for that hyphen.

NEIBERT: Hyphen? Is that what it comes down to? I've lived amongst many tribes on this continent: the Fulani, Kabye, Tuareg. I have been called brother by a Nuba warrior, who despised all white people. He gave me this necklace, and said it was the symbol of the lion: strength, endurance and brotherhood. I may not be a black man outside, but I am a black man. Here. *(Points to his heart)*

(Joaquim laughs heartily. Ama, who has been standing quietly, intercedes.)

AMA: You can't just become an African, a black man, because you want to be. There is much more that binds us together than the eye can see. How dare you appropriate our culture. Shame. You are no better than Mr. Blake. *(Pointing at Mr. Blake)* You pillage as well.

(Joaquim studies them with great amusement.)

NEIBERT: No, you are wrong there. I love this culture. I despise everything European, everything that it stands for.

MR. BLAKE: Does it matter how he chooses to lead his life? That's what you told me.

AMA: It is our culture. Our culture. You may admire it, study it, but you can't travel here, put on a robe and take possession of it.

NEIBERT *(Pointing at Mr. Blake)*: What about him?

MR. BLAKE: Don't bring me into this. I've never claimed to be a black man. I am an African, which means I have a connection to this ravaged continent, but I have no illusions about my race. In fact, I quite enjoy being a white man.

DAVID *(Shouts)*: Kenya, Nigeria, Egypt, Morocco, Ghana, South Africa, Somalia and . . . and . . . Togo. That's eight countries. I named eight African countries! *(Smiles)* THERE!

(Joaquim slams down his feet.)

JOAQUIM: None of you belong here! *(Snaps)* No more talking of this!

(A moment. Joaquim sips his drink.)

SARAH: Refresh my memory, what are the approved topics?

JOAQUIM: The weather. "Has the rain stopped?" "Ah, look at the rain" . . . such as that. Family. "I miss my mother." "Do you have brothers or sisters?" . . . such as that. Politics, sports and *(Looking at Sarah)* complaints are strictly forbidden. So is anything I don't know about or understand.

MR. BLAKE: I must say what remarkable rain we're having today. I don't think I'll be able to visit my Auntie.

JOAQUIM: No talk of weather and family now. You may thank Mr. Blake.

SARAH: What does that leave us with?

JOAQUIM: Nothing!

MR. BLAKE: He's worse than the government! Makes you sentimental for Bokassa . . . Say there Lieutenant Sir, I'd ease up on the spirits.

JOAQUIM: Would you?

(He gulps down the last drop of liquor and slams down the glass.)

NEIBERT: We should be comfortable with silence, there is an old proverb in the Yoruba tongue. It is said that—

JOAQUIM: Please respect my rules. Those who don't will be punished.

(Neibert places his finger over his mouth. He nods. Ama goes to the bar.)

AMA: I'm not speaking, I'm helping myself to some brandy wine.

(She passes her hand across her lips. David looks at his watch. A moment.)

DAVID *(Sarcastically)*: It's noon!

(There is a huge commotion heard outside. They all cluster around the window and look out into the audience.)

JOAQUIM: ATTENTION!

(Lights fade.)

Scene 2

Hotel lobby. Rain continues.
Joaquim keeps his gun trained on Simone Frick, a nervous woman who speaks incredibly quickly with a European accent that is difficult to place. She has the tendency to be frazzled and a bit flighty when overwhelmed. Simone carries an umbrella and a briefcase. In addition, she wears a bottle of water strapped around her waist. The others stand at attention in a poorly formed line.

SIMONE *(Nervously)*: Hello, I hope you are safe and comfortable. Allow me to introduce myself, I'm Simone, Simone Frick. I have come on behalf of the . . . the United—

MR. BLAKE: My dear have you brought grain and a blanket so we can get on with our lives?

SIMONE *(In rapid succession)*: I have explained to Lieutenant Sir that we did not feel it was advisable to enter into negotiations prior to evaluating the situation and making a determination as to the character of the participants. It is not our practice to negotiate with captors, be they government or NGOs, but given the fact that foreign nationals are involved, they felt the situation might best be handled by an international body. I sympathize with your predicament. I would also like to assure you that we are very much in control and by the end of today we should have matters safely resolved.

(She collects herself, adopting an official posture. The sound of a plane taking off.)

MR. BLAKE: Madam, it sounds as though your plane took off.

(Simone gasps.)

SIMONE: Oh dear.

(Flabbergasted, she re-collects herself, once again adopting an official posture.)

JOAQUIM: Where is my food? Back in line! Where is my blanket?

SIMONE: Ah . . . It is not our practice to fulfill demands until we have entered into a dialogue and determined that it is the only resolution, so to speak, to a, a, a—

SARAH: Dilemma.

SIMONE: Yes.

AMA: It's not as though Mr. Joaquim asked for the release of political prisoners or some other potentially volatile demand. You could have at least brought one blanket for his mother and made our lives that much easier!

SIMONE: And who are you?

AMA: I am a hostage! More specifically, an aid worker. I've been in this damn hotel for too long. I came to use the telephone to request the same thing as Mr. Joaquim. Now, I've been through two bottles of brandy wine and I'm beginning to eye some of the harder liquor!!! Does that answer your question? Ms. Frick, what is your plan?

(A moment. They stare incredulously at Simone. She fumbles for words.)

SIMONE: We find that when were are in the midst . . . of . . . of . . . I'm sorry I lost my train of thought—

SARAH: I hope you're good at what you do.

SIMONE *(To Joaquim)*: I wish you wouldn't point the gun at me, Lieutenant Sir. I'm here to help you. I want what is best for all of us.

JOAQUIM: Sit down! *(Simone squats)* Not there, over here. *(Points at the couch and Simone quickly maneuvers over to it. Unhinged)* I have already told you what I want. TELL ME MY GRAIN AND BLANKET ARE ON THE WAY!

SIMONE: You don't have to yell. I don't care for yelling. It . . . it. Ah . . . It's just not that simple, Lieutenant Sir. Caution is . . . well . . . Your country is at a pivotal juncture . . . There are soldiers up north . . . since the revolution . . . and one can not make decisions without . . . *(Once again losing her train of thought)* Excuse me, does anyone have a headache tablet?

JOAQUIM: ENOUGH! I am drowning in words.

NEIBERT: Indeed!

SIMONE: I'm sorry. But. *(Timidly)* How am I to know whether the blanket is an actual demand or a "symbolic" demand? And, what . . . wha . . . what is the communication of such a demand? After a war there are so many parties claiming to be the legitimate representatives of the people. It is difficult to know who is in control. *(Takes a sip from her water bottle)*

JOAQUIM: At the moment, I am in control. *(Pulls Simone to her feet by her collar)* If I kill someone, will you understand more clearly?

SIMONE: That's not necessary. I can certainly communicate your seriousness to my colleagues.

MR. BLAKE: How? By telepathy?

SIMONE: You make a joke, but it's all quite complicated, I assure you.

DAVID: It really isn't that complicated. Trust me. He wants some grain and a blanket. There! We've all figured that out without a master's degree in conflict resolution. God damn.

(Joaquim sits Simone back down. She takes a tissue from her briefcase and wipes her brow.)

SIMONE: All I ask is that you permit me to do my job. I am here to protect you. You may not appreciate that. There are people that care!

SARAH: I'm sure. There are also people that don't care. None of that really matters as long as we don't have access to a decent meal and a bathroom with running water.

(Simone manages a smile.)

SIMONE: I'm sorry . . . I understand. How are you holding out?

SARAH: S-H-O-W-E-R! I am sickened by the smell of my own body. We need showers. Even a simple walk in the rain. You're here to ensure that we're being treated humanely, the stench in this hotel is inhuman.

NEIBERT: It is a natural odor that we've learned to be ashamed of, she does not speak for all of us.

SARAH: You are the worst offender. Oh yes, it's gotten that bad, Neibert.

SIMONE: But, are the other hostages safe?

JOAQUIM: They are all present and accounted for.

SIMONE: I thought there were . . . *(Gasps)* Oh Lord.

MR. BLAKE: It was my idea to inflate the numbers. I didn't think that anyone would take notice otherwise. A few broken down tourists and several perpetual forest dwellers would hardly draw international attention.

(A moment. David stares at Sarah, who appears completely and absolutely distressed. Ama remains calm. Neibert stoops, observing, as he puffs lackadaisically on his zillionth cigarette. Mr. Blake fans himself with the section of the Herald Tribune. Simone struggles to say something.)

SIMONE: It's hot isn't it?

(Joaquim grabs Simone's briefcase and slams it to the floor. Simone is thoroughly disarmed by the abrupt assault.)

JOAQUIM: Shut up! Attention! *(They all snap to attention)* Give me one hundred deep knee bends. Now!

MR. BLAKE: You're going to give me a bloody heart attack. Absolutely not!

JOAQUIM: Now! *(They begin to do deep knee bends. Simone Frick watches incredulously)* I'm counting. Four, five . . .

SIMONE: What's going on? Mr. Joaquim—

JOAQUIM: Shh.

(Without warning Joaquim moves toward the veranda. Simone starts to follow, but Joaquim stops her. Joaquim goes out onto the veranda and begins to pace. Simone doesn't know whether or not to comply with Joaquim's orders.)

SIMONE *(Whispered)*: What is he doing?

DAVID *(Whispered)*: He goes to the veranda to think up other humiliating rituals to perform.

MR. BLAKE *(Whispered)*: Can you tell me who won the Rugby finals? Miss Frick?

AMA: Shhhh. You'll upset him.

SIMONE *(Whispered)*: I don't know. And it's Ms. Frick.

MR. BLAKE: Not married?

SIMONE: I prefer not to divulge that information for obvious reasons.

MR. BLAKE: I bet not. You're a good looking woman. Yummy. *(Flashes an indecent smile)*

SIMONE: I see you've been mining the ancient pits of misogyny.

(Neibert toys with the beads around his neck. Simone retrieves her briefcase and nervously rearranges some papers.)

JOAQUIM *(Offstage)*: TWENTY-ONE, TWENTY-TWO . . .

(Mr. Blake walks toward the bar, bumping into Neibert, who diligently performs his deep knee bends.)

MR. BLAKE: Will you get out of my way.

NEIBERT: Go around.

SARAH *(To Mr. Blake)*: He'll see you!

MR. BLAKE: Let him! I'm too old for this MAOIST nonsense.

JOAQUIM *(Offstage)*: THIRTY, THIRTY-ONE, THIRTY-TWO . . .

NEIBERT *(Yells)*: Take your time! Don't give in, comrade! Stand your ground!

DAVID: Oh that's brave and noble of you. No skin off your back, you have all the time in the world. A bad day for you is stepping in monkey shit.

NEIBERT: No my brother, a bad day is an infection that won't heal and having to walk seventy kilometers to find a student with a year of medical school who doesn't know the difference between gangrene and a little pus, but nevertheless wants to amputate your leg up to your testicles with a pair of garden shears. That's a bad day. Cigarette? *(Offers everyone a cigarette)*

SARAH: Must you smoke?

NEIBERT: It is the one freedom I have!

(Simone takes a cigarette.)

SIMONE: Thank you. *(Struggles to light the cigarette, her hand shaking ever so slightly. She eventually gives up)* Is . . . the Lieutenant Sir dangerous?

SARAH: I didn't travel this far to do calisthenics in this wonderful spa-like atmosphere.

SIMONE *(Whispered)*: Is he alone, then?

MR. BLAKE: Completely.

(Ama, David and Sarah rest.)

SARAH: I don't want to be the one to ask, but without a plane how do you plan on getting us out of here?

SIMONE: A simple phone call will solve that problem.

MR. BLAKE: Simplicity is not an option. Our friend, in his fervor, rearranged the radio in my plane and the telephone has become an interesting showpiece.

SIMONE: This isn't what I expected . . . expected. *(She laughs nervously. She tries again to light her cigarette. The matches keep breaking)* How far is the next village?

MR. BLAKE: Don't you think we've considered all possibilities, Ms. Frick. Unfortunately, they haven't found a cure for his form of paranoia. And by now this forest is probably teeming with soldiers. Do you think we would be better off in their care?

(David chuckles.)

DAVID *(Sings)*: "Fly me to the moon and let me play amongst the stars."

JOAQUIM *(Offstage)*: SIXTY-FIVE, SIXTY-SIX, SIXTY-SEVEN . . .

(They all return to doing deep knee bends. Neibert lights a cigarette and continues his deep knee bends.)

NEIBERT: YOU MEAN SIXTY! . . . I support his struggle. Who am I? A man that crossed into his forest. I am a guest. A guest accepts the rules of the house.

DAVID: Or leaves, which of course we can't do.

MR. BLAKE: It's easy for you to be cavalier, your great purpose in life is the search for the agogwe.

(Joaquim continues to pace on the veranda. They watch him through the window.)

224

NEIBERT: Perhaps this is my purpose. No? We all have been disappointed, given over our common sense to desires. I admire that he has acted. Done. Committed. This could be a beginning. No? Our friend could be on the verge of staging a great grassroots movement, a rebirth. Joaquim could be Jomo Kenyatta, Julius Nyerere, Kwame Nkrumah. And why not? At what moment is a revolution born? Look at him. He's fomenting change, as we speak.

DAVID: Stop mythologizing him. In the U.S. he'd be a gangsta, plain and simple. This is the equivalent of a mugging. A sucker punch.

NEIBERT: You have no vision. We are the problem, not him! You have no vision!

SIMONE: Look, there are a lot of hungry soldiers—we can't bend to all of their demands.

AMA: Then why are you here?

SIMONE *(Defensively)*: To gather information of course; it's a matter of verification!

(They bombard Simone with questions.)

DAVID:	MR. BLAKE:	AMA:	SARAH:
What the hell is that?	We just wait for the soldiers?	Will there be grain?	Verification?
He's crazy!	*(Laughter)* Ha!	Will there be grain?	Are you here to help us?

(A moment. Simone slowly backs away.)

SARAH: Are you here to save us?

(A moment. Simone glances out at Joaquim on the veranda. Finally:)

SIMONE: Well . . . a supply plane is scheduled to stop through here perhaps as soon as tomorrow.

SARAH: Thank God.

AMA: My sweet angel, you couldn't have spoken more beautiful words. Will there be grain?

(A moment.)

SIMONE *(Lying)*: Ah . . . yes.

DAVID: Why didn't you say that in the first damn place!

(David and Sarah hug. Ama laughs with delight. Neibert stops his deep knee bends. Simone edges toward the window. Mr. Blake follows her.)

MR. BLAKE *(Discreetly)*: You don't sound convinced.

SIMONE: He's so young.

MR. BLAKE: Why did you lie to them? They don't intend to meet his demands, do they? You haven't got a plan!

(Simone glances over at the others celebrating. Joaquim stares off into the distance.)

SIMONE: Um-um . . . If I tell Mr. Joaquim that his demands have been met, it will buy us some time. Everything will be resolved before he realizes what has happened.

MR. BLAKE: A tourniquet, I see, bless your heart. But how can you be so sure that someone is coming back for you?

SIMONE: I have been assured. *(Mr. Blake bursts into laughter. A moment)* You concede once and you've created a monster. It's not our policy.

MR. BLAKE: We're in a part of the country where one good storm can do more damage than a military coup. What would you have him do?

SIMONE: Go through legitimate channels. Local government. I'm sorry. What more can I do?

(Joaquim pops his head into the lobby.)

JOAQUIM: Ninety-one, ninety-two . . .

(They momentarily return to doing deep knee bends. Ama approaches Simone.)

AMA: Ms. Frick, it's hopeful that you have come. If they knew what has been going on in this region they'd—
MR. BLAKE: Ah sister, you could find virtue in a mudslide.

(Joaquim reenters unseen by the others.)

She . . . she didn't come to save us, she . . . she came to pick up the pieces. It's an inconvenience, that's all. A fly in the ointment. Her colleagues would like to forget this part of the world, but our . . . our friend has made it difficult. He has reminded them of broken promises and . . . *(Realizes that Joaquim is standing behind him and falls silent.)*
JOAQUIM: No talk, talk means trouble. That is how everything begins. Talk leads to shouting to stones being thrown and death. No talk, you talk too much.

(He cocks the gun and points it at Mr. Blake. Simone steps into the line of fire.)

SIMONE: Mr. Joaquim, I have carefully mulled over your demands. I promise you a supply plane will be arriving um, soon . . . well soon. It is our . . . our full intention to meet your demands at that time. Everything will be okay. Everything will be okay.

(Silence. Rain. The lights fade on all but Joaquim.)

JOAQUIM: And if you're lying, one of you must die. I am to be taken seriously. You are laughing at me. All I want is what I was promised years ago.

(The lights slowly fade.)

Scene 3

Hotel lobby. Dawn. Rain continues.

Mr. Blake sits at the bar and smokes the very end of a cigar. Neibert stands looking out the window into the distance. Ama thumbs through the ledger on the front desk. Sarah and Simone sit talking softly.

David watches Joaquim as he fights sleep. He succumbs. Suddenly he is jerked awake by a stream of gunfire heard in the distance. He grabs hold of David. They are all startled by the gunfire.

JOAQUIM *(Whispered)*: SHH! Hear! Guerrillas, foraging. Hear it? Guns in the distance. They are close close. *(A moment)* Mr. Bradley, how long does your watch say since Ms. Frick promised the plane?

DAVID *(Reluctantly)*: It could be the rain—

(Joaquim wipes his eyes and peers longingly at the rainy sky.)

JOAQUIM: Yes. Rain! That watch won't tell you when the plane comes.

DAVID: No.

JOAQUIM: Why do you keep looking? What good is this time?

(He lets go of David. David starts to walk away; he reconsiders.)

DAVID *(Ventures)*: Lieutenant Sir, we're beginning to get hungry. The crackers are stale. We just want to go home.

JOAQUIM: Home is no longer. It is my memory now.

DAVID: What about your mother?

(A moment.)

JOAQUIM: She live with my sister and she husband in a village near the river. She say, "When you reach the city, get me a blanket like the missionaries have. Soft, soft. Pretty, bright red." The hotel don't even have blankets. That's all she wanted. Ten years a soldier and I can't even get my mother a blanket. I won't go home until then. *(Shakes his head)* For a poor man, a farmer, there is no respect. You must take respect.

DAVID: You sound like my father in the early seventies.

JOAQUIM: He was a farmer?

DAVID: No, but he was poor.

JOAQUIM: There are poor people in America?

(David laughs.)

DAVID: Sorry, I'm not laughing at you. Hell yeah, we got poor folks in America all right.

JOAQUIM: You?

DAVID: Well, no. Not anymore.

JOAQUIM: Really? Tell me this, you live in a city?

DAVID: Yes.

JOAQUIM: What is your city like?

DAVID: A huge stone village with lights strung as far as you can see, a constant hum of complaints and aspirations, of ills and decadence. It's . . . incredible and complicated.

JOAQUIM: Why you come here?

DAVID: That is the question I will ask for the rest of my life . . . Peace of mind. Curiosity. You may not understand, but as an African-American I don't think I would have felt complete until I'd made the trip to the motherland.

JOAQUIM: Are you complete?

DAVID: Well, I still want my marriage to be the way it was when we were in graduate school. I regret that I didn't fight for a promotion. I still harbor the illusion that one day I'll take a posting as a foreign correspondent. Am I complete? I am in process.

JOAQUIM: All I want is to be a civil servant, have a suit and ride the bus to my office building. Seven stories, the tallest office building in the city. Have a telephone and an ink pen. A commode. I could have read good, but the war came to my village. And took me away. Ten years, you know. My father was a farmer. His father. His father. It was my destiny. But the war was all around us, in the stories of men who spoke of it with respect. The war was a distant monster, too far away to make me scared. Then men without limbs began to appear and beggar children wept for food. The sound of gunfire rippled through the forest. Rat, tat, tat, tat. And the war was upon us. I was the youngest son, I was given up to the rebels to fight for freedom. It was either bullets or children. And children are less valuable. Ten years later, we are victorious, and I am not a child. My village is a clearing in the forest, taken by the war. And the land is barren, there are no farmers left. This peace is a curse. There is too much time to think. *(A moment)* I was a good soldier. Do you know what it means to have been a good soldier? I was told that things would be better if we won. That the man with the glorious voice spoke the truth.

DAVID: "You got to fight for what you believe in . . ." my dad used to say.

JOAQUIM: What is that?

(A moment.)

DAVID: I don't know. Season tickets. A decent table in a restaurant. A cover story. *(Glances down at his watch)*

JOAQUIM: I don't understand.

DAVID: How old are you? Nineteen, twenty?

JOAQUIM: Maybe. I don't know.

DAVID: Don't you think your mother would want you to come home with or without the blanket? I'm sure there's a pretty young woman waiting for you, wondering where you've been. *(Joaquim cracks a smile. A broad glorious smile. His face relaxes, even brightens for a moment)* You didn't lose your smile after all . . . Then you have a special lady friend?

JOAQUIM: No. I have no livestock, no land . . . What girl will have me?

DAVID: With a smile like that I know a few sisters that might be interested.

(Embarrassed, Joaquim covers his mouth with his hand. David moves closer to Joaquim.)

JOAQUIM: Please don't try to be my friend. I don't need friends. It is too hard to watch friends die.

DAVID: A friend protects a friend.

(A moment.)

JOAQUIM *(Barks)*: I didn't hear you say Lieutenant Sir.

DAVID *(Snaps)*: Lieutenant Sir.

(The others freeze.)

SARAH: What did he say to you?

DAVID: Nothing. Nothing. It's okay. It's okay.

(David walks away from Joaquim, who stares after him. Gunfire is heard in the distance. An animal crying out. Neibert goes onto the veranda and looks out into the distance. He wanders away. Joaquim wanders onto the veranda and looks out into the distance.
    Lights fade.)

Scene 4

Hotel lobby. Night. Rain continues.

Ama and Mr. Blake play cards. Simone sleeps on the couch. Sarah leans against the window smoking a cigarette. David walks over to Sarah.

The lights flicker.

SARAH: I am in a crisis.

DAVID: What now?

SARAH: Feel. Feel the roots. *(David feels the roots of Sarah's hair)* Growth. My perm is going at the roots . . . This has not happened to me since I was child in summer camp.

DAVID: You wouldn't have this problem if you let your hair grow out naturally.

SARAH: You don't see many women with naturals in the corner offices. "The horror." *(David laughs)* I hold you responsible.

DAVID: I'm glad we're here. Well you know what I mean. He's not a bad person. He's just a—

SARAH: You can't rationalize this. I've never had to ask permission for anything in my life, let alone using the toilet.

(David walks over to the desk, tests the telephone.)

DAVID: Well, we've seen things none of our friends have. We came here looking for something. If—

SARAH: No ifs from you. I wanted what everyone else gets. This is way too deep for me.

DAVID: I wish you wouldn't smoke.

SARAH: I don't want to hate him, I want him to get what he wants . . . These are our people David, our ancestors, and before now I never gave this village, region, or country a thought. They're starving. And right now I'm resenting the fact that they're starving because it's ruining my vacation. And I am progressive. *(Laughs)*

DAVID: We haven't had to take a breath and look inward in years.

SARAH: Why are you always so prescriptive?

DAVID: I don't know what to say to you anymore.

SARAH: Everything will be all right.

DAVID: Everything will be all right.

SARAH *(Snaps)*: When? . . . I'm sorry. You really are caring. *(David strokes her face; he leans in to kiss her)* Do you love me?

DAVID: . . . Yes. I do, but sometimes when—

SARAH: Now is not the time. Good thoughts. Freedom! Chocolate! Espresso! *(A moment. She glances over at a sleeping Simone)* It's too quiet.

DAVID: Good. I like this quiet.

SARAH: It scares me. We may die here and nobody will know. *(David stands abruptly)*

DAVID: Oh God . . . I hope not. *(He begins to laugh)*

SARAH: Why are you laughing?

DAVID: He's a child one minute trying on his smile and in the next moment he's Tyree Simmons with the bad-ass attitude ordering me to give up my handful of bubble gum. Which of course I always did. I wish I wasn't afraid, Sarah.

SARAH: But you said he wasn't a bad person. I heard you say it. And now you're afraid. How is that supposed to make me feel?

DAVID: It is *my* feeling, Sarah. You can't hold me responsible for yours as well.

(A moment.)

SARAH: Why don't we all say it! No supply plane is coming! We're stuck here! He's going to kill us!

(She laughs at the absurdity. The others awaken.)

SIMONE: Not so! It's only a matter of time. That plane must be coming.

MR. BLAKE: Yes, keep telling yourself that, if it's helpful. *(Laughs)*

AMA: Don't you see? They abandoned us long ago.

SIMONE: NOT SO! They will adhere to procedures. Stop laughing. I am confident that everything . . . Then what . . . what is it you propose we do?

AMA: Pray for an end to the rain.

(Sarah and Mr. Blake stop laughing.)

SIMONE: I promise you they're not going to leave us out here! They wouldn't.

MR. BLAKE: They have. Things are never what they seem. False hope is the fabric that holds this continent together. You are naïve if you think that bottled water and a rain slicker will protect you from the elements out here. They sent you with a briefcase full of documents which are useless to a man who cannot read. My dear, you speak the language of détente, which in theory might be quite beautiful but it is no match for men that are hungry and willing to do anything to ensure victory. They should have sent a soldier. It's not your fault, I'm sure.

(A distant scream is heard, perhaps a monkey. Silence. Another scream, clearly a man's voice. They all stir.)

SIMONE: What the devil?

(David peers out the window. Sarah stands alert.)

DAVID: It was an animal or something.

SARAH *(Unsure)*: Yes.

DAVID: That's it.

SIMONE *(Convincing herself)*: Yes.

SARAH: Someone should go and see.

SIMONE: It sounds so close, so human.

MR. BLAKE: It is human.

SIMONE: Are you sure?

MR. BLAKE: Yes.

(A moment.)

AMA: Where is Neibert? *(Rushes to the window)*

MR. BLAKE: Fool! He probably tried to run off.

DAVID: Should we go look? *(Looks at Mr. Blake)*

MR. BLAKE: What's the point of getting soaked? We'll know soon enough.

(David reluctantly heads toward the door.)

SARAH: So we just sit here and wait? I'm not going to just sit here patiently awaiting my own death. Jesus Christ, in the movies there is always one hero in the bunch. A take-charge sort of person . . . David?

DAVID: Well hell, I'm on vacation! I won't be forced to make difficult decisions. What about you? You get paid the big bucks for your ideas. Isn't that what you always say?

AMA *(To Sarah)*: Yes, you're so good at delegating orders, why don't you go see!

SARAH: Unlike you, I'm not a saint or a martyr.

(A scream. Silence. Another scream is heard.)

DAVID: I'll go.

SARAH: No—stay here! I hope it's "him" out there. Him: stuck, trapped, dying! Screaming for our help!

DAVID: Sarah!

SARAH: Don't "Sarah" me, if you had—

DAVID: Had what? Become editor of the magazine, president of the co-op board, delivered the ultimate vacation, the Africa of our imagination. IT DOES NOT EXIST!

(Sarah sinks into the couch. Neibert, soaking wet, comes tumbling into the hotel lobby. His hands are bound with vines and his face bruised and covered in mud. Joaquim, also soaking wet, pushes Neibert from behind.)

MR. BLAKE: What is going on?

(Ama goes to aid Neibert.)

AMA: Oh goodness.
JOAQUIM: Get away from him.
AMA: He's bleeding. He needs attention.
JOAQUIM: That is his punishment. *(He shoves Ama away)* You see this man. He thought he could outrun me. He forgets that this is my forest. I can call up these trees to do my service.
NEIBERT: I swear to you, I was not trying to run. I heard the clarion voice of the agogwe. It was singing to me, imploring me to follow it into the jungle. When you have been searching for something as long as I, nothing will stop you from the chase. You heard it, didn't you?
JOAQUIM: Maybe I did, or maybe it is just a tale for children.

(Neibert, disappointed, struggles to his knees.)

NEIBERT: Did you?
JOAQUIM: You think I am stupid?
NEIBERT: No! I swear on my life. I am a warrior like you.
JOAQUIM: Stop mocking me! *(He kicks Neibert. Neibert falls on his side)* You are a Belgian. How can you want what I want? You think I want your help. Then you'll turn around and tell me that I owe you something. I have a debt to you. NO! You! Sarah! *(Points at Sarah)* Bring me some whiskey. *(Sarah takes a deep breath and retrieves the bottle of whiskey for Joaquim)* Where is my glass? You! *(Points at David. David balls up his fist, hesitates, then acquiesces to*

the demand. David brings Joaquim the glass and pours him a drink) More. *(To Mr. Blake)* You!

DAVID: We are hostages, not servants. You should treat us with a little more respect, my brother.

JOAQUIM: You mongrel, weren't you bred to serve?

(David lunges for Joaquim. Mr. Blake steps between them.)

MR. BLAKE: Don't.

JOAQUIM: I just joke to see how much fire you have inside you.

(David looks away and nervously fidgets with his watch. Joaquim rips the watch from David's arm.)

DAVID: It was a gift. A gift—

MR. BLAKE: Lieutenant Sir, do you have a better use for time than David Bradley?

JOAQUIM: I am in control. That is reason enough. He keeps looking at the watch like something is going to happen. Like he's expecting someone to come. NOBODY IS COMING TO SAVE YOU!

SARAH: Lieutenant Sir, that watch was a gift I gave my husband. Please give it back to him.

(Joaquim is fascinated with the watch. He listens to it tick.)

DAVID: Sarah, don't start with the man.

JOAQUIM: Listen to your husband! *(He laughs and drinks down the whiskey. He grabs the bottle)*

SIMONE: This is not the way you get what you want. If you kill any of these people, you will get nothing.

JOAQUIM: Then you tell me what is best. What I can expect? It has been days.

(Simone looks to the others.)

SIMONE: I am merely a messenger, Lieutenant Sir. I volunteered for this assignment. I can't conjure your desires out of this forest wall, no matter how many times you ask me. They put me on a plane and told me I'd be home in a day. "Be firm," they said. "It's probably some local people who will bend at the sight of authority. A little charm goes a long way. Don't make any promises you can't keep, and don't drink the water." Goddamn them! Good intentions and protocol are all I have Lieutenant Sir and you are welcome to that!

JOAQUIM: Protocol, is it worth a lot?

MR. BLAKE: Absolutely nothing.

SIMONE: You must let these people go. A little good faith will not go unrecognized.

MR. BLAKE: Very good, you're demonstrating some authority.

JOAQUIM: No . . . no . . . no . . . *(He marches around the room)*

SIMONE: Keep me here. I don't mind. If . . . If the rain stops, if a plane lands, if I'm able to return to the city, you will be given an audience. I will guarantee that your concerns will be heard. A handshake and it's sealed.

JOAQUIM: A handshake from a woman.

SIMONE: It is all you have.

(Joaquim thinks. He places the gun on the table. Simone eyes it. He pours himself a drink.)

JOAQUIM: And that would be the end?

SIMONE: Yes.

JOAQUIM: What if I know that grain will last only a season. What if I want more? *(Picks up the gun)*

MR. BLAKE: Don't get greedy, Lieutenant Sir.

JOAQUIM: Are you accusing me of being greedy? You with your wide flat ass and Cuban cigars. What if I was to ask them for weapons?

MR. BLAKE: If you enjoy this game, ask for something practical. Don't waste your time.

JOAQUIM *(Savoring)*: I want weapons to defend myself.

SIMONE: Against what?

JOAQUIM *(Drunkenly)*: The war. This hunger. I want it to end! I want it done! I CAN'T STAND—

(He walks over to Neibert and cocks the trigger. They all close their eyes.)

NEIBERT: Please don't!

SIMONE: Don't!

JOAQUIM: Are you ordering me?

SIMONE: No, I'm begging you. *(Gets down on her hands and knees)* I am begging you.

(Joaquim withdraws the gun. A moment.)

JOAQUIM: Are you lying? Your eyes lie. Close them!

(Simone closes her eyes. Ama gathers strength.)

AMA: When I first saw you I thought you looked dignified.

JOAQUIM: And now?

AMA: I think you look pathetic and spoiled.

JOAQUIM: I don't think much of you. You Nigerians are so superior to everybody. Think that we are backward out here in the bush. I have been to the city. I know how men live. *(Drunkenly maneuvers his way over to Sarah)* What about you? What do you think? You think this white woman is here for your life or theirs?

DAVID: Leave it alone.

JOAQUIM: ANSWER!

SARAH: I think you enjoy scaring us.

MR. BLAKE: Lieutenant Sir, we've indulged you enough.

JOAQUIM: Mr. Blake thinks you've indulged me enough. Belgian.

239

(Neibert squats on the floor.)

NEIBERT: Yes . . .

SARAH *(Screams)*: What do you want from us? All of us want things! Life sucks! I'm sorry about that.

JOAQUIM: But do any of you wake up hungry?

(A moment.)

AMA: I have been hungry. I have stood where you are.

JOAQUIM: With your education from London and your big words?

AMA: I also have made sacrifices.

JOAQUIM: Words.

AMA: Not words: feelings, frustrations, desires, needs. When did you become general? You run from the soldiers, but they have already caught up with you.

JOAQUIM: How can you say? Not true. I am fighting for what I am owed.

AMA: Against who? Who owes you? Me? Her? Him?

(Joaquim walks toward Ama, who backs away from him.)

JOAQUIM: I'm not going to hurt you. *(Ama backs away)* Why are you backing away? I'm not going to hurt you. *(Grabs Ama's arm too tight)* Look at me. Should I have fled my home in terror like Maximo?

SARAH: Stop, you're hurting her.

AMA: Look at what you are doing to us.

JOAQUIM: What will you have me do? Go back to my village and hunt for yams in the muddy ground until my hands are chapped, beg in the streets of the city from the men I fought against? What?

AMA: You're too impatient! Things will get better. I promise you.

JOAQUIM: Will that promise grow fruit? When?

AMA: Soon . . . soon.

(*A moment. Joaquim takes a drink of whiskey. He lets the bottle slip to the floor, disheartened.*)

JOAQUIM: This is not what I wanted. I just want to set things right. That's all. Simone Frick?

SIMONE: Yes?

JOAQUIM: It's not wrong to set things right?

SIMONE: No.

(*Joaquim sits down.*)

JOAQUIM (*To Sarah*): You come here.

SARAH: What are you going to do?

JOAQUIM: I said come here. (*Sarah, frightened, walks over to Joaquim. Joaquim examines her, then reconsiders*) Not you, him. (*Pointing at Mr. Blake. Sarah backs away. Mr. Blake slowly walks over to Joaquim*) Kneel down.

MR. BLAKE: Don't do it.

AMA: Please.

MR. BLAKE: Lieutenant. This is not how a military man—

JOAQUIM: KNEEL DOWN! I must set things right.

(*Mr. Blake refuses. Joaquim forces him to his knees.*)

SARAH: Oh God.

JOAQUIM: If I may have any satisfaction Mr. Blake. So much time and I do not know your first name.

MR. BLAKE: Basil.

JOAQUIM: Basil, you offer everyone a drink, but never me. We should be friends so much time we've spent in the same room. Together. We pass no words. Do you recognize these shoes? Basil?

MR. BLAKE: Yes, those are my shoes.

JOAQUIM: Do you know what I'm going to ask you to do?

MR. BLAKE: I can imagine.

JOAQUIM: Then do it. (*Mr. Blake bends down and kisses Joaquim's feet. Joaquim laughs long and hard*) I was only going to ask you to shine them . . . But I see how your mind works. (*Laughs*) Oh, but you give me so much more pleasure than I hoped. Basil. It will never be the same . . .

(*In a burst of energy, Mr. Blake charges Joaquim. He wraps his fingers around the young man's throat and begins to choke the life out of him. He pushes Joaquim onto the coffee table. David retrieves the stone from next to the front desk. He raises it. He hesitates, trying to decide how to strike. He lowers the stone across Joaquim's head and knocks him out. Joaquim's gun drops and he goes limp.*)

DAVID: Oh God, did I kill him?
SIMONE: I don't think so.

(*They gather around Joaquim. David hovers over him.*)

AMA: Get the gun.

(*Sarah retrieves the gun. Joaquim, dazed, manages a smile. Joaquim laughs. They all stare, hard and contemptuously.*)

MR. BLAKE: Joaquim, all you had to do was place that gun down on the coffee table and walk away and no one would have thought any less of you. I'm sure the Missus would have gladly kept you on and by next month everyone would have returned to their respective places in the universe.
JOAQUIM: That is why I did it. I was going to let you go.

(*Sarah begins to pass Mr. Blake his gun.*)

SARAH: David, what should I do?
JOAQUIM: Throw the gun away . . . You keep it!

(David looks at Sarah, uncertain.)

SARAH: Even now, you're barking orders at me?

(She slowly passes Mr. Blake the gun; he examines it.)

MR. BLAKE: Joaquim, I don't recognize you. *(He fires one shot at Joaquim, who slumps to the ground. Mr. Blake returns his gun to the holster at his side)*
AMA: Sweet Jesus.
SIMONE: Mr. Blake!
MR. BLAKE: I had no choice. He had a gun to our heads. You, Mrs. Bradley, you said you wanted him dead.
SARAH: But I didn't mean it.
MR. BLAKE: What can I say?
DAVID: You could say I'm sorry. For God's sake, he was going to let us go.
MR. BLAKE: He was a soldier, he should have known better. You will go home and talk about your trip to Africa at some dinner party. Don't forget to tell them how beautiful the countryside is, Mr. Bradley. And about some of the wonderful people you met. But also tell them the truth. Tell them what a man is willing to do for some grain.

(Lights begin to fade on all but Sarah and David.)

SARAH: It rained for another week and then it stopped.
DAVID: Yes, this is the stone.
SARAH: A reminder.

*(The rain stops.
Blackout.)*

END OF PLAY

Las Meninas

A Yoruba proverb states:

"The white man who made the pencil
also made the eraser."

Memoirs of Madame la Marquise de Montespan,

WRITTEN BY HERSELF

The poor Queen had had several daughters, all divinely well made and pretty as little Cupids. They kept in good health up to their third or fourth year; they went no further. It was as though a fate was over these charming creatures; so that the King and Queen trembled whenever the *accoucheurs* announced a daughter instead of a son.

My readers remember the little negress who was born to the Queen in the early days—she whom no one wanted, who was dismissed, relegated, disinherited, unacknowledged, deprived of her rank and name the very day of her birth; and who, by a freak of destiny, enjoyed the finest health in the world, and surmounted, without any precautions or care, all the difficulties, perils, and ailments of infancy.

M. Bontems, first *valet de chambre* of the *cabinets*, served as her guardian, or curator; even he acted only through the efforts and movements of an intermediary. It was wished that this young Princess should be ignorant of her birth, and in this I agree that, in the midst of crying injustice, the King kept his natural humanity. This poor child not being meant, and not being able, to appear at Court, it was better, indeed, to keep her from all knowledge of her rights, in order to deprive her, at one stroke, of the distress of her conformation, the hardship of her repudiation, and the despair of captivity. The King destined her for a convent when he saw her born, and M. Bontems promised that it should be so.

Director's Note

How does one recapture an erased history?

In the library of St. Genevieve in the Latin Quarter of Paris, there is a simple unsigned portrait of an African woman in nun's habit: Louise Marie-Therese, the Black Nun of Moret (1664–1732). Cloistered all her life, this African-featured nun took the veil at the late age of thirty-one in 1695. Journals and diaries attest to her having been visited throughout her life by important personages from the royal Court. A folder at St. Genevieve bears the title, "Documents Concerning the Princess Louise Marie, Daughter of Louis XIV and Marie Theresa." The folder is empty.

On November 1664, after a pregnancy marked by "dark forebodings," Marie-Therese, the pious and devoted Queen of the notoriously philandering Louis XIV, gave birth to a baby daughter. Laughter is said to have greeted her birth. Rumors ran wild in the court. The child was said to have been born "black as ink from head to toe," covered with hair, a monster. Shortly after birth, the child was pronounced dead by a grief-stricken King.

It was rumored at Court that the child was fathered by an African dwarf named Nabo, a young man from Dahomey presented to the Queen by relatives in Spain. Soon after his arrival, Nabo had become the Queen's favorite companion. Perhaps, it was discreetly suggested, a penetrating glance from this slave had corrupted the royal womb. Nabo was sent for by the King. He disappeared.

—John Emigh
Brown University, March 1997

This note was written for the accompanying program to Brown's 1997 production.

Production History

Las Meninas received its world premiere at San Jose Repertory Theatre (Timothy Near, Artistic Director; Alexandra Urbanowski, Managing Director) in March 2002 under the direction of Michael Donald Edward. The set design was by Gordana Svilar, the lights by Robert Jared, the sound by Jeff Mockus and the costumes by B. Modern. Choreography was by Carolyn Houser Caravajal and Marcus Cathey. The dramaturg was Nakissa Etemad, the dialect coach was Lynne Soffer and the stage manager was Nina Iventosch. The cast was as follows:

LOUISE MARIE-THERESE	Rachel Zawadi Luttrell
MOTHER SUPERIOR	Carol Mayo Jenkins
QUEEN MARIE-THERESE	Mercedes Herrero
KING LOUIS XIV	Mark H. Dold
NABO SENSUGALI	Daniel Bryant
LA VALLIERE	Bren McElroy
PAINTER	Ken Ruta
QUEEN MOTHER	Carol Mayo Jenkins
DOCTOR	Ken Ruta
COURTIERS/SERVANTS	Justin Buchs
	Scott Nordquist
	Eryka Raines
	Kim Saunders
	Megan Smith
	Brian Trybom

Characters

LOUISE MARIE-THERESE

MOTHER SUPERIOR

QUEEN MARIE-THERESE

KING LOUIS XIV

NABO SENSUGALI

LA VALLIERE

PAINTER

QUEEN MOTHER

DOCTOR

LADY SERVANT

COURTIERS, SERVANTS

Time

1695, looking back on 1664

Place

France

Act One

Scene 1

The year is 1695, looking back on 1664. Louise Marie-Therese, a light-complexioned black woman, kneels on the floor of her cell in the convent Moret. She wears the austere clothing of a novice and a highly ornate gold cross around her neck. It is a sharp contrast to her unassuming attire. The Mother Superior, a striking older woman, pours a pitcher of steaming water into an old bath tub.

MOTHER SUPERIOR: It is almost time, child. Are you prepared?

LOUISE: Already, Mother? May I have final words with my sisters?

MOTHER SUPERIOR: You don't have much time. Your bath is ready. I will call on you shortly.

(The Mother Superior tests the bath water and exits. Louise listens for a moment, then slowly rises.)

LOUISE *(Nervously; to audience)*: Shhh! Close the door! *(Looks around suspiciously)* Shhh! I'm not demented as the Mother Superior might have you believe, and no you won't go blind if you listen . . . Now quiet, sweet sisters, and I will tell you again. *(Smiles gloriously)* This *is* the *true* story of the seduction of Marie-Therese . . . the Queen of France.

(Lights rise on Queen Marie-Therese, a plump blond, dressed in the exquisite clothing popular in the French court during the 1660s. She sits and sips a glass of wine. Next to the Queen sits King Louis XIV, a lovely young man more elegantly clad and adorned than his wife. He covers his mouth with a handkerchief to keep down a belch. It erupts. They sit for a portrait, which is being painted by an expressionless man. Members of the court adoringly watch their King and Queen.)

It started with a box.

(Lights rise on an ornate box, neither too big nor too small.)

A gift from the Queen's cousin Monsieur De Beaufort, to take the Queen's mind off of her husband's improprieties, which had yielded several healthy children who wandered the court freely like plumped wild pheasants.

(The Queen curls her upper lip and sips her wine.)

Yes, it started with a box. The day after the King belched up a most prodigious worm, a foot in length, following his afternoon ride. The Queen took the worm as a powerful sign and readily accepted the gift.

(The Queen speaks with a rough Spanish accent.)

QUEEN: You see now! Mi primo give me a gift. Look at the size of the box . . . Louis, it could be treasure, gold, from the New World . . . He been there you know, my father sent he. How could I not accept it?

KING: I'm sorry, did you say something, Marie? Speak French, for God's sake I do not know what you are saying. (*He belches*)

QUEEN: I'M TALKING OF DE BOX DAT ARRIVED FOR ME DIS MORNING!

KING: Not louder Marie, in French. Please, my ears are dying!

LOUISE: The scandal, oh the scandal that was to follow this Queen, the princess of Spain.

(*Lights fade on Louise.*
The Queen traipses over to the box and examines it for a moment. The Painter throws his arms up in frustration.)

QUEEN: A gift! What is the best gift that you ever received? Did it come in a box dis size or bigger? (*The King shrugs his shoulders*) Do you remember whether that gift was given to you by someone you love, or someone you did not know? (*She places her ear to the box and giggles*) Mercy, supposing it is so splendiferous that I cannot repay it. Oh dear! Now I'm afraid to open it. (*The Queen smells the box*)

KING: Oh for God's sake, please open it.

(*The Queen finally opens the box. A very short African man raises his head over the edge, gasping for air. Horrified, he peers at the powdered members of the court. He is a "little person," petit. The Queen claps her hands with unbridled pleasure.*)

QUEEN: Ay Dios mio. Es un African. A little one at that. Look Louis, es fantastic.

(*The King, disinterested, can't be bothered to look.*)

Isn't he lovely? No?

KING: If you like. Now come sit, my dear, so we can finish —

QUEEN: —I like very much . . . *(She claps her hands again)* Oh goodness, I wonder what he does. Should I say something to him?

KING: If you like.

(The Queen isn't sure what to say. She looks to members of the court for guidance. Madame de La Valliere, the King's lovely, haughty mistress, speaks.)

LA VALLIERE: Perhaps the little moor will give us a song, Your Majesty.

QUEEN: Ah yes! Bueno . . . Sing for me!

(Nabo, the African dwarf, does not respond. He stares incredulously at the Queen.)

Well? . . . Sing, little man!

(Nabo still does not respond.)

SING! COMPRENDE?

NABO *(Timidly)*: I can't!

QUEEN: Oh?

(A moment.)

Give us a dance then!

NABO: I don't.

(The Queen, mortified, searches her mind for another prospect.)

QUEEN: . . . Then what is it dat you perform?

NABO: What can one perform after being in a box for three days? I was promised six goats and some beads, and I closed my eyes and I had crossed the ocean. And now I'm scented, powdered and stuffed in a box. If I perform, it's functions of the body, and that Your Majesty is private. Each place I go, they expect me to perform. What? I do not know. And they pack me back in a box and send me on. I've traveled halfway across the world in this box. And I'm tired, tired, tired . . . of it!

KING: Oh?

(The King sits erect, quite surprised by Nabo's frankness.)

QUEEN: He's tired, Louis! Delightful! *(Approaches the box again, with a balance of caution and curiosity)* Are you hun-gry?

NABO: Yes, yes.

(The Queen's eyes grow large with enthusiasm.)

QUEEN: Is it true?

NABO *(Apprehensively)*: What?

QUEEN: What they say, of course . . . is it true dat human flesh tastes like wild boar?

NABO: I wouldn't know.

QUEEN: Sweet Mother, you've probably never had wild boar. *(Claps her hands)* Den you will have.

NABO: I won't have to eat human flesh as well? What kind of barbarous place is this?

(The Queen roars with delight. The court joins in her laughter.)

QUEEN: Did you hear dat, Louis? Barbarous! What a wonderful fool I have.

(The King rolls his eyes.)

KING: Lovely gift my dear, but be careful . . . remember what happened to the last one. *(Winks at La Valliere)* I'm bored. I'm tired of sitting, I feel like a ride or fete or something.

(He yawns, stands, and gazes at Nabo in the box, then prepares to leave.)

QUEEN: Where are you going?
KING: Pardon me, I have pressing affairs of state to attend to.

(The King takes La Valliere's hand. The entire court stirs.)

QUEEN: But, Louis—
KING: Shhh!
QUEEN: But—
KING: Smile. *(The Queen smiles to reveal a mouthful of rotten teeth)* There, now that's where your charm lies. You needn't strain yourself with anything else.

(The King exits, followed by La Valliere and his entourage. The Queen's ladies remain at a distance.)

QUEEN: That es your King, not nearly as impressive as his portrait. *(Nods to the patient Painter)* My compliments! *(The Painter nods)* Louis, his work es of a nefarious nature, wrapped in lace and velvet . . . and extremely productive . . . But what of me, left to have my portrait painted alone. *(To Nabo)* You, sit with me.
NABO: I can't!
QUEEN: WHY?
NABO: I can't get out of this box.
QUEEN: Oh? I'll call someone to help . . . Naturally I can't really be . . .

(She signals to her ladies, but they're useless. Nabo frantically waves his arms, desperate to be free.)

Sweet Mother, I'll . . .

(She struggles to lift Nabo out of his box. After considerable effort she manages to free him. They tumble head over heels. The Queen's ladies quickly straighten her clothing. Nabo, dressed as a French nobleman, bows.)

Please, no need for that. I'm bored by formalities. Save it for Louis. If you can't relax with a fool, who can you relax with?

NABO: You call me fool, but it isn't my name.

QUEEN: Well? I will give you a name then.

NABO: I have one!

QUEEN: You do?

NABO: Nabo Sensugali. *(He bows again)*

QUEEN: I don't like it! I can't say it! Jorgito or Pedro, you like Pedro?

NABO: No!

QUEEN: You're indignant for a man that came in a box. I could put you back in dere and ship you home.

NABO: Indeed? I welcome such punishment, for this liberal tongue deserves no mercy. Send me home!

(A moment. The Queen roars with delight.)

QUEEN: Pedro . . . You don't mean dat of course! You're teasing me! Besides, you do what I say . . . Pedro!

NABO: Nabo!

QUEEN *(Whispered)*: Pedro . . .

NABO: Nabo!

QUEEN *(Furiously)*: DON'T TAKE AN IMPERIOUS TONE WITH ME! *(Whispered)* Pedro . . . Please? Por favor? *(Smiles)* You're no fun, are you? You know I can force you! But dat would poison our friendship and dat's not any way to begin. *(Grins)* Come here . . . Come and sit by me . . . *(Nabo begins to kneel by her side)* . . . in de King's chair.

NABO: If I must.

QUEEN (*Growls*): YOU MUST!

(*The Queen strikes an elegant pose for the Painter. Nabo reluctantly takes a seat next to the Queen.*
Lights rise on Louise.)

LOUISE: And there it began in the King's chair with a Painter re-shaping her likeness, molding that haphazard smile into an enigmatic smirk. With the image of Nabo lightly drawn in, uncommitted . . . a mercurial impression barely perceivable.

(*The Queen smiles at Nabo. Lights fade on the Painter and Nabo.*)

And so, sisters, sat the Queen many years later, sipping wine, trying, as she did, to remember beyond her illness. And I, a child in the company of a Queen, charity's ward.

(*The Queen, now worn and tired, turns to Louise. She coughs uncontrollably, then regains her strength. The Queen lets a few drops of wine from her glass fall to the floor.*)

QUEEN (*Whispered, barely audible*): Dios de Salve, Nabo.
LOUISE: What was that you said?
QUEEN: Did I say something? Oh sweetness, forgive me I can't remember now . . . Oh yes, shall we have more wine? (*Louise pours wine for the Queen. The Queen gets lost in a memory*) So many lavish rooms and faces and words I couldn't understand. It wasn't my home until I could invite someone else in. Comprende? And I laughed and laughed and—
LOUISE: And laughed?
QUEEN: Yes, how did you know?

(*She begins to laugh loud and robustly, but is suddenly overcome by a wave of melancholy.*)

What was I saying? Oh yes. You really should see our gardens? I've been told they're the most beautiful in de world.

LOUISE: And the King, is he as handsome as they say?

QUEEN: Yes, to many.

LOUISE: Are there truly celebrations that have no end?

QUEEN: They always end, my child, even in Versailles.

LOUISE: Indeed. I'd very much like to see Versailles, Your Majesty, but these walls are my home. And dreams are a beggar's fortune, that's what the Mother Superior says. So why tell me these things?

QUEEN: I enjoy your innocent conversation. Having little wit, the court offers small comfort.

LOUISE: But, Your Majesty, your gift of friendship is a small cruelty. I'd rather not be your confessor if I must listen to your tales with such eager resignation. Perhaps it would be better to torture some other novice with your beautiful stories. Why have you chosen me?

QUEEN: My dear child, everything happens according to a divine plan. And each time I ask why, I move a little further away from God.

LOUISE: You uphold ignorance as a virtue?

QUEEN: Shall we not ask questions of one another? Yes, I think it best. Don't you? (*Strokes Louise's face*) You're so pretty. I was never pretty.

(*The Queen begins to cough. Mother Superior enters and places her hand on Louise's shoulder.*)

MOTHER SUPERIOR: Look Louise, you've upset the Queen. Naughty girl. Say you're sorry.

LOUISE: I'm sorry.

QUEEN: Louise, I want you to know—

MOTHER SUPERIOR: You are not well, and it's so cold in here. Perhaps on another visit, Your Majesty.

(*The Queen coughs.*)

LOUISE *(To audience)*: And she left . . . never to return. Did I take wine with the Queen? you ask. Was I her confessor? you ask. Am I mad? you ask. Well, judge not dear sisters and allow me to speak on this eve of my wedding to the Lord for these words shall never again pass my lips, and these truths have an audience.

(The Queen's cough transforms into laughter.
The lights rise on the Painter and Nabo.)

QUEEN *(To Nabo)*: I think more wine is absolutely necessary . . . Don't you?

(She turns back to Nabo, smiling.
The Mother Superior and Louise retreat into the darkness.)

NABO: If Your Majesty pleases.

(A servant pours wine for Nabo. He sips it and pours a quick libation on the ground.)

QUEEN: What was that?
NABO: A libation for an ancestor I wish not to forget.
QUEEN: Oh? Libation? How silly to waste good wine on an ancestor.

(They share an awkward silence. Nabo and the Queen steal glances at each other. The Queen touches Nabo's hair. He recoils.)

QUEEN: Bueno! Much different . . . May I?

(She reaches out her hand like a child.)

NABO: No!

QUEEN: Well. With my other fools I do as I please. Aren't you supposed to entertain me?

NABO: How does one entertain Your Majesty?

QUEEN: HOW DARE YOU ASK ME A QUESTION! . . . *(Whispers)* I don't know.

NABO: Perhaps that is the problem!

QUEEN: Oh no! I can't bear de embarrassment of a fool without wit. It's like a truffle without sugar or a day without gambling. It's a wonder how—

NABO: In my country we tell stories, we have a tradition of sharing tales to—

QUEEN: A story? *(Disappointed)* No, no, no! You tumble delightfully! You sing some silly little song that rhymes! Like, like, well, anyway . . . A story? But surely you must be acquainted with one of our new dances—

NABO: No, not really Your Majesty. I am—

QUEEN *(Exasperated)*: Not even the chaconne? But everyone knows it. Where are you from? . . . Give me your hand.

(She stands. Nabo stands, she clumsily leads him through the steps of the chaconne, he is unable to follow.)

No, no . . . Or . . . Something short and rhythmic like de orientals.

(She demonstrates, performing a clumsy approximation of an Asian dance. She loses herself in the dance. Nabo watches, amused and bewildered. The Painter merely looks away with embarrassment. As the Queen's frenzied dance ends, Nabo and the attendants applaud. The Queen, momentarily flustered, curtsies. She smiles, emphatically, revealing her mouthful of rotten teeth.)

Sweet Mother, I've never done dat before. Was I good?

NABO: You had energy.

(The Painter coughs.)

QUEEN: Indeed . . . Not like Louis. He danced a ballet last night. De role of Apollo, my favorite. All the court was dere, even los niños. I haven't seen a showing like dat since I arrived in Paris drawn by a hundred grey horses. *(The King appears with two dancers)* Apollo in his full glory. *(The King dances a short ballet and exits with two dancers)* It was beautiful. I haven't de grace or de delicacy. Que Lastima . . . Now, tell me your—

NABO: Nabo.

QUEEN: I prefer Pedro.

NABO: It isn't—

QUEEN: Voila! I'm pleased you've come, my little friend. I tire of my wicked Dona Molina, she forgets what good friends we were in Spain. I like having someone to spend time with me until I close my eyes and sleep, and when I awaken you'll be dere to help me with all the things dat I do during the day. Wouldn't dat make the ladies jealous. *(Savors the notion)*

NABO: What is it that you do, Your Majesty?

QUEEN: I do whatever I like.

NABO: Which is?

QUEEN: Oh I see . . . I'm queen of France, I don't know . . . I rule.

(The Queen smiles fatuously.)

NABO: Forgive me for asking, but why am I here?

(A moment.)

QUEEN: Why? Don't you like your wine? . . . Mi primo, my cousin gave you to me. He knows how much I love little . . . back in Spain we had a number of . . . but none of dem were . . . De court was always filled with laughter and little people.

NABO: I see. But as you may have observed I am at the end of my wits. I'm afraid I can't make myself or anyone laugh.

QUEEN: Over time you can acquire a sense of humor, I've seen it happen.

NABO: Dear me, does it mean I'm to stay here?

QUEEN: You're mine . . . aren't you?

NABO: No. He said that if I—

QUEEN: Oh yes, I'm sure of dat.

NABO: But that implies that at some point I relinquished my own will, which I have not. And therefore I belong to no one, unless that someone is me.

QUEEN: I'm confused.

NABO: You are.

QUEEN: No, I've changed my mind, it's you dat is confused. (*Without a pause*) Painter, he came in a box addressed to me, you saw. I let him out, didn't I? But now he says he belongs to no one. But clearly he was given to me, which makes him mine, even if he didn't belong to mi primo. And my goodness if every man had a free will, then imagine the chaos that would be imparted. Dat's finished, let's move on to other things . . . What was your—

NABO: Na-bo!

QUEEN: Nabo. Dat's right. De name is growing on me. It floats very quickly off de tongue. Not like dese French names dat take so long to get out, dey ferment in your mouth and leave a bad taste. (*Protracted*) La Valliere! Ha!

(*She walks over to the canvas and studies the painting.*)

That's not me! You've given me a healthier, more masculine look dan I appreciate. (*Sucks in her cheeks*) Thin me out, more color in the cheeks, and extend my chin. How come Louis gets color and I don't.

PAINTER: Your Majesty, I paint what I see.

QUEEN: No, you paint what I see! *(She steps up to the canvas)* How can you be so insensitive to my needs? Must your brush also favor the King's whore, La Valliere? What about me?

PAINTER: Your Majesty—

QUEEN: Enough! If we were in Spain I'd have you executed, but de French are so caught up in decorum. *(To Nabo)* Don't you find that?

NABO: Yes, decorum . . .

(The Queen corners Nabo.)

QUEEN: I am beautiful, Pedro, yes?

NABO: You're asking me?

QUEEN: Yes. I want to know whether you find me beautiful.

NABO: As Queen you define what beauty is and by that standard I imagine that, yes you are.

QUEEN: Really? *(Shoots a vicious look at the Painter)* Thank you, Pedro. You'll have a fine room, I'll see to dat, with a view of the garden. Do you like the garden? Should we look now? I love the garden. Can you smell it? I like the idea of the garden smelling aromatic all year-round, don't you think? I've been finding the court to be particularly rank this season, a change in the sensibility, comprende? *(Walks up to Nabo and touches his hand)* De things we give up for peace in the land. I carry my duty out admirably, the pious Queen. On my knees half the day, praying . . . Do you know what I'm praying, Nabo?

NABO: No.

QUEEN: Dat he'll contract syphilis from one of his whores and die and I'll rule . . . Now we have a secret between us and dat makes us friends. You give me one and it's sealed. *(A moment)* Go on.

NABO: . . . When I said you were beautiful, I lied. I find you plain.

(The Queen sits.)

QUEEN: I don't find you beautiful either. True!

NABO: Beauty is not the only virtue in the world.

QUEEN: I'm so short on dem, I should like possess at least one.

(Nabo walks over to the Queen and places his hand on hers.)

Bittersweet words, you're de only one dare tell me the truth. And who are you?

NABO: Someone not unlike yourself.

QUEEN: Are you equating yourself with a queen?

NABO: No, with a sad woman a long way from home.

QUEEN: You have no shame!

NABO: You, Your Majesty, own it.

QUEEN: What a miserable fool you've become.

(She throws herself into the chair, covering her face with her hands, and pouts. Nabo takes her hand down from her face. She brightens up suddenly.)

Yes? Not even a little beautiful?

NABO: A little.

QUEEN: Indeed. Beauty is overrated. Beauty? We'll have no more talk of this, I think so. Now won't you make me smile a tiny bit even? I demand that you do! . . . please . . . Tell me one of your stories den . . .

(Nabo enacts his tale.
    Lights rise on Louise.)

LOUISE: And he began . . .

NABO: This is the story of a family, not a heroic tale, but a simple story of four souls bound by their love; a mother, a father and two sons.

LOUISE: And he wove a resonant tale of a small ancestral plot from which all the world could be seen, a vast mat of quivering trees. He carried her through the crevices and contours of the terrain, from the burial rites to the harvest, to the arrival of an intruder who claimed the eldest son as his own.

QUEEN: Oh no!

LOUISE *(Savoring the telling)*: He marched her across the savanna, through the forest to the ocean. In the port city he took her through the streets, where the smell of singed flesh, frankincense and stewed goat overwhelmed the Queen, who gasped just once at the telling. *(The Queen gasps. Louise closes her eyes)* He told of the terrible struggle that ensued, and the son's attempts to flee, to find his way home. Then of the unpleasant trip to the place where—

NABO: —the sun was covered over and the damp air formed mold on the young man's clothing, and the wind blew cold.

LOUISE: A land where tufts of smoke came from people's mouths as they spoke—

NABO: Where he was treated like an animal . . . a goat on a string, led about—

QUEEN: Shame!

LOUISE: The young man's family waited for one day, then one month, and then one year. He never returned.

NABO: But it didn't stop him from dreaming of home—

QUEEN: STOP! It's too sad. Pedro. Imagine if something like that were true.

NABO: It is.

QUEEN: Wretched . . . I'll pray for dat young man.

NABO: Would you help that young man get back?

QUEEN: Yes, of course.

NABO: I am he.

QUEEN: You? But if I sent you back, I wouldn't have you. And I've grown very fond of you, my friend. We share a secret, dat bonds us. *(Places her hand on Nabo's shoulder)* Don't you like me?

NABO: If I must.

QUEEN: . . . You must! We can be friends. Yes?

(She bends in front of Nabo. She goes through the motions of taking a string from around Nabo's neck and placing it around her own.)

. . . You've just begun to entertain me.

(Nabo registers the horror.)

LOUISE: This Queen who only the night before damned God for her creation.

Scene 2

The ladies in waiting prepare the Queen for bed.
Louise stands on the Queen's bed.

LOUISE: And what will be said about of our Queen Marie-Therese? Who will dare speak of the unfortunate alliance that brought peace between Spain and France, but no peace to the bedroom? What whispers will become record? And whose word history? Will it be the clever Madame de Montespan, who once told me that the Queen always retired first having spent a good part of the day roaming the court in search of the King. Her King was always tender, stroking his wife's side before falling off to sleep.

(The ladies exit.
Louise climbs off the bed. The Queen seductively spreads herself across the bed. The King enters in his lavish night clothing. He hurries quickly into bed and rolls over on his side feigning sleep. After a few moments, the Queen sits upright in the bed.
Louise giggles.)

QUEEN: You're not a sleeping. *(The King does not respond)* Where have you been? *(The King still does not respond)* Do you know what night it is? *(The King rolls away from her)* You're not a sleeping.

KING: I'm exhausted, Marie. And if I'm not "a" sleeping now it is because I must endure your miserable dismantling of the French language.

QUEEN: I recognize dat smell!

KING: Of ennui.

QUEEN: La Valliere.

KING: Hisssss . . . I thought we forbade that in this bedroom.

QUEEN: It's La Valliere. I smell her, I smell her, I smell her, I do.

KING: You know how it is—you rub up against a woman these days and wear her scent for the next month or so. It could be anyone that I'm wearing at this moment.

QUEEN: INSOLENCE!

KING: My God woman, learn something new for a change! Like subtlety, now that's a word of beauty when spoken by a woman of breeding.

QUEEN: You promised me tonight.

KING: It's my prerogative to will my own intentions. And I choose not to keep my promise.

QUEEN: Damn you to a fiery hell, keep going back on your promises. Just wait and see.

KING: I'm afraid I prefer the wait. Have you been eating sweets in bed again?

QUEEN: No.

KING: 'Tis a shame, you did have a full set of teeth when you arrived.

(The King peels a piece of candy off of his face.)

QUEEN: May I kiss you?

KING: Must you?

QUEEN: It has been—

KING: I know—

QUEEN: We're not out in de court you needn't be coy with me.

KING: Good night Marie!

QUEEN: NO, no, no!

(The Queen jumps up and down on the bed. The King climbs out of bed.)

KING: I'm tired. Tomorrow I have a full day of pageantry and whatnot. One of those damn barons, dukes or marquis or something from up North is coming. It's only appropriate that I out-show him . . . But I need my sleep if—

QUEEN: I want another baby . . . I es lonely, Louis. Please, por favor.

KING: You just got a new fool, didn't you?

QUEEN: He isn't a fool. He's my companion.

KING: Well, you should try and make friends with one of the ladies if you're lonely, wouldn't that be more befitting . . . They're all over the place for God's sake just choose one . . . Madame de Montespan is pleasant, wouldn't you enjoy spending time with her in the country? They're always asking after you.

QUEEN: Dey are?

KING: Yes.

QUEEN: Dey pretend as though dey don't understand what I say. Dey whisper.

KING: It's not whispering Marie, it's etiquette, *savoir faire*, a lady needn't be heard in every room of the palace.

QUEEN: It seems a lady doesn't have a place in dis palace. Did La Valliere beg you for her last child. Did she?

KING: La Valliere didn't eat sweets in bed. Good night Marie. Maybe tomorrow morning I'll find this conversation charming.

QUEEN: I'm going home den.

KING: To start a war? . . . Oh but would I love to go south this summer . . . *(Kisses the Queen, then pushes her aside)* There! No war.

QUEEN: I hate you, Louis. I'm going to tell my auntie.

KING: Don't tell Mama.

QUEEN: Will!

KING: Then tell her! Good night!

(The King rolls over and pulls the covers over his head. Louise sits on the bed.)

LOUISE: She told the Queen Mother.

(The lights suddenly rise on the majestic Queen Mother. The Queen goes to her side.)

QUEEN MOTHER: I didn't sleep with Louis's father until I was nearly forty, and I only did so because I had grown bored with my other . . . experiences.

QUEEN: Other experiences?

QUEEN MOTHER: Yes.

QUEEN: Sweet Mother! Did you love de King's father?

QUEEN MOTHER: . . . At times. He was dying for most of his life, which didn't make for a gratifying companion, but gave me fodder for plump conversation. In the end he had an erection twice, Louis and Phillipe. Maria, we Queens have but one function, produce a king and then love whomever, whenever, why ever. You'll die young if the King is the great love of your life, because you will always be chasing the scent of his mistress, and there is nothing less pleasant on a man's breath. I tell you because you are my niece, my daughter, my cousin and a Spaniard!

QUEEN: I would never take a lover! Are saying that I should?

QUEEN MOTHER: It wouldn't be Christian for me to say it aloud.

(The Queen Mother nods yes.)

QUEEN: De King would never approve.

QUEEN MOTHER: It is no fun if he does.

QUEEN: Sweet Mother! Can you love two?

QUEEN MOTHER: Only if you're adventurous. *(Laughs robustly)* Anyway. Let me sleep, Maria. I'm old and growing sentimental with the remembrance of more fecund times.

QUEEN: I would never take a lover and forsake my chance at heaven.

QUEEN MOTHER *(Patting the Queen on her hand)*: My dear, we'll stroll tomorrow. Bring along your boy. They carry him everywhere, I'm afraid his legs will atrophy if he doesn't walk. It happened you know to one of the Bavarian princes.

QUEEN: Really?

QUEEN MOTHER: Yes . . . During one of those ugly peasant insurgencies, the wretches stormed the castle. Everyone managed to escape, but that poor unfortunate prince. My dear he'd been carried so often he simply never learned how to walk. It was then that he discovered that the power of name was not necessarily enough to carry him to safety. He was killed by an Italian actor by the name of Fabrezio, who'd been insulted by . . . anyway, bring the child . . .

(The Queen Mother slowly retreats into the darkness.)

QUEEN: Good night Auntie.

(The Queen Mother disappears. The Queen continues to wander through the night.)

LOUISE: The Queen wandered the court, absently. Once even bumping into a drunken courtier who grabbed her bosom, kissed her chin and traveled on. *(The Queen gasps. Louise laughs)* Shhh. Say nothing yet, and I'll conjure their faces. We're free, but a moment, in their memory. Sisters, these walls, our prison and savior, tonight are a palace. This tongue a door, and behind it a bed chamber.

(Lights rise on Nabo asleep in a small bed, designed for a man of his modest proportions. Next to his bed is a small makeshift altar with cowrie shells, a small clay pot and several burning candles.)

QUEEN: Nabo? *(Shakes Nabo awake)* NABO!

(Nabo, still half asleep, gazes at the Queen. She sits on the edge of his bed.)

I couldn't sleep.

NABO: Uh?

QUEEN: Wake up!

NABO: Yes, Your Majesty.

QUEEN: I always thought dat life was continuous here, dat the games never ended, you just join in when you're ready. But my goodness, everyone sleeps.

LOUISE: But according to Comtesse de Clagny, the Queen says.

QUEEN: I am surprised dat the court isn't awake when I am, you'd think they'd be more considerate then dat.

LOUISE: And in Madame de Arnaud's diary—

QUEEN: 'Tis a pity de court hasn't learned to stay awake all night. If so, they'd realize that the sun rises from the east even when Louis is asleep.

NABO: Do you wish me to dress?

QUEEN: Oh? *(Thinks)* No need. I think your attire is charming.

(Nabo starts to get out of bed.)

NABO: As you please.

QUEEN: So formal.

NABO: You are Queen.

QUEEN: Yes, of course.

NABO: Is there something that you need? Is there a reason why you are here, Your Majesty?

QUEEN *(Snaps)*: Reason? Why shouldn't I be?

NABO: Well—

QUEEN: Yes?

NABO: I'm afraid how it may appear. Please, Your Majesty, I don't wish for trouble.

QUEEN: What trouble do you speak of?

NABO: Oh . . . I've heard stories about the sort of things that happen when certain lines are crossed. If you understand what I'm saying?

QUEEN: I don't! Which means this conversation should probably end!

NABO: I didn't mean to overstep, Your Majesty. But—

QUEEN *(Singsong)*: Lines, lines, where are dese damn lines dat everyone keeps talking about, so many drawn I can barely remember where to stand, sit or shit! It's a ridiculous French notion. Nonsense! I can do as I please!

NABO: That's what frightens me.

QUEEN: You! Afraid of me?

NABO: Yes.

QUEEN: What a thrill, no one's ever been afraid of me. *(Moves closer. Nabo modestly pulls the covers up around his body)* You pull back, why?

NABO: You're sitting on my bed . . . *(The Queen bounces up and down on the bed)* It's not very big.

QUEEN: Oh come, you don't mind that I'm sitting with you?

NABO: You are Queen.

QUEEN: If I wasn't would you want me to? *(Pause)* WELL?

NABO: At this moment, in the middle of the night at the edge of my bed with this cold breeze blowing in from the door which was left ajar sending a chill down my back, Your Majesty?

QUEEN: Well?

NABO *(Forcing out the word)*: YES!

QUEEN: I thought so. You know I sensed it, from the moment I saw you. I knew we'd be friends. Can I tell you a secret?

NABO: Another one?

QUEEN: Yes . . . *(Whispered)* When I couldn't sleep, I thought, who will I go to for comfort? And you're the only one I could think of, my little African man.

NABO: Surely that's not true.

QUEEN: Yes. It is de truth.

(The Queen moves closer to Nabo.)

NABO: I didn't know that I was to perform both day and night.

QUEEN: Oh? NOT LIKE THAT! YOU'RE A DWARF! You're black like night. *(She roars with delight)* How could you think? *(Stops laughing abruptly)* Would you want me like that?

(The Queen awaits a response. Nabo climbs out of bed.)

Of course you would, I don't need to ask.

NABO: Perhaps the Queen should go back to bed. I will take you. We'll get you something sweet and then back to your room. You'll catch a cough dressed up in your night clothing.

QUEEN: But, I don't want to go! No! No. I'll stay here with you, si! We'll let Louis wonder where I am tomorrow.

(The Queen climbs into Nabo's bed. Her feet dangle over the edge. Nabo curls up on the cold floor.)

LOUISE: And his face touched the cold, and he knew there'd be little sleep for him in this land.

(Nabo sits up.)

NABO: Are you sleeping?

(Nabo stands up and creeps toward the Queen. He slips the pillow from beneath her head and holds it above her face,

*as if to smother her. He struggles with the notion of suffo-
cating the Queen for a moment, then gently lifts her head
and places the pillow back under it. He does a warrior
dance as if evoking a distant spirit for strength. He kneels
before his makeshift altar.)*

Please mighty Legba, why am I here? If I do as she says
will she let me go? If I'm very funny will they give me
more food? If I kiss her will she free me?

LOUISE: In his small room facing the darkness, he stood wondering how he had gotten so far from home.

*(Louise blows out the candle.
Blackout.)*

Scene 3

*The King strolls with La Valliere by his side. He addresses several
members of the court, who laugh generously.*

KING: I simply grew tired of his constant braggadocio and
asked him to prove his assertions. When he couldn't, the
embarrassment was too much and he placed poison in his
brandy. He lived, much to my delight, because I get such
a chuckle when I see him. *(The court roars with delight)*
Without his shoes he couldn't be much taller than Marie's
fool, with them he was a virtual giant. It took him years to
properly learn how to balance on the heels. I did see him
once walking alone in the garden, when a tremendous
gust of wind whipped up and tipped him over. I watched
for hours from my window as he struggled to stand, which
he could not do. It was not until evening that he was finally
rescued by the gardener. Alas, when he showed up for dinner with the English ambassador, he told those supping

that he had been attacked by highwaymen and dirtied in battle. *(The court roars with delight)* I'm still going to appoint him as an ambassador, I admire his gumption and willingness to challenge the natural order. But he does believe in God and Louis, which makes him more than fit. *(One member of the court laughs. The King cuts him with his eyes)* Who are you? *(The courtier does not respond)* GET OUT!

(The courtier exits quickly. The Queen enters with Nabo trailing behind her.)

So, you've finally found me?
QUEEN: Who says dat I was looking for you?

(The King glances over at La Valliere.)

KING: Anyway, the other day I was speaking with him in this very room and—
QUEEN: I thought that I'd come for my final sitting with the Painter. Am I wrong to think dat the portrait must be complete in time for the fete? Really, I had no idea I'd find you here. None whatsoever!
KING: I was telling a story. Now I've lost my concentration. I'm growing impatient with you, Marie. The other day I was—
QUEEN: A story? Nabo told me de absolutely most funniest story this morning. I nearly spoiled myself with delight.

(Nabo takes a few steps back.)

KING: You interrupted my story again to tell me one that Nabo told you . . . that Nabo, Nabo? Who is . . . ?
QUEEN: Silly, he is my companion, of course.
KING: Where is this companion? Show yourself!
NABO: I am here, Your Majesty.

KING: Oh? You? So Nabo, you have a story that is better than mine?

NABO: Oh no, Your Majesty.

KING: The Queen seems to think so . . . tell it!

NABO: I'm sorry, Your Majesty.

KING: TELL IT!

NABO: I . . . I was explaining to Her Majesty that when I first arrived in France, I'd never seen white powdered makeup or a wig. As fate would have it, I . . . I was engaged by a patron who was quite beautiful, oh yes! Finely dressed with his white powdered face and a high standing wig, which gave him the illusion of a glorious head of hair. I must confess the ladies found him very comely and often visited. He inspired some of the finest poetry in this country. *(The King raises his eyebrows)* I mean the world. So you can imagine my surprise one evening when I went into his sleeping chamber to say good night and found an old balding man tucked in my patron's bed. "Who are you?" I demanded. For what was this shriveled old man doing there? I tried to pull him out of my patron's bed. But he refused to budge, insisting that he was my patron. "Oh no," I said, "my patron is a beautiful man with a full head of hair, a man who is still in his golden years." He slapped my face, I slapped his. "Fool!" he said. "Indeed!" I said. So I found my patron's sword and drove this man triumphantly from the house. That evening as I was searching for signs of my patron's disappearance I came upon his wig placed lovingly in a cradle as if a child. Next, I found my patron's face in a jar of rouge and a compact of powder. Oh dear. I could still hear the old man yelling from the cold. I thought, Should I let him in to give me a thorough beating or should I let him freeze to death and claim he went mad?

KING: What happened?

NABO: He went mad.

*(The King laughs; the members of the court join in.
Louise enters the light.)*

KING: An amusing story! Tell another.

(The Queen smiles.)

LOUISE: At that moment the dinner bell chimed.

(The dinner bell.)

KING: Oh! Dinner time. Bring the fool around later, Marie.
He amuses me.
QUEEN *(Excited)*: I'm glad he pleases you.
KING: Will you be joining me for dinner?
QUEEN *(Beaming)*: Yes.
KING: I didn't think you'd miss that.

*(The King and Queen exit, followed by the court and
Louise. La Valliere scowls at Nabo as she leaves.)*

PAINTER: I heard that story before. Performed by the Italian
commedia in Abruzzi. They did it better. I was painting
some overripe Italian nobles who had a love for the theatre
and engaged me to paint them as classic characters from
the Greek and Roman tragedies. Agamemnon, Lysistrata.
My favorite was Medea, clutching her babies in arm.
NABO: I heard the story in Lisbon as I was traveling with the
Sultan from Alexandria. One of the Portuguese seamen
kept telling it over and over again. The Queen is easily
amused. I cough and she laughs, I fart and she laughs.
PAINTER: Yes. It doesn't surprise me. I've been here so long
I'm beyond surprise. Years ago I'd be immobilized with
astonishment, but, now all I feel is—

(He can't find the right word.)

NABO: Numb.

PAINTER: Precisely.

(The Painter takes out a flask of wine.)

NABO: Until this evening no one other than the Queen had spoken to me. For a while I thought I was a figment of her imagination. Imagine that horror.

PAINTER: I've lived worse while serving this court. For a while I thought I was invisible. I'd speak and no one would respond, it was almost a year before I was acknowledged. And those first words were "IDIOT, you made me look like a moor!" I'd grown so accustomed to being ignored that I was overcome by emotion and fainted.

NABO: What you must hear.

PAINTER: The hell. Some days I worry that I will be put to death for what I've heard. But I make them look magnificent, despite my better judgment. They all look the same, you know. Or haven't you noticed. They're all related, you know. The same grandfather and grandmother. It's disgusting! All of them! But! I am a Painter, a fine Painter. I do what I can.

NABO: Indeed.

PAINTER: You know, I have been studying you. You have a remarkable complexion. You should let me paint you.

NABO: Me?

PAINTER: You're as fine a subject as any of them. *(Passes Nabo the flask)* Nabo, have some wine with me. Come, come they won't be back for hours. *(Giggles)* What would you say if I told you that she likes you?

(Nabo takes a quick swig.)

NABO: The Queen?

PAINTER: Yes, indeed. There'll be a portrait yet. I've already composed it in my head. So, tell, what do you think of our Queen of France? Do you like her?

NABO: Do you?

PAINTER: I don't like any of them. In fact, I hate them all. And in every portrait that I paint I write in tiny letters in the lines of their forehead or the sides of the eyes: "I hate you." Come and look.

NABO: I don't read.

PAINTER: Pity . . . It's no fun having this secret alone. So what is it like in the palace beyond these public rooms?

NABO: It's magnificent. No detail left to the imagination.

PAINTER: Have you been to her bed chamber?

NABO: No, of course —

PAINTER: Forgive me, I only ask because I've often wondered what color scheme they've chosen. I imagine green and gold, with allegorical sketches. That's what I see!

(Louise enters.
The lights fade on Nabo.)

LOUISE: I met the Painter many years later, when he was older and fading in memory. He painted a portrait of the Mother Superior, turning her craggy face into one of an angel of mercy . . . *(To Painter)* Is it true, Monsieur, that you were in the court of Louis XIV?

PAINTER: Yes . . . you look so familiar to me.

LOUISE: Perhaps we've met before.

PAINTER: I think not! *(Laughs, studies her face)* No, you know who it is you remind me of, an African, yes, a dwarf of very fine character from Dahomey. He served the Queen about seventeen years ago. Funny man. You resemble him.

LOUISE: Me? Resemble an African? *(Laughs)*

PAINTER: It had always been rumored but I would never have guessed. They grew close, you know.

LOUISE: Surely you joke with me, monsieur.

PAINTER: Forgive me, perhaps I've said too much.

LOUISE *(To audience)*: He told me he had a portrait, but he never came back to show me . . . *(To Painter)* What was the African's name?
PAINTER: Bobo . . . I believe.

(Lights rise on Nabo.)

LOUISE *(To audience)*: He remembered a few stories, vague at best.
PAINTER *(To Nabo)*: Let me paint you, Nabo. Without the adornments. Your face.

(Nabo takes off his wig.)

NABO: I hope I'm not here long enough for you to finish.
PAINTER: I've seen fools come and go from all over the empire. You'll be here.
LOUISE: A sketch, colors selected, hues blended. Frustration. And finally found in a damp cellar, a portrait of a nameless African man.

Scene 4

The King and La Valliere lounge on the sofa, whispering intimately. The members of the court sit, alert, attempting to glean bits of conversation.
Louise walks amongst the courtiers.

LOUISE: And then there was La Valliere: pretty, fertile thing. *(La Valliere laughs; Louise laughs, mockingly)* She was the King's diversion, skilled in the art of—

(The Mother Superior suddenly appears, a daunting presence looming in the background.)

MOTHER SUPERIOR: Masturbation! Do you like masturbation? You must! Why else tell such tales? It is untrue, no matter who told you otherwise. Silence your tongue, child! I won't hear of it! What are you doing? Is this how you prepare for your vows on this blessed evening? Sisters, I beg you to close your ears to this insanity.

(The Mother Superior walks briskly into the darkness. Louise hesitates before defiantly resuming her story.)

LOUISE *(Hushed)*: Please, stay if you will, for what does she really know of desire? If my tale surprises you, then let it be the surprise of a warm hand upon your thigh. What is the danger of a story, if it offers up such divine contentment? But now the Queen awaits us in the courtyard, darkness encroaching—

(The Queen enters wearing hunting attire, trailed by Nabo similarly dressed. The Queen taps her foot, awaiting acknowledgment.)

QUEEN *(Without a breath)*: I've been waiting outside in the carriage for nearly an hour. Do you know what that means? I could have caught my death, dere's such a terrible wind. It's dark. I hate to travel at night. We'll arrive at the Chateau and nothing will be prepared. I'll have to sleep on de floor like a peasant. Do you want me to sleep on de floor like a peasant?

(Nabo peers at the King from around the Queen's skirt.)

KING: Oh? Marie. What is it? Calm yourself. If you're having trouble, I'll summon Doctor Fagon.

(The Queen throws her hat and gloves on the floor.)

QUEEN: Are you coming?

KING: Were we scheduled to leave this evening? Perhaps my secretary failed to notify me. Anyway, I've decided that I won't go to the country this month.

(The Queen stops short. Nabo takes the Queen's hand, attempting to calm her.)

QUEEN: But Louis—

KING: La Valliere has persuaded me to stay. It appears a troupe of Italian—

LA VALLIERE: Performers.

KING: Yes, are booked for next week. La Valliere says it's fabulous and shouldn't be missed.

QUEEN: La Valliere says? La Valliere says? I'll play no role in this farce. I've all my bags packed and loaded, I've assembled my household and closed off my apartment. There are nearly thirty people standing outside dese window awaiting you in the cold.

KING: Then I'll have my valet fetch them capes. I'm afraid I'm not going.

(La Valliere claps her hands.)

LA VALLIERE: You won't be disappointed. Better than Molière, I'm told.

QUEEN: Putana.

(La Valliere yelps, retreating behind the King.)

KING: Marie!

NABO: Temper, temper. Let it go and one will always be chasing it.

KING: Marie! *(Aside)* You've embarrassed us. *(To court)* My apologies to all. *(Grabs the Queen's arm and leads her toward the door; aside)* I want you to board that carriage and leave tonight. Now get out!

QUEEN: Have you forgotten your duties? Daddy won't like it. ¿Pero, quién te has creído que eres tu? Eres un paleto Borbón. Nosotros los Hapsburgos hemos sido emperadores mil anos.

(The Queen throws a tantrum, stomping across the room in an undignified manner.)

KING: What sort of primitive dance is this?

QUEEN: Te Mandará con La Vallière a los infiernos.

(The Queen storms out. Nabo follows.)

LOUISE: The gentle Queen rampaged through the palace in a rage that's still legendary. Tearing portraits from the walls and shredding tapestries with her bare hands. A most unchristian display for such a devout Catholic. Possession was blamed, a trance induced by proximity to an infidel. It was Nabo who finally calmed her.

(The Queen pushes open the doors to her bed chamber. Nabo scrambles behind, attempting to calm his Queen. The Queen shoves her servants out of the room and slams the doors shut. The Queen fumbles about the bedroom searching for something to destroy. Finally, the Queen flings herself on her bed.
  Louise retreats into the darkness.)

QUEEN: If Louis is not going to the country, then I'm not going either. I defy you, Louis! Look Nabo, I'm not shaking.

NABO: That's right, Your Majesty, don't let him take your pride. Once he has that you're bankrupt.

(The Queen holds out her rock steady hands.)

QUEEN: I wish I were not so cowardly.

NABO: And I wish I had longer legs. If I had longer legs I'd have been gone. We don't always get what we want as you well know.

QUEEN: Shame! I have suffered my fifth insult of the day. I will not tolerate another. I'm going to bed and don't wake me until spring when my garden's in bloom. I don't think I can bear one more indignity this season.

(The Queen begins to weep.)

NABO: Your Majesty frightens me, are you all right?

(He dries her tears with a handkerchief. He hugs her. She closes her eyes and rocks, pressing her face against his.)

QUEEN: What kind of Queen am I that quivers in the arms of a fool?

NABO: What kind of fool am I that cradles in my arms a queen? Shall I let you go, Your Majesty?

QUEEN: Only if you like?

NABO: Pardon me if I say that I like very much holding Your Majesty.

QUEEN: And I like very much being held.

NABO: Shall we go on sitting this way?

QUEEN: No bells have tolled and no bolts of lightning have struck.

NABO: My God does not punish for such acts.

(A moment. The sound of laughter is heard from the corridor. Nabo and the Queen quickly release their embrace. They stare awkwardly at each other, attempting to find appropriate words. The laughter ceases and they immediately re-embrace. The Queen lets out a long sigh, which transforms into a moan. She turns her face into Nabo and they kiss spiritedly and passionately. Nabo pushes the Queen away.)

There is danger around this corner.

QUEEN: We pay the price for the things we desire. I've offered my teeth for my excesses.

NABO: Now look good. Your anger shouldn't drive you to places from which you'd otherwise run.

QUEEN: Nor should your desire to be free rob me of my virtue.

(They embrace.)

NABO: In all my travels I've never held someone as close as I hold you now.

QUEEN: In all my life I've never been held by one as tenderly.

NABO: Not even the King?

QUEEN: Not even the King. Dear God, what should we do?

NABO: You are Queen.

QUEEN: Yes. No. Wet your finger.

(Nabo wets his finger. The Queen leads his hand beneath her dress.
Louise enters the light.)

LOUISE: With a kiss he now possessed the Kingly prize. With a kiss he tasted empires past and future. With one tender kiss she drew him in and they faced the possibility of freedom.

(Blackout.)

Act Two

Scene 1

Lights rise on Louise's decrepit cell. She sits on the edge of a tub, slowly unbuttoning her gown as she speaks. She wears a simple undergarment.

LOUISE: Well, well, sweet sisters, I detect some disbelief. How could I have conjured so elaborate a tale on this, the eve of my wedding? Are you still contemptuous of my story? What further evidence do you need? Have you had tea with the Queen and shared intrigues with nobility?

(The Mother Superior, dressed in black from head to toe, moves from the darkness into the light. She walks across the space slowly, punctuating her statements with the gentle rise and fall of her elbows, like a young bird preparing for flight.)

MOTHER SUPERIOR: I held you in my arms not long after your birth. You came with the storm clouds that lasted a full week, colicky and hungry for a swollen nipple. It was the night that the great tree fell against the rectory and tore a hole in the roof. Father Josephus nearly drowned in rain water. He coughed up a river of water for days.

LOUISE: I'm not listening.

(The Mother Superior smiles.)

MOTHER SUPERIOR: It's my turn. It was I who carried you in
and placed you in a bundle next to my bed. I, who put
aside a multitude of questions for a homeless child.

LOUISE: And that three hundred livre bestowed to the order
annually. Yes Mother, I came with an excellent dowry.

(Louise laughs.)

MOTHER SUPERIOR: My final reward is to have you join us.
But, if you're to take your vows with us you must first
purge your imagination of these exaggerations. How can
you wed God, when you still harbor the tales of the devil.
The Queen? The King? *(Crosses herself)* Do you know
what your assertions could do? Shall we pray? *(Closes her
eyes and rattles off a quick prayer)* AMEN!

LOUISE *(Whispered)*: Amen!

(The Mother Superior wipes her brow and sighs.)

MOTHER SUPERIOR: Avert catastrophe! That's the message
I'm receiving from the Lord! More a command actually
than a message. AVERT CATASTROPHE GOOD SIS-
TER! *(Whispered as though confessing a sin)* Why, at
Moret we have such a simple life, we are women of virtue.
Women of noble birth enter our ranks in numbers far
greater than any convent in France can boast. If we were a
royal court it would be the finest in this nation. There's no
place for your perfidious tales of *bastards, fornicators* and
drunkenness. Tales of Moorish infidels weaving vulgar
jokes, unchristian even before their execution. I am nau-
seated. *(Moans as though wounded)* AVERT CATASTRO-

PHE! Words! Words! Sickening and potent like some potion to rid the body of vapors. Queens! Kings! Cursed! Malediction! How did our ranks swell with such pernicious tales of debauchery and niggerdom. *(She begins to weep)* I can't stop weeping. I shall drown in the sea of licentiousness. I'm praying now for your soul. *(She prays in Latin, picking up her pace while traversing the stage as if in search of some answer. She suddenly stops)* You've left me no choice. I must beat this demon from within you. Drive this dark homunculus out before it can do any more harm to our reputation. How can you wed God unless you have purified your soul?

(The Mother Superior removes a black leather whip from beneath her robes. She lifts the whip to strike Louise. She mimes delivering the strokes.)

LOUISE: Sweet sisters, what demon resides within, and when did my life become a sin? And tell me, what troubles her so deeply that to look upon me is to beat me?

(Mother Superior fades into the darkness.

Louise strokes the ornate cross hanging about her throat as the stage swells with a chorus of female voices singing somber, sacred music. Louise dreamily crosses out of the light as the music shifts from sacred to secular. A loud gasp is heard. The lights rise on the Queen gasping. She is surrounded by her ladies in waiting, who tug the strings of the stiff corset about her waist, trying to conceal her swollen stomach.)

QUEEN: PULL! Pull! I say pull!
LADY SERVANT: It is no good, Your Majesty. Perhaps—

(Two young maids attempt to pull the Queen's corset tighter and tighter. The Queen screams with pain.)

QUEEN: Don't say it! Tighter! Tighter I say! . . . .

LADY SERVANT: Your Majesty I'm afraid we will hurt you.

QUEEN: I must get into this dress. It's my costume for tonight's fete! Louis is Apollo and I'm to appear as his twin, Artemis. I'll spoil everything. The dressmaker spent over two months refining dese costumes. The beads were imported from the Orient. We are to make a grand entrance through the garden, it's been rehearsed since the beginning of the spring. Ay!

(The Queen lets out a wretched cry. One of the servants begins to weep.)

LADY SERVANT: I'm sorry Your Majesty, but I can't do this any longer . . . I'm afraid my Queen will die.

QUEEN: If your Queen dies then she will be buried in dis dress as the Goddess Artemis. Deo Volente! Now pull by God! You worthless wenches!

(The women pull the corset so tight the Queen cannot utter a word. Waving her arms wildly, she struggles to indicate to them to loosen it, but they misread her instructions and pull tighter. The women slip the elaborate dress over the Queen's head, and then proceed to powder her face. Fully adorned the Queen looks like a fragile porcelain doll.)

(Gasping) How do I look?

LADY SERVANT: Magnificent, Your Majesty.

(The women applaud. The Queen attempts to bow, but cannot.)

QUEEN: You see! *(The sound of chamber music from outside)* The music! *(Recounting what she must do)* I step out, bow to the King, he bows to me, he takes my hand and . . . and

. . . and we move to the barge . . . and . . . and . . . Quick! Help me to the door.

LADY SERVANT: Are you sure, Your Majesty?

(The Queen shoots a look at the Servant. She moves with great difficulty, sidling back and forth. Before they reach the door, the Queen grows weak and faints. The women, unable to support her weight, let the body slide to the floor.)

We've murdered the Queen!

(The women furiously fan the Queen. She slowly comes to and they lift her to a chair.)

Are you all right?

(The Queen takes in air.)

QUEEN: No! Ah! Quick! Quick, wench! Go through mi closet and see if there's another Goddess I can appear as. Juno maybe! Something large and flowing. Loosen me quick, I can feel the mushrooms and barley wine coming up.

(The lady servants disrobe the Queen, who lets out a tremendous sigh of relief. One Lady Servant ventures to speak.)

LADY SERVANT: Has it not been four months since Your Majesty last bled? *(The Queen shoots a quick disapproving glance at the young woman)* Sickened by the sunrise and the ring of the dinner bell?

QUEEN: What are you suggesting?

LADY SERVANT: That you're in the family way, so swollen suddenly. It would be glorious news! Something grand to announce at the height of the fete as the toast is being made. It would be a true celebration!

QUEEN *(Horrified)*: *Imposible!* And you won't repeat that again. Foul vapors fill my belly and a simple emetic will purge dis bloat.

LADY SERVANT: If that's how you'll have it, Your Majesty, but there will come a time when you can no longer hide it.

QUEEN: Insolence! Would you talk to . . . to . . . to Louis dat way? I have it on authority that the desserts are richer and more prone to linger in the belly dis season. Now find me something else to wear.

(The fete music grows louder. Nabo enters ringing bells and dressed as Bacchus/Legba for the fete. He wears an African mask and a huge phallus strapped to his front. The Queen stares at him, covering her mouth with disbelief. She races off the stage, trailed by her servants. A simple drum beat sounds for his performance.)

NABO: Ananse spider had roamed the earth for many years, when suddenly he felt the presence of death pursuing him. Oh no, not yet, he thought. He hadn't had time to spread his seed, to keep his tradition of trickery alive. So from village to village he roamed, his erection swelling and growing. But every woman that he encountered was married or barren or withered or old. Finally, in a tiny village at the foot of a great mountain he spotted the most beautiful woman he'd ever seen. Her hair twisted in spirals, reaching for the sky and her skin blackened and glowing with a shea butter sheen. As he hung in a baobab tree lazing in the midday sun, he decided she would be the woman to bear his child. As fortune would have it, she was the wife of the moon. How opportune, he thought, All I need to do is slip into her hut at night when the moon's hanging high in the sky. So Ananse spider crept into the moon's hut that night and seduced his wife. He used the Moon's slippers to hide his footprints so there'd be no record of his visit. When the moon returned in the morning to sleep with his wife, he found that she was already satisfied. This happened day after day until the moon finally sensed some deception. So the next night the moon decided to go only three quarters of the way into the sky, and the night after that only half way into the sky. But it was too late, for Ananse had been sated and the moon was forever to be suspicious, only rarely returning completely to the sky, in order to keep an eye on his wife at night.

(Nabo bursts into laughter. A burst of seeds shoot out of the head of the phallus. All others are silent. Lights rise on the King dressed as Apollo.)

KING: Vulgar! Moon? Spider? Why did the spider speak? Does a spider have an erection? Nonsense! It's a barbaric tale and I found it hard to follow. It smacks of paganism! Where's the humor? A most inappropriate tale and now that it's been told I declare that it should never be spoken again. Bring on another fool to start these festivities. I've grown bored with this one.

(A battery of trumpets sound. The King departs.)

NABO: Yes sire. Yes sire.

(The lights fade on all but Nabo.)

Yes, Spoiler. Yes, Spineless. Yes—

(The lights rise on the Painter cleaning his palette and packing his belongings.)

PAINTER: Ah! And you thought no one was still watching!
NABO: That was my Nana's tale. Where I come from a spider can speak, a rock can dance and a tree can weep.

PAINTER: I'd like to see that place some day. Yes, indeed. If I could walk in your tiny shoes and purge my feelings before the King. Oh the stories that he'd be forced to endure. *(Makes retching sounds)*

NABO: You wouldn't wear those shoes for very long if you knew the places where they've been. Rolling, tumbling, tortured daily with their ticklish needs. You'd trade my shoes for a pair of worn sandals.

(Nabo removes the phallus.)

PAINTER: Oh you're wrong, I wouldn't be caught dead in a pair of sandals. *(Laughs, then stops himself; whispers)* I imagine you've heard.

NABO: Nothing that need be whispered.

PAINTER: Come closer. *(Whispers)* She's with child, you'll soon have another to entertain.

NABO: With child?

PAINTER: You must know.

NABO: I do not. I swear.

PAINTER: These ears are never wrong. It is the truth, spoken by a lady of repute. Only this morning the Queen relinquished her meal in the chapel.

NABO: Pregnant? Performing for the King during the festival, I've seen little of the Queen.

PAINTER *(Whispers)*: I'll tell you something, she can't bear a child more ghastly than her first. *(Makes an apelike face. A moment)* It's no secret, the Queen's the ugliest woman in all of this court. If she wasn't Queen they'd turn her out to pasture. Moo! It's a wonder, you know, that the King . . . *(Grabs a hold of Nabo's phallus)*

NABO: Come. She's not without charm. In the late afternoon light she can be thought to possess a few pleasant features.

PAINTER: In the late late afternoon perhaps. *(Laughs, then grows suddenly melancholy. He packs his brushes)* I thought

I'd lost the ability to laugh. If I may say, I'm going to miss you.

NABO: Am I to be sent away?

(The Painter laughs.)

PAINTER: No, I am. It appears this painter couldn't transform the man into a God. The Apollo of my imagination wasn't to the King's satisfaction.

NABO: But it is a remarkable painting, my friend.

PAINTER: You think so? But nevertheless, I am being released. And suddenly I feel at ease.

NABO: Now, I were in your shoes.

PAINTER: But Ananse spider wears the shoes of the moon . . .

(The trumpets sound. The Painter disappears as quickly as he appeared. Nabo rings his bells, resuming his festive dance. He stops abruptly.
Lights rise on Louise.)

LOUISE: A child? A child.

Scene 2

The Queen Mother and the Queen stroll down the palace corridor. Courtiers bow as they pass.

QUEEN MOTHER: What news, dear child. What news! You glow! Pregnancy does have the tendency to bubble the blood in the cheeks. Don't look so frightened, the first is always the most difficult. You'll have no trouble with this one. Kaplunk!

QUEEN: How'd you find out?

QUEEN MOTHER: How? How? I thrive on such precious gossip. You spend all your mornings in your bed chamber and all your evenings in chapel. The signs are there.

QUEEN: Does everyone know then?

QUEEN MOTHER: Everyone! Who is everyone? Of course not! I pay dearly for news that intrigues me. I recommend that you find help that's more discreet. I'm thoroughly disappointed; I didn't even have the pleasure of a good old fashioned barter. Regrettably, when you reach my age, you must take short cuts in this sport of gossip. When I tried my hand at governing, I found gossip to be the most incisive tool. I was well-seasoned then. Alas, they weren't quite ready for me. (*Kisses both of the Queen's cheeks*) You're so slow at learning the ways of the French court, without intrigue we might as well be English: humorless, passionless and without reason. (*Stops and fans herself*) Maria, I'm hurt.

QUEEN: Where, Auntie?

(*The Queen Mother slaps her chest.*)

QUEEN MOTHER: I thought I'd at least be the first to know. Ha! Does Louis know?

QUEEN: Not yet, Auntie.

QUEEN MOTHER: That's right, spring it upon him at just the perfect moment. Everything is political and there's nothing more potent than a Queen's womb.

QUEEN: I didn't want to say anything until I could be sure. Dere's no need to get him excited for nothing.

QUEEN MOTHER: Hmmmmm?

QUEEN (*Half-hearted*): I will tell him dis evening.

QUEEN MOTHER: Is there some information that has no price? (*She lifts her eyebrows*)

QUEEN: I don't understand what you're asking.

QUEEN MOTHER: If you don't understand, then perhaps I am mistaken.

QUEEN: Maybe this once, Auntie.

(*The Queen Mother takes the Queen's hand.*)

QUEEN MOTHER: All is well?

QUEEN: Yes.

QUEEN MOTHER: Sometimes we make mistakes, but none that are too big to fix, it is the power of our rank. There are explanations for everything in this age of science, but still little can be stated with certainty. Don't look so worried, I'm here.

QUEEN: I'm afraid for what grows in my belly. I've dreamt of a child unnatural. It's not yet the fourth month and I feel it moving in my stomach as though it wants to get free. ¡Ay! ¡Dios mio! What if I give birth to a basilisk or some other horrible creature like the women from the Far East who sleep with pagans.

QUEEN MOTHER: We all have our fears. We all have our problems, some are solved with prayer and others with vinegar, mustard seed, a rat's liver and ginger root. *(The Queen gasps)* Yes. *(Bows to a passing courtier)* Maria, some day I will tell you all. *(Slaps the Queen's hand)* But today I prefer to stroll and enjoy the lovely men, ah yes, and women. The times have changed. Heed my advice: send your fool away, Maria. *(Resumes walking)*

QUEEN: Nabo? Why, Auntie? *(She does not follow)*

QUEEN MOTHER: So much time spent with an infidel could give rise to talk. I've heard that a soul as black as his could permeate your womb.

QUEEN: No! I'm going to the chapel dis moment to pray. And each morning from now until the birth I will spend on my knees. It isn't the case.

QUEEN MOTHER: It wouldn't be the first case, you know. *(Whispers)* The de Medicis.

(The lights fade on the Queen Mother as they rise on Louise. The Queen falls to her knees.)

LOUISE: She prayed for a healthy beautiful boy without the dull eyes of her first-born son. She prayed that she'd awaken from her dream in the Spanish palace with her circle of tiny ladies and the little wicked Dona Molina at her bedside stroking her hair. She prayed that the gentle Nabo was of princely proportions. What a cruel predicament.

(Louise and the Queen are on their knees swaying back and forth in prayer.)

QUEEN: I will repent! I will repent!

(The West African drum sounds. The Queen sways to the rhythm, fighting the impulse to move. Louise begins to dance.)

I will cleanse! I will cleanse!

(Louise's dance becomes more impassioned. The Mother Superior appears from the darkness.)

MOTHER SUPERIOR: Where'd you learn such a preposterous dance? Stop!

(Louise collapses to the ground.)

LOUISE *(To audience)*: So I'd planned my wedding to a Spanish prince, more comely than the gardener's son. We'd escape these stone walls on his dappled horse. So I waited day one, so I waited day two, so I waited day three, day seventy, day four hundred, day one thousand.

(The Mother Superior cracks the whip and disappears.)

I waited and waited, but he never did come.

(Chamber music plays.)

Scene 3

The King, the Queen, La Valliere, Doctor Fagon and members of the court play cards in an antechamber. The Queen belches, a monstrous belch.

KING: It's not your turn, Marie!

(La Valliere laughs flirtatiously as the King places a card.)

LA VALLIERE *(To King)*: I'm not going to play cards with you, you're too clever for me.

(The Queen throws a card down.
  Louise enters.)

LOUISE: As the Queen's belly grew, they worshipped all day at the card table.

LA VALLIERE: Lovely day, don't you think?

DOCTOR: Special for this time of year. I look forward to a ride in the country, do you?

QUEEN: Yes.

LOUISE: And they gossiped.

LA VALLIERE: She's not his daughter from what I was told. His wife was barren, an accident involving an ox. Yet he traveled up north in the child's company.

KING: At his age he deserves applause not chastisement. I've known many a man that was seduced by the luster of a child's cheek. *(The Queen bitterly throws down a card)* It's not your turn, *Maria. (Picks up the card and shoves it in the Queen's hand)* I will remove you from the game if you cannot follow the rules. Do you have money to wager? Or is this another exercise that shall cost me?

(The Queen Mother enters assisted by a supple young man. The craggy-faced woman does her best to remain upright,

*though gravity pulls her forward and she occasionally has
to be straightened out.*
   Louise exits.)

QUEEN MOTHER: Grand afternoon to all. Please don't stand
   on my account. *(She waits for all to rise before continuing.
   The men stand. The women bow their heads)* Ah! There
   you are Marie. Have you shared the *news? (The Queen
   looks down. The Queen Mother shoots a piercing glance at
   La Valliere)* Perhaps Madame de La Valliere is curious to
   hear the Queen's news? No? *(La Valliere smirks)* I believe
   that Maria has something to share.

(The Queen Mother claps her hands for emphasis.)

KING: Can't it wait, Mother. We're in the middle of a game.
QUEEN: Yes.
QUEEN MOTHER: No!
KING: I'm not in the mood for talk. Save your thoughts for sup-
   per time. Concentrate on your cards, *Marie.*
QUEEN MOTHER: And once the news has been told you will
   scold her for not sharing it sooner. It is good news.
KING: Which will make it all the more pleasurable over a good
   meal.
DOCTOR: There!

*(The Doctor lays down a card, quite pleased with himself.
The King acknowledges the defeat with a nod of the head.
He quickly scribbles out an IOU note.)*

KING: I now owe you two hundred livre. Collect it from the
   Minister of Finance tomorrow morning.
DOCTOR: Sire, it was my pleasure.
KING: Don't display too much glee, Fagon. It is un-sportsmanlike.
   But I forget, you physicians do so enjoy the pains of others.

(He rises and pulls out the chair for the Queen first and then La Valliere. Doctor Fagon stands and nods.)

You see what happens, Mother, when you and *Marie* strain my concentration. You're used to defeat, but I—

QUEEN MOTHER: No speeches for God's sake, we're not in a session.

KING: Don't start, Mother. Stay out of my affairs.

QUEEN MOTHER: Your affairs are mine, a mother's prerogative. Don't ever forget how and why you sit where you are! NOW TELL HIM MARIA!

QUEEN *(Tongue tied)*: I—

LA VALLIERE: Oh go on now, I'm dying to know what news could bring such light into the Queen Mother's eyes.

KING: Should I sit or stand *Marie*?

QUEEN: I—

KING: I'll sit therefore I won't be disappointed if I had bothered to stand and it wasn't worthwhile.

QUEEN: Maybe I should wait until supper. Nothing better than good news on a full stomach.

KING: So it is.

(The King leads his entourage toward the door. They follow at an appropriate distance behind him. The Queen Mother pinches the Queen.)

QUEEN *(Yelps)*: I'M PREGNANT!

(The King stops short. The courtiers applaud. The King silently counts the number of months on his fingers.)

KING: Pregnant? *(Again, he silently counts the months on his fingers)* Fagon, can this be confirmed?

(Fagon shrugs his shoulders.)

QUEEN MOTHER: Nonsense. A woman's body tells her what she needs to know.

KING: Hysteria is not uncommon, particularly during these spring months. It is not unknown for maladies and other disorders to be contrived for mere entertainment. Remember that poor Duchesse, lovely thing she, well, remember. Can this be confirmed, Fagon?

(The Doctor examines the Queen, gently rubbing her belly, looking into her mouth and stroking her hair. He smells her breath.)

DOCTOR: She's all the signs of early pregnancy, sire. Her tongue is a solid pink and protrudes slightly. Her breath sour. Her hair is coarse and her hands warm and moist. I'd say she's pregnant.

(The King once again counts on his fingers the number of months.)

QUEEN: Are you pleased?

KING *(Hesitantly)*: Yes, wonderful news. Fagon. Fagon. *(Summons the Doctor to his side; whispered)* Could it be some other sickness that causes these symptoms?

DOCTOR: I'm delighted that all the outward signs are there. She is pregnant.

KING: Is there some way, other than the *usual* way that the Queen could be ripe? If you understand what I'm saying. I can't recall when I rested with the Queen last, but I'm sure this child is mine. She's a pious Queen.

DOCTOR: Of course. Have you eaten food from her plate?

KING: Yes.

DOCTOR: Kissed her lips after seven?

KING: Yes.

DOCTOR: Dried her tears or touched her saliva.

KING *(Thinks)*: Yes, yes! That's it!

(The King steals a glance at the Queen clutching her belly. His face grows long and troubled.)

DOCTOR: These are all quite scientific considerations, sire. Congratulations are in order.

KING: Yes of course. *(Returns to the company of the women)* We'll have the church bells rung and a feast for all who can fit. *(He throws his arms in the air and gestures wildly. He stops to think, suddenly inspired)* I'll commission a musical extravaganza, which will be played as the boy is being delivered. The first sounds that he hears will be the celestial bellow of the horns drawing him from his watery sanctuary. *(Muted French horns play a pastoral melody)* No! *(The music stops)* It should be silent so his cries can echo throughout the palace. All the doors of the Louvre flung open so the sound will carry out into the air. I'm to have another son!

(The court claps. The King acknowledges the applause with graceful bows of the head, suddenly delighted. He kisses the Queen's hand, then exits in a flurry with his entourage following behind at an appropriate distance. Louise traipses on stage carrying a glass of burgundy wine.)

LOUISE: Cheers! Louis! Another son to inherit the empire. Cheers! Marie! Another son to be tutored, pampered and plumped up for leisure. His mind afflicted with inherited madness. Matri, Patri, Avus, Avia . . . still years after that first celebration, they'd send his mistress and some pastries.

(La Valliere, with a basket in hand, sheepishly approaches Louise. She overextends her arm in a hollow gesture of politeness.)

LA VALLIERE: Louise Francoise de La Baume Le Blanc, The Duchesse de La Valliere.

LOUISE: Pleased. Louise Marie-Therese.

(La Valliere eyes Louise, inspecting her clothing.)

LA VALLIERE: Dear child, you're not so black as they say.

LOUISE: Nor do you resemble the witch so described. Lovely dress.

LA VALLIERE: I'll give you the name of my dressmaker, wondrous creature. *(Gasps in feigned disbelief)* If the window were larger you'd get glorious light in the morning. It would actually be quite lovely. Oh dear, I couldn't bear the confinement of a convent with prayer as the central event of my day.

LOUISE *(Aside)*: She retired to a Carmelite house not soon after our meeting, it seems the King took another lover.

LA VALLIERE: Should we take our meal in the garden? Spiced mutton and stuffed plums in anisette. A treat.

LOUISE: It sounds delicious, but I'm not permitted outside these walls no matter how tempting the offerings.

LA VALLIERE: Even on a day like today? That's ridiculous. Someone should speak to the Mother Superior.

LOUISE: Someone already has, I'm afraid. *(Laughs)*

LA VALLIERE: Then this will do. *(Inspects the cell with abrupt twists of her head. She spreads a blanket across the floor)* The Queen asked me to come in her stead. A fever took hold three days ago and it rages through her body. Doctor Fagon says it will pass after a complete bloodletting.

LOUISE: Give her my well wishes.

LA VALLIERE: Yes, I will. I think the Queen is most generous to give charity to one such as yourself. I know how much she looks forward to visiting the convent. She always seems reinvigorated after conversations with you. I've come to try my hand. I too need to be uplifted. I understand that you have a magician's touch. *(She awkwardly lowers herself to the blanket)* Come child, it will be like a picnic in the meadow.

LOUISE: Picnic in the meadow? It sounds lovely, but I wouldn't know.

(A moment. Louise bows her head. La Valliere can't stop herself from staring. Louise catches her and La Valliere averts her glance.)

LA VALLIERE: I've come so far. Don't you want to see what I've brought?

LOUISE: If you haven't brought me freedom, it is of little interest to me.

(Louise knocks the basket out of La Valliere's hand. A loaf of bread and some wild flowers spill out.)

LA VALLIERE: I'm sorry. If I could have brought—

(Louise drops to her knees and kisses the hem of La Valliere's skirt.)

LOUISE: You have persuasion with the King. I thought at least you'd bring something more inspired.

LA VALLIERE: My influence is no longer in fashion.

LOUISE: But you could still plead my case. Ask him why I have been punished. Ask him to come, so I can present my case directly. *(Takes hold of La Valliere's dress)* By my age, most of the young women here have been promised to men and those that haven't are given a trade. I must know whether there is some plan for me. I must know whether I am to grow old here.

LA VALLIERE: Don't you know? Hasn't anyone ever told you?

LOUISE: Told me what?

(La Valliere giggles to herself.)

LA VALLIERE: This is going to cheer me up.

LOUISE: What are you saying?

LA VALLIERE: The Queen is your mother, Louise. You are never going to leave here!

LOUISE: My mother? Then it is true. Is the King my father?

LA VALLIERE: Oh no! Has the Queen never uttered a word? Have you never looked in a mirror?

LOUISE: Not since I was a child. Then surely, my blood must be worth something to somebody.

LA VALLIERE: Don't you know? Your blood?

LOUISE: Am I that different from you? I bleed. I laugh. I weep. I feel no difference when I touch my face.

LA VALLIERE: Where the royal blood ebbs, the African blood flows. Your face is that of disgrace.

LOUISE: African? Me?

LA VALLIERE: Have you never asked yourself why your skin is brown, though you see no sun? Why you live here, so neatly tucked away from the world? Clever girl—

LOUISE: What questions do your bastard children ask of you?

LA VALLIERE: They know when to bow their heads, and when to hold them high. They too will never inherit what is rightfully theirs, though their blood flows directly from the throne. I understand— *(She stands and straightens her clothing)*

LOUISE: Do they worship simple pleasures and know their father's touch?

LA VALLIERE: It is getting late and I don't want to make the journey back in the dark.

LOUISE: Royal blood? What use is this blood if it makes a prisoner of me?

(Louise grabs the bread knife and slashes it across her wrist.)

LA VALLIERE: No! MOTHER SUPERIOR! MOTHER SUPERIOR! MOTHER SUPERIOR!

(La Valliere gathers her basket and exits hastily. The Mother Superior enters and wraps Louise's wrist with a handkerchief.)

MOTHER SUPERIOR: You bleed again, so devoted are you to our suffering. You've a few more liters to meet the saintly requirement. Purify, my sweet virgin. Purify!

LOUISE *(Weakened, struggling to stand)*: Cheers! Papa! I'd never seen an African other than the stained glass windows of Balthazar bending over Christ with a gift, wearing his azure turban more magnificent than the others. As the light shone through the window at noon I imagined he was my father, casting purple hues across my forehead. I'd pray to him, a King from a far off land who ruled countries more beautiful than France. A King who'd been in the very presence of Christ. In Madame de Montespan's version my father was not a King. In mine, sometimes he is.

(Lights up on Nabo, who sits by his altar with a bottle of wine, drunk. He pours a libation before the altar.)

NABO: Wine wasted on an old friend that has abandoned me. Well Legba, wine used to make you rise up. Dance. I can't hear you, too far from home now. Look at me with a foolish heart that has grown too large for my body. Legba, do me this one last favor and point in the right direction home. I don't know anymore.

LOUISE: The good Cure said that the Virgin Mary is black from head to toe, and is most beautiful in the eyes of God. As a child, I ran from the taunts of children. "Gyspy swine, Gypsy girl." But God sees nothing but the naked soul, said the Cure, and he taught me how to read the gentle words of the Bible. Sweet sisters, when did blackness become a sin?

(Nabo stands. He walks in circles; his pace grows quicker as he speaks.)

NABO: I know that Dahomey is to the south and I know the great river runs east past my village and I know the palace faces . . . Well I know when the sun rises . . . well I know that when my uncle bowed to Mecca he always turned . . . *(Turns in circles)* Well I know poor Nabo, you will never get home at this rate.

QUEEN *(Offstage; echoing)*: NABO! NABO!

NABO: Well well Legba, tomorrow will be the day that we have another discussion.

(He pours another drink as an offering.)

QUEEN *(Offstage)*: Nabo! Pedro! *(Nabo rolls his eyes)* Nabo!

LOUISE: The Queen summoned him to the countryside where she was convalescing. She'd acquired too much fluid in the ankles and needed to be carried everywhere like an Oriental princess. Eight months pregnant, ghastly!

(The Queen sits by the country hearth, warming her feet. She drinks brandy wine from a silver chalice. Her eyes grow large as she hears stirring outside her chamber. One door panel swings open. Nabo tumbles in. The Queen does not respond. Louise leaves the light.)

NABO: You're not surprised?

QUEEN: Of course not, I called you here. I missed your company—

NABO: And I, yours.

QUEEN: Really? What took you so long? Did anyone come with you? What did you bring me? Where is everyone? Did dey come? *(Nabo shakes his head)* The Queen Mother? *(Nabo shakes his head)* Ladies from the court? *(Nabo shakes his head)* Musicians? *(Nabo shakes his head)* Anyone?

NABO: The King thought it best that you have a companion and believes none gives you more pleasure than myself. *(He bows graciously)*

QUEEN: How thoughtful of the King. I'm surprised that he knows I'm still alive. Has Louis really asked after me?

NABO *(Lying)*: He's pale with worry.

QUEEN: Liar! Have the decency to lie with some panache.

NABO: If you'd like.

QUEEN: Yes, very much!

NABO: The King sighs at supper, he cries out for his Queen whenever—

QUEEN: Stop! Cries? Louis never cries. Try again!

NABO: The King has been heard to whisper after his morning treks. Maria! *(The Queen leans forward)* Maria! He is sickened by the news of your illness.

QUEEN: Yes, go on.

NABO: And, and, and—

QUEEN: Regrets that—

NABO: That he cannot be at your side at such a delicate time. He sent me to convey this message.

QUEEN: So thoughtful. And my child?

NABO: As robust as when you left.

QUEEN: Does he miss his mama?

NABO: At three, he barely takes the nipple of the wet nurse.

(The Queen lies back and sighs with relief.)

QUEEN: Bueno! I had thought that all had forgotten, left me to rot and wither in dis sedate countryside. Even the ladies are abandoning me one by one, afraid that such a prolonged absence from the court will destroy their rank. Nonsense! Bring me my powder! I suddenly feel better. *(Nabo fetches the Queen's compact of powder)* Let's do something!

(He douses her face with the white powder, giving her a ghoulish glow.)

NABO: Shall I begin with a story?

QUEEN: No, all of your stories have sad endings.

NABO: Oh, the Queen is in a mood today. I thought you'd given up Nabo for some other entertainment. But I can see my competition has been sweets and wines and puddings.

QUEEN: Silence! I'm not fat, I'm fecund. Si? . . . Nabo, tell me the truth, did Louis send me here to die? I've heard from my little wicked Molina that as I rode north, the King went south with his mistress. She's pregnant again. And here I am with his child from a few tears I shed and shared with him. I know this to be so.

NABO: Of course, I dare not cry for fear of spreading my seed, my sadness could yield an empire.

(The Queen weeps slightly, collects herself and carries on as if nothing happened.)

QUEEN: Please, I sent for you for merriment.

NABO: Merrymaking is perhaps where our problem lies.

(Nabo sinks down next to the Queen. The Queen's face is contorted with horror.)

LOUISE: And there they sat for almost a full day: frozen, paralyzed by the possibility. Can you imagine? He was going to father a child with the Queen of France, the Princess of Spain, the divine vessel; he, a man no larger than a child. A court jester. A fool.

(Nabo laughs hysterically, to the irritation of the Queen.)

QUEEN: Stop it! *(A moment. Silence)* I'm so cold, I can barely summon a servant to stoke the fire. And there's no one to help me in and out of my chair to circulate the blood in my ankles. I'm practically a prisoner, confined to this chamber full of portraits. I'm carrying the royal heir, for God's sake. RIGHT? CLARO QUE SI.

NABO: Can you be so sure?

QUEEN: Hush. It is the King's child, of that the Doctor is certain.

NABO: Are you?

QUEEN: Don't even say aloud what I know you are thinking.
   I don't want to see you now! GET OUT! Blackie!

NABO: Fattie!

QUEEN: Little Man.

NABO: Ugly cow!

QUEEN: FOOL! FOOL! FOOL!

NABO: Inbred, big jawed, thick-ankled, wench!

(The Queen falls back in her chair and howls like a wounded animal.)

QUEEN: GET OUT!

(A moment.)

NABO: You've forgotten the kind words you had for Nabo not
   so long ago.

QUEEN: Forgotten yes, my memory is like cheesecloth.

NABO: Do you want me to remind you? *(The Queen shakes her head)* You are my sweet little Nabo.

QUEEN: NO!

NABO: You touch me as the King does not.

QUEEN: NO!

NABO: Ay dios mio! TE AMO, TE AMO!

QUEEN *(Ecstatic)*: NO!

(Nabo moves close to the Queen and plants a kiss on her neck.)

NABO: You—

QUEEN: You are wicked, Nabo. Tempt and taunt me. I should
   be above such devilish seduction. STOP!

NABO: Would it be so horrible if the child bore Nabo's face?

QUEEN: It would be impossible for me to be with your child. You can't be virile at your size. Why, your seed is incompatible with royal needs. NO! *(Suddenly horrified by the question, she turns her back on Nabo)* Be thankful that you're not its papa, it would mean your end! It would mean my end! And I'm fond of your insolent presence.

NABO: You're right. Let us pray it isn't true. What am I thinking?

QUEEN: I am the vessel of empires to come. I can't afford to bring anything other than a royal child into dis world. It's what I'm bred for, Nabo. My sole purpose. If I cannot provide that, then what will become of Maria? You were shipped in a box and I, a carriage. When you first peered up over the edge of that little box I recognized you. Look at me, Nabo. They think I'm stupid. They think I've no feelings, no cares. They think I can be treated like spoiled meat. *(Presses her fist into her stomach)* I could pound my belly and let the King know that I HAVE SOME POWER TOO. I have some say in the shaping of this nation. I deserve to be treated decently, instead of shipped off to Fontainebleau and quickly forgotten. I came with a most excellent dowry. I brought peace to this land and I will take it away. Oh, what havoc this child could bring!

(The Queen raises her fist to pound her belly. Nabo stops her and presses his face against her stomach.)

NABO: No! Don't!

QUEEN: You are mi Angel, Nabo. Sometimes I feel that we are in love. Is that strange? Could we be in love?

NABO: In desperation.

*(Nabo kisses the Queen as lights fade on them.
Louise enters smiling.)*

Scene 4

Louise stands alone in a circle of light; she slowly unbuttons her novice clothing.

LOUISE: On this, my wedding night, with not a relative alive to bear witness to my testimonial. And this story is almost complete save for my birth and when it occurs, so will the death of Louise Marie-Therese. Be patient, sisters, and allow me this sweet selfish remembrance. *(She peels off her novice clothing, revealing a crude slip beneath. She steps into the tub, slowly lowering herself into the water)* The night before my birth everyone had a dream. They all sat up in their beds sweating out fears. It was a birth most anxiously undesired. What manner of beast would burst from between the Queen's legs if dreams be purveyors of the future?

(Nabo screams. Lights rise on him in a little bed, his chest heaving up and down.)

NABO: Oh dear Legba, I dreamt of my end which came with a child bearing my face. I dreamt this child was bound in cloth and couldn't breathe. The child was gasping and I couldn't free her.

(The Queen yelps. Lights rise on the Queen sitting in her bed chamber. The Queen Mother wipes her forehead with a cloth.)

QUEEN: It was a most terrible dream.
QUEEN MOTHER: Your screams shook the palace.
QUEEN: Is there any way to stop this birth?
QUEEN MOTHER: You are no more than a day from delivery.
QUEEN: How many sins can one commit before admission to Heaven is impossible?

QUEEN MOTHER: It is a question for the clergy, I've never cared to know the answer myself.

QUEEN: I've had a premonition that dis child will be born grotesquely disfigured, without a face, a monster.

QUEEN MOTHER: These signs change their meaning at will, what you see now may mean something different tomorrow. Only an oracle, pagan or a butcher can read these signs with clarity.

(*A labor pain hits, and the Queen doubles over in pain.*)

It is time!

(*The Doctor rushes to the Queen's side with a number of servants. The Queen is stretched across a bed. The Doctor and the ladies crowd around the Queen.*)

DOCTOR: Push! (*The Queen cries out*) Push!

LOUISE: Push!

(*With one final scream the Queen's cries are drowned out by the sound of a baby crying.*
Louise, soaking wet, suddenly rises in the tub.)

DOCTOR: She's here.

(*The Doctor takes a close look at the child and immediately wraps her in a blanket. The ladies burst into spontaneous applause, as they struggle furiously to get a glance at the child. Their whispers swell into a chorus of "Let me sees." They fall suddenly silent.*)

LA VALLIERE: Let me see. Let me see.

(*La Valliere bursts into laughter. The Doctor attempts to stifle the laughter.*)

QUEEN: Let me see her! What? Why are you laughing? Let me see her! *(She begins to laugh herself and then stops)* What? Why are you laughing?

(She reaches for the baby. The Queen Mother peeks at the child, shrieks, and faints.)

My baby! Can I hold my baby! My baby! My baby!

(Laughter drowns out her cries. Church bells ring. The lights fade on Louise and the Queen as they rise on the King and Doctor Fagon. The King takes a pinch of snuff, sneezes and wipes his nose in his blouse.)

KING: Tell them to stop ringing those damn bells. I didn't hear what you said.

(The church bells continue to chime.)

DOCTOR *(Reluctantly)*: Brown, brown . . . Your Majesty. The child is brown.

KING: Brown? Are you sure? What does that mean? Is it a good sign? Is it a scientific term?

DOCTOR: No, no I'm referring to the color of its skin.

KING: BROWN?

DOCTOR: We fear that the Queen's fool, having *looked* upon Her Majesty so often, transformed the infant's complexion through a trauma during the pregnancy. This shouldn't last long, perhaps a month or two and then her true color will return.

KING: I see. A look! It must have been a very *penetrating* look. It's not the first I've heard of such an affliction, it did pass with the de Medicis not long ago. The royal womb tends to be more fragile, a divine vessel is more susceptible to out-side irritations. It is why I'm told so many perish at birth.

DOCTOR: Oh yes! Quite right! How do you wish me to handle this?

KING: She'll need a name nevertheless! We will call her Louise Marie-Therese. Did you take that down?

(The Doctor pretends to take down the information on his hand. He bows obsequiously.

The Mother Superior crosses the stage holding a child in her arms. She gently rocks the infant, intermittently blowing kisses. Lights rise on Louise.)

MOTHER SUPERIOR: You know, you'll have to take another name when you take your veil.

LOUISE: Yes, I know.

MOTHER SUPERIOR: I am your mother and the Lord is your father. I am your mother and the Lord is your husband.

(The Mother Superior continues to rock the child as she moves across the stage and disappears.)

KING: When can I see the child?

DOCTOR: The Queen rests. I haven't yet told her. The child—

KING: Can I see whom she resembles?

(The Doctor clears his throat.)

DOCTOR: Perhaps the King would care to wait. Until—

KING: Nonsense. Prepare the child for a viewing.

(The Doctor goes to the door.)

DOCTOR: BRING OUT THE CHILD!

(A nursemaid rushes in with the baby and shows her to the King. The King, aghast, loses his balance, nearly tumbling

to the ground. A courtier brings him a glass of wine, which he drinks down quickly.)

May I recommend that she be placed elsewhere until her affliction heals? Someplace where her complexion won't be affected by so many curious eyes. I know an excellent little Benedictine convent.

(The bells stop ringing.
Mother Superior grabs Louise from behind.)

MOTHER SUPERIOR: My dear Father Josephus nearly drowned in rain water. At Moret we have such a simple life, we are women of virtue. Women of noble birth enter our ranks in numbers far greater than any convent in France. If we were a royal court it would be the finest in this nation.
KING: Will this affliction clear?
DOCTOR: Not to my knowledge, but—

(A moment.)

KING: She is a girl after all, she wouldn't be . . . I'll have my valet, Bontems, deliver her this evening. We'll make arrangements to have her baptized in the convent. She must be baptized, I insist. The Queen is as pious as they come, that must be known by all. It is a pity that from now on she's to spend so much time in prayer, so young.
DOCTOR: Sire, I could announce the child's death if—
KING *(Louder)*: It was stillborn you say? It always saddens me to prepare for a birth and a death on the same day.
DOCTOR *(Whispered)*: They are excellent nuns and will care for the child well.
KING: I must have them prepare my mourning clothing. *(Whispered)* The good sisters must be informed that the child is to know nothing of its birth. She is to be sequestered from

the rest of the world until her death, or until her discoloration mends itself. I'm sure the Benedictines will be sympathetic if I let my generosity be known.

DOCTOR: And if the Queen insists on knowing the truth?

KING: Excuse me, I must dress for the funeral. And go and comfort my wife.

(The King exits. The courtiers burst into laughter.)

LOUISE: It was whispered, my nose was broad and flat. It was whispered that my hair was kinky and tight. It was whispered that I was born with two horns and hooves for hands. They whispered as they prepared for a royal funeral. Hysteria seized the Queen and it took three women to hold her down.

(Lights rise on the Queen being strapped to the bed by three women. She pulls at her hair, shrieking and crying.)

LADY SERVANT: She's dead, Your Majesty.

QUEEN: I heard her cry!

LADY SERVANT: She was born still!

QUEEN: I heard her cry!

LADY SERVANT: Calm, and drink this. In all of the excitement you are confused.

QUEEN: No! I want to know where my baby is! I want the King! I want him to tell me where my baby is. She isn't dead, I heard her cry. I heard her crying. I heard her crying! You tell the King that if anything has happened to my baby I will start a war that will take generations to pass. Now get out of here you LIARS!

(The Queen hisses at the women, who scramble quickly out of the room. She twists and turns attempting to loosen the restraints. Nabo emerges from beneath the bed carrying a withered flower.)

NABO: The flower stood through most of the night, it was only your yelling that gave it a fright.

QUEEN: Come, come. Untie me! *(Nabo unties the Queen's arms)* They've taken my baby, Nabo. They said she was grossly deformed and I should not look upon her. They said she was born still. It was for my own good, Fagon said. For my own good, nursemaid said, but nothing good has come of this day.

NABO: She was mine too, not the King's to give away. I heard the cries of a child this very morning echo through the palace.

QUEEN: She was brown from what I could see and they laughed and laughed like in my dream. She was beautiful from what I could tell. Tiny. Let's find the child and run away.

NABO: Where? Where can a Queen run with an African dwarf? If I could get away I'd have been gone long ago.

QUEEN: We'll go to the land of your stories. To Africa?

(Nabo laughs.)

NABO: You wouldn't survive there.

QUEEN: Why not? You've survived here.

NABO: Some of me, but not all.

QUEEN: To the New World.

NABO: Old values have taken root.

QUEEN: Then I'll kill myself. *(Screams violently)* I am Queen of France.

NABO: And what does that mean? You are so innocent, Maria. *(Kisses her forehead)* When you could love the whole world. You choose to love me. A truly noble heart.

QUEEN: No, you chose me. I'll bear the shame if only they will let me have my child.

NABO: She has no place in this court. No, Maria.

QUEEN: We can go elsewhere.

NABO: Where? With what?

QUEEN: I have jewels.

NABO: I once asked you to let me go and you refused.

QUEEN: You are free, I know this now. Please, take me away from this place.

NABO: I wouldn't be free if I did. Where I go I'm not a fool, I don't think you yet understand that. I'm not servant or slave. And if you came I'd be all of those things.

QUEEN: Please, I can't have two losses in one day.

NABO: I've had many, you'll survive the pain . . . but as things stand, I'm lucky if I survive this day. We can spend all night making plans, but don't you know, Your Majesty, my fate was sealed when I foolishly sold my life for six goats and some beads.

(La Valliere enters and taps Louise.)

LA VALLIERE *(Laughing)*: No one told you?

LOUISE: My father was—

LA VALLIERE: An African dwarf.

LOUISE *(To Queen)*: Why didn't you ever tell me?

QUEEN *(To Nabo)*: We can run away.

(The Queen's servants and Doctor Fagon appear and lead the Queen offstage. Louise follows them. Nabo picks up the wilted flower as two guards seize him.

Lights rise on the King pacing. He stops and sits behind a desk. Nabo is brought before the King, who makes a show of going through a pile papers. Nabo bows.)

NABO: A joke for the middle of the day, sire? Something to take the edge off the affairs of state?

KING: No. It is a pity, I really do like you, more than I like her in fact. I'm sorry . . .

(He glances at the document in his hand searching for Nabo's name. He speaks casually.)

Nabo Sensugali, I have before me a warrant for your execution. I've passed my judgment, I hope you don't mind too much, but I promise I won't make an event out of it and you'll have a Christian burial. You are Christian?

NABO: Actually I—

KING: Yes, then I imagine you are.

NABO: Perhaps the punishment does not befit the crime. Sire, may I know what I have been charged with?

KING: Treason.

NABO: Treason, I see. Of what nature?

KING: A penetrating look that threatened the welfare of the royal heir.

NABO: The gallows? It's so large a punishment for one so small. If you factor in my height, I'm one half the size of an average man and therefore I've committed only half the crime. Sire, you could always exile me to a far off land, like Africa.

KING: The thought has crossed my mind, but I believe execution is more demonstrative in this instance. It's the Queen's honor that's at stake. *(Sips his wine)* Talk has already reached epidemic proportions. I can't have the Queen's reputation tarnished any further.

NABO: Yes, you can't have that.

KING: We both know it's talk. You and the Queen—what a foolish notion. Why, you're half the size of an average man. I'm three inches taller than that. *(Coughs)* This child does not exist as far as I'm concerned. I wish it had died at birth and then its odd discoloration could be explained away. But it survived, I'll not pretend otherwise. I . . . I care for my wife, despite what many think. She is my innocent angel, whose love has been unconditional. Familiarity is often more comforting than true love, which makes the heart violent and is accompanied by fits of rage, great passion and ultimately hurt. I know with Marie I will never suffer that great hurt.

NABO: Is it necessary to take a man's life twice? As is my case. You've taken mine once when I entered this court, which means I'm already dead and therefore your judgment has been enacted. Can a dead man be killed, and if so, by what means? Redundancy is not a kingly trait.

KING: Then you're familiar with kingly attributes.

NABO: Oh yes, Your Majesty.

KING: Hmmm?

NABO: May I ask another question?

KING: Go on!

NABO: May the Queen see her child? Her sanity hangs by a thin thread.

KING: I—

NABO: My life for hers and the child's.

KING: That's not possible. Officially this conversation is not even happening, I'm out for a ride.

NABO: If we never had this conversation, is it possible that I never existed? The Queen never did give birth, which means she has no child, which means no crime has been committed.

KING: That is true. The truth. No crime committed.

(He signs the paper before him.)

NABO: So you signed me out of existence and tomorrow I will never have been here.

KING: Yes.

NABO: I gave a woman a few moments of love. I should be thanked for that. I was shipped to and from empires bizarre and unwelcoming in a box no full size man could survive. Bought, sold, bartered and brokered until I do not know who I am. Laughed at, kicked and disgraced, I've learned more than most men about this human race. And if my tongue were acid you'd now be dead. I've made kings weep with joy and queens whine with delight. Months of pleasure I've given your court, and I am to pay for the one moment I stole for my own.

KING: Yes, unfortunately, that seems to be the case. *(He folds the warrant)* You did make me laugh. *(Laughs)* That story you . . . well perhaps now isn't the best time. You've given me a few moments of laughter and that won't go unrecognized. The child will live, and let it not be said that I was without a heart. And yes, in time I might find my way to grant the Queen some privileges. All of that said, I'm afraid you're not quite fool enough for this place.

NABO: Sire!

KING: Yes.

(Nabo laughs and shakes his bells furiously.)

Take him out.

(The lights go to black on all except Louise. She slowly begins to unbutton her slip.)

LOUISE: Taken to the woods and decapitated in one quick stroke to the back of the neck. Buried as a Christian beneath a great flowering tree. His name never spoken by anyone in court again. Nabo Sensugali. At the moment his neck cracked and split, Bontems carried me in his arms through the violent rainstorm.

(Lights rise on the Mother Superior.)

My mother sat . . .

(Lights rise on the Queen in bed, cradling the air. These lights quickly fade.)

I'm not yet finished. My mother sat . . .

(Lights rise once again on the Queen in bed cradling the air.)

In her bed singing and waiting for Nabo.

QUEEN *(Singing)*: Go to sleep little one.

LOUISE *(To the Queen)*: Are you my mother? *(The Queen continues to sing the lullaby)* Is my father an African?

QUEEN: Go to sleep little one.

(The lights fade on the Queen. The Mother Superior slowly makes her way toward Louise with a wedding gown in her hands. Nuns enter.)

LOUISE: And my father's neck cracked and split, his head tumbling to the ground with a grin still on his lips. And now I will stop waiting. I have no family other than you, my sisters, and God. The King decreed them out of existence.

(The nuns take off her wet slip and place her in the wedding gown.)

And now I too will be lost to history.

(She lies, spread-eagle, face down on the floor as the lights fade.)

END OF PLAY

Crumbs
from the
Table of Joy

and Other Plays